VALIANT HEARTS

ATLANTIC CANADA
AND THE VICTORIA CROSS

D1525338

JOHN BOILEAU

FOREWORD BY
MAJOR-GENERAL (RET'D) LEWIS W. MACKENZIE

NIMBUS
PUBLISHING LTD

Nimbus Publishing Limited
PO Box 9166
Halifax, NS B3K 5M8
(902) 455-4286

Printed and bound in Canada

Design: Cover: Heather Bryan
                Text: Arthur Carter, Paragon Design Group
Author photo: Mark Doucette

Library and Archives Canada Cataloguing in Publication

    Boileau, John,
    Valiant hearts : Atlantic Canada and the
    Victoria Cross / John Boileau; includes bibliographical
    references and index.
    ISBN 1-55109-548-3

1. Victoria Cross 2. Soldiers—Atlantic Provinces—Biography 3. Heroes—Atlantic Provinces—Biography 4. Canada—Armed Forces—Biography 5. Atlantic Provinces— Biography I. Title

CR4885.B63 2005   355.1'34'0922715   C2005-905771-8

Canadä   The Canada Council | Le Conseil des Arts
              for the Arts | du Canada

We acknowledge the financial support of the Government of Canada through the Book Publishing Industry Development Program (BPIDP) and the Canada Council, and of the Province of Nova Scotia through the Department of Tourism, Culture and Heritage for our publishing activities.

DEDICATED TO THE MEMORY OF

THE TWENTY-ONE "VALIANT HEARTS"

WHOSE STORIES ARE TOLD IN THIS BOOK.

"FOR VALOUR"

O Valiant Hearts, who to your glory came
Through dust of conflict and through battle flame;
Tranquil you lie, your knightly virtue proved,
Your memory hallowed in the Land you loved.

—John Stanhope Arkwright, from *The Supreme*
Sacrifice and Other Poems in Time of War, 1919

ACKNOWLEDGEMENTS

The research and writing of this book have been a labour of love for me, and many people have helped me bring it to fruition. When I began, I only intended to tell the stories of the ten Victoria Cross recipients who I knew were born in Atlantic Canada. However, my research soon discovered there were eleven. Canadian authorities have consistently ignored one individual, apparently because he served in the British Army. Yet those same authorities recognize several other recipients with similar backgrounds and experiences.

I also quickly found out there were a number of other gallant men who, although they were not born in Atlantic Canada, had close associations with the region and equally deserved to be included in the book. I must thank Dave Danskin for bringing Valentine McMaster to my attention and providing excellent information on him, as well as Joan Cervin for telling me about her father, Claude Dobson, and providing photographs of him. Other children of VC recipients also assisted. Armed with an obscure clue from me, Urban Hughes performed outstanding detective work in tracking down Brenda Wood, daughter of Robert Ryder. Wood graciously supplied photographs and stories of her father. Similarly, Dr. Thomas Ricketts and Dolda Clarke, son and daughter respectively of Tommy Ricketts, helpfully provided photographs and family stories. Terry Hissey, who has researched Ricketts in some detail, kindly reviewed the chapter on him.

The staff of several museums also contributed photographs and interesting details. These include Bruce Gilchrist, John Harrison and Gary Melville at the Army Museum–Halifax Citadel; Chuck Coffen at the Shearwater Aviation Museum; and Marilyn Gurney at the Maritime Command Museum. At Halifax's Cambridge Military Library, librarian Jeanne Howell and custodian Master Corporal Michaela Brister were most helpful and understanding, in particular giving me lots of leeway in returning books from the library's outstanding collection.

In England, several friends provided assistance beyond the call of duty. Major (ret'd) Ronnie McDuell put me in touch with the Leicestershire Museum and Philip Bent's story through his many contacts, and helped with research at the National Army Museum in London. Retired Captain Ian Condie, who probably knows everyone who ever served in the Royal Navy, discovered information on Frederick Peters in the Admiralty's Historical Section. At the Army Medical Services Museum, Captain (ret'd) Peter Starling could not have been more helpful in providing information and illustrations of William Nickerson and Valentine McMaster. Finally, my long-time friend Jim Dickinson, a retired Essex Assistant Chief Constable, was my faithful companion, researcher and co-driver as we toured the First World War battlefields and cemeteries of France and Flanders on four separate occasions over the past few years.

In Ottawa, Lieutenant-Colonel (ret'd) John Price unstintingly undertook photographic research for me at the National Archives and Library of Canada, working his way through their sometimes confusing filing system. I must also thank Major-General (ret'd) Lewis MacKenzie, arguably Atlantic Canada's best-known living soldier, who kindly agreed to write the foreword, putting a very personal and regional stamp on his comments.

At Nimbus, Sandra McIntyre and Dan Soucoup deserve my thanks for agreeing to publish *Valiant Hearts*, as do Robert Plowman and James MacNevin for their outstanding work in making my words read that much better. The interpretation of events, of course, remains strictly my own.

Lastly, as always, my wife Miriam has been a great support in letting me get on with writing, even when there was snow to shovel and grass to cut.

JBB
"Lindisfarne"
Glen Margaret, Nova Scotia
August 15, 2005
Sixtieth Anniversary of Victory
in Japan Day

PREFACE

This is a book about heroes.

It is not a book about those who are so frequently portrayed as heroes by the media: people such as athletes, actors, rock stars, financial wizards, businesspeople or politicians, among others. This is a book about real heroes, men who fulfil the original and often seemingly forgotten meaning of the word today. This is a book about men in war, men who displayed outstanding valour and courage in action against their country's enemies, men who unquestionably, unhesitatingly and unselfishly were prepared to give their lives in battle.

And several of them did.

The twenty-one men profiled in this book have at least two things in common: they all have strong connections to Atlantic Canada (eleven of them were born in the region) and they all received the Victoria Cross (VC), the supreme British Empire (and later, Commonwealth) award for bravery in battle. Apart from that, they share very little. They range from the uneducated son of dirt-poor black ex-slaves to the product of the English public school system, from civilians caught up in the enlistment fever of the times to career military men, from farmers to fishermen, from young to old.

Much has been written about VC recipients over the years and new books continue to be published about them on a regular basis, attesting to an enduring fascination with that rare decoration and the mystique surrounding it. Unfortunately, a great deal of what has been put down on paper over the years is inaccurate, with unsubstantiated newspaper articles often later becoming accepted facts. This book attempts to correct such errors, at the same time as it delves deeper into these courageous men's stories by filling in the details of their lives before and after (at least for those who survived) the award of the VC.

This book also goes beyond the lives of the eleven VC recipients born in Atlantic Canada by telling the stories of another ten awardees who had various connections with the region, usually through having lived or served in it. A few of these men are commonly referred to as being "associated" with

Atlantic Canada, while in other cases their links to the region have never before been detailed.

Before reading their stories, one point requires clarification. The men who received the VC should never be referred to as "winners," or as having "won" the VC, as such terms are generally regarded as inappropriate when referring to any of the selfless acts that resulted in the award of the medal.

The stories of these gallant men, these brave souls, these "valiant hearts," provides an object lesson for us all.

The heroic deeds they accomplished should never be forgotten.

—John Boileau

ABBREVIATIONS

ADC	Aide-de-Camp	KCB	Knight Commander of the Order of the Bath
AMC	Armed Merchant Cruiser		
Anzac	Australia and New Zealand Army Corps	MB	Medal of Bravery
		MC	Military Cross
BCATP	British Commonwealth Air Training Plan	MM	Military Medal
		MMV	Medal of Military Valour
BEF	British Expeditionary Force	MO	Medical Officer
		MP	Member of Parliament
BNA	British North America	NCO	Non-Commissioned Officer
BPF	British Pacific Fleet		
CB	Companion of the Order of the Bath	OC	Officer of the Order of Canada
CEF	Canadian Expeditionary Force	PIAT	Projector, Infantry, Anti-Tank
CMG	Companion of the Order of St Michael and St George	PPCLI	Princess Patricia's Canadian Light Infantry
CO	Commanding Officer	RAF	Royal Air Force
CPR	Canadian Pacific Railway	RCAF	Royal Canadian Air Force
CV	Cross of Valour	RCN	Royal Canadian Navy
DCM	Distinguished Conduct Medal	RCNVR	Royal Canadian Naval Volunteer Reserve
DSC	Distinguished Service Cross	RCR	Royal Canadian Regiment
		RN	Royal Navy
DSO	Distinguished Service Order	RNR	Royal Naval Reserve
		RSM	Regimental Sergeant-Major
FAA	Fleet Air Arm		
GCB	Knight Grand Cross of the Order of the Bath	SC	Star of Courage
		SMV	Star of Military Valour
HMCS	Her/His Majesty's Canadian Ship	UN	United Nations
		UNB	University of New Brunswick
HMS	Her/His Majesty's Ship		
HQ	Headquarters	USN	United States Navy

TABLE OF CONTENTS

FOREWORD

Shortly after my return from the Balkans in 1993 I was in St. John's, Newfoundland, to deliver a speech at Memorial University. Word reached me that the premier, Clyde Wells, would like me to drop by his office. Early in our conversation he asked, "Why is it that the majority of the Canadian casualties in Yugoslavia to date have been Atlantic Canadians in general and Newfoundlanders in particular?" "Well sir," I said, "that's easy to explain. There is a monthly quota for every Canadian Forces Recruiting Centre in the country. When a potential recruit from Toronto is told that this month's quota has been filled, he goes home and waits for next month to roll around. Now, when someone from your province is told the same thing he starts hitchhiking! It might be Winnipeg before he finds a vacancy, but he will keep heading west until he finds one."

It has always been thus. Atlantic Canadians have always made up a disproportionate share of the men and women in uniform serving their sovereign and their country. Those who observe this phenomenon from outside the region erroneously deduce that it's the lack of job opportunities that causes the military option to be so popular. This condescending opinion fails to recognize patriotism when it sees it. The statistics clearly show that military service tends to run in families for multiple generations. With Atlantic Canada's outstanding record of military service for the past century, it is highly likely that this trend will continue well into the future.

Not surprisingly, acts of bravery by soldiers, sailors and airmen from the region are legion. Indeed, their disproportionate share of the British Commonwealth's highest award for valour in the face of the enemy, the Victoria Cross, deserves to be singled out for special recognition.

The *Concise Oxford English Dictionary* definition of heroic does not include "sacrifice" or "risk" as prerequisites. I disagree. Scoring three goals in a single hockey game or forty points in basketball are extraordinary acts but these don't qualify as heroic in my book. On the other hand, deciding, in a split second, to put your life at a degree of risk where the odds are solidly against your survival sets you apart from the rest of us.

Twenty-twenty hindsight frequently attributes acts of bravery to love of God, Queen, country and regiment, in that order. It makes for emotional nostalgia, but is untrue and misleading. A soldier's world under fire is tiny and usually restricted to a few buddies on each side of him. It is the camaraderie and respect borne of sharing so much together that causes one soldier to take the lead in risking his life for the others. Today we jeopardize that key motivator of bravery and sacrifice by patching together units just before we despatch them to an operational theatre.

John Boileau has done a great service by bringing together, under one cover, the accomplishments of twenty-one unqualified heroes, all of whom had a connection to the Atlantic region. As the reader marvels at their unselfish bravery it's important to remember that unseen and unrecorded were thousands of other individual heroic acts, obscured by the confusion and agony of war. The sacrifice of these unrecognized heroes was equally generous and they too are honoured by those who are recognized here.

—Lewis W. MacKenzie, OStJ, OOnt, MSC, CD, Major-General (Ret'd)

Lewis W. MacKenzie was born in Truro and raised in Princeport, Nova Scotia. He served Canada as an infantry officer for thirty-six years and retired in 1993. A veteran of nine peacekeeping tours, he is best known for his tour as Commander of Sector Sarajevo for the United Nations Protection Force in Yugoslavia.

General MacKenzie is the author of *Peacekeeper: The Road to Sarajevo*, a highly regarded account of his peacekeeping experiences around the world. Since his retirement from the Canadian Forces, he has become a much sought-after—and outspoken—columnist and commentator on world affairs. He is unquestionably Atlantic Canada's most prominent living soldier.

INTRODUCTION

FOR VALOUR

The simple bronze cross bearing the words "For Valour" is one of the rarest gallantry awards in the world. Since it was instituted by Queen Victoria in 1856, the Victoria Cross has been awarded only 1,355 times to 1,351 men. (Three individuals earned it twice and it was also conferred upon the American Unknown Warrior.) On just ninety-eight occasions it has been awarded to men closely associated with Canada, as well as to several others with some link to the country. Twenty-one of these courageous individuals had connections to Atlantic Canada—eleven of them were born in one of its four provinces, while the remaining ten had various associations with the area.

During the Crimean War, when Queen Victoria decided to honour the bravery of her sailors and soldiers, there were very few existing means of recognizing gallantry in action. In particular, as the preamble to the Royal Warrant that established the VC states, there was no way of "adequately rewarding the individual gallant services either of officers of the lower grades in Our naval and military service, or of warrant officers and petty officers, seamen and marines in Our navy, and non-commissioned officers and soldiers in Our army."

THE VICTORIA CROSS, THE HIGHEST AWARD FOR GALLANTRY IN THE BRITISH EMPIRE/COMMONWEALTH, WAS INSTITUTED IN 1856. AS OF MID-2005, ONLY 1,351 MEN HAVE EARNED IT, THREE OF THEM TWICE.

From the outset, everyone in the armed forces was eligible for the Victoria Cross. "Neither rank, nor long service, nor wounds, nor any other circumstance or condition whatsoever, save the merit of conspicuous bravery" was to be considered. The campaign to recognize gallant service was, in many ways, instigated by the media of the day, a result of the war against Russia in the Crimea, which saw some of the earliest incidents of reporting from the front. Indeed, William Howard Russell, who provided the British public with many eyewitness accounts of the conflict in his column in *The Times*, is considered the first modern war correspondent. His articles helped garner public support for the idea of an award to recognize gallantry in the field.

A British Member of Parliament, Captain G. T. Scobell, appears to have been the first person to publicly demand such an award, when he raised the matter in a speech in the House of Commons in December 1854.

QUEEN VICTORIA AND HER CONSORT, PRINCE ALBERT, IN MARCH 1861. THE QUEEN AND ALBERT WERE DIRECTLY INVOLVED IN THE DESIGN AND DEVELOPMENT OF THE VICTORIA CROSS.

Following this lead, a number of senior government members and other influential persons took an interest in the creation of a suitable award. One of the most active was Victoria's husband, Albert, the Prince Consort.

In fact, Scobell's speech may have been the impetus that caused the British Secretary for War, the Duke of Newcastle, to write to Albert in January 1855 reminding him of an earlier conversation in which the subject of a new medal for gallantry at sea or in the field, and for which all ranks would be eligible, was discussed. After the courageous yet disastrous Charge of the Light Brigade in the Crimea on October 25, 1854, Queen Victoria herself saw the need for such an award and the medal which resulted was, in many ways, of her design. Indeed, the idea of a medal for which all ranks would be eligible was regarded as something of a novelty, and it initially encountered opposition from some senior officers.

Albert threw himself wholeheartedly into the effort. He made numerous suggestions about the Royal Warrant to establish the award, the design of the medal itself and the motto it was to bear. Throughout this period, the queen also showed great personal interest in the details of the new honour. The medal, and its name, went through a few iterations before its final form was decided. It was Prince Albert who came up with the simple designation "Victoria Cross," a definite improvement over the name originally proposed—"The Military Order of Victoria." Furthermore, when the medal was originally submitted to the queen, it bore the motto "For the Brave." However, she rejected this, feeling it implied "that only those are deemed brave who have got the Victoria Cross." By royal command the wording was changed to "For Valour." The queen signed the original Royal Warrant establishing the Victoria Cross in January 1856.

Simplicity is a hallmark of the Victoria Cross. The medal is a cross pattée (although heraldry experts have never agreed on this designation for its shape and the Royal Warrant that established it describes it as a Maltese Cross, which it clearly is not), thirty-five millimetres square, made of bronze. In the centre of the obverse, in relief, is the royal crest of a crown surmounted by a lion, above an

DETAILS OF THE OBVERSE AND REVERSE OF THE VICTORIA CROSS OF JOHN BERNARD CROAK, WHO EARNED THE MEDAL DURING THE FIRST WORLD WAR AT THE BATTLE OF AMIENS. BECAUSE OF THE CASTING METHOD USED, EACH VICTORIA CROSS IS UNIQUE IN SOME SMALL WAY.

escroll bearing the inscription "For Valour." A wide "V" descends from the centre of the suspender bar—which is emblazoned with the symbol of victory, a laurel sprig—supporting a plain round link to the medal itself. The reverse of the medal is plain and has an indented circle in its centre, inscribed with the date or dates of the act that earned the VC. The name of the recipient is engraved on the back of the bar.

It was decided that the medal would be struck in a base metal, and the new Secretary of State for War, Lord Panmure, took the design to London jewellers Hancocks & Company to make a prototype, although the firm's expertise was in silver. They made a sample in copper, but the queen was not pleased with the result. As an alternative, she suggested bronze, as it is a very hard metal with a rich colour. It was subsequently proposed that the bronze be taken from the cascabel—the large knob found at the rear of a field gun to hold ropes when the cannon is being manhandled—of two Russian guns (later found to be of Chinese origin) captured at Sebastopol during the Crimean War. However, this bronze was of such inferior quality that it would not cool evenly, resulting in a sand cast medal instead of one made from a die, requiring individual handcrafting of the details on the obverse and making each medal, in some small way, unique. It also appears that some of the medals presented later in the First World War were made of another metal.

Today, the British Army's 15 Regiment, Royal Logistic Corps, stationed at Donnington, holds the remaining bronze for any future VCs. Slightly more than ten kilograms of the metal—which resembles a lump of cheese and is secured in special vaults—remain, enough to make eighty-five more medals. In 1959, just under a kilogram and a half of the bronze, enough to make twelve medals, was given to Hancocks in the most recent issue. The cannons from which the cascabels were taken currently stand outside the Officers' Mess at Woolwich, near London, the home of the Royal Artillery.

The Victoria Cross hangs from a ribbon which is slightly wider than the medal, at thirty-eight millimetres. Originally, the ribbon was blue for the navy and red for the army. However, when the Royal Air Force (RAF) became a separate service on April 1, 1918, it was felt there was no colour particularly suitable for RAF VCs. As a result, King George V decreed that henceforth the ribbon would be red (actually, a dull crimson) for all three services. When the ribbon is worn on a uniform without the medal, a miniature cross is set in its center. A second award of a VC (to date there have only been three) is indicated by a bar on the ribbon, or a second miniature cross on the ribbon when it is worn without the medal. Originally, all VC recipients, except for commissioned officers, received a pension of £10 a year, plus an additional £5 for a second award. This was increased to £100 for all ranks in 1959, to £1,300 in 1995 and to £1,495 in 2002, tax-free.

Queen Victoria conducted the first investiture of the medal that bore her name in Hyde Park, on June 26, 1857, presenting awards to sixty-two of the eighty-five original recipients. These awards had been announced in the *London Gazette* of February 24, and were made retrospective to cover the Crimean War. Fifty-eight of these went to the army and the remaining twenty-seven to the navy and marines. The medals of those who were not able to attend due to service abroad were forwarded to local commanders overseas for investiture.

Though not present at the ceremony, a Canadian was among these first recipients of the VC. Alexander Roberts Dunn, from York (now Toronto), joined the 11th Hussars (Prince Albert's Own Regiment of Light Dragoons) in 1852, when he was nineteen. Tall and handsome (his sword was specially made to accommodate his 1.9-metre height), Dunn fit the image of a dashing cavalry officer, and—sent to the Crimea as a lieutenant in charge of a troop of cavalrymen—he soon had the opportunity to prove his valour. On the morning of October 25, 1854, Dunn rode in the fateful Charge of the Light Brigade at the head of his men. When it was over, only twenty-five of the 110 Hussars who charged the Russian guns survived. Dunn was one of them.

After riding around the enemy cannons, slashing at the Russian gunners with their heavy cavalry sabres, the Hussars were finally forced to withdraw. As Hussar Sergeant Robert Bentley struggled to escape on a horse that was near collapse, the Russians singled him out and knocked him off his steed. The enemy were about to finish Bentley when Dunn wheeled his horse about and rode back to help him. With his giant sabre Dunn cut down three Russian soldiers, then dismounted from his own horse, lifted Bentley onto it, and sent it off towards the British lines. Now on foot, Dunn went to the aid of one of his troopers who had lost his mount, dispatching another Russian in the process. He and the soldier then made their way back to their own lines. For his gallantry, Dunn was awarded the VC, the only officer in the Charge of the Light Brigade and the only cavalry officer in the Crimean War to attain this distinction. By the time of the first investiture in 1856, Dunn had resigned his commission and returned to Canada.

He soon rejoined the army and became a full colonel in 1864—the first Canadian to command a regiment, the 33rd Duke of Wellington's, and the youngest colonel in the British Army. In late 1867, the 33rd was sent to Abyssinia (modern Ethiopia) where Dunn lost his life in 1868 in mysterious circumstances, while hunting. His death is still surrounded by conjecture— accident, suicide or murder. The truth will never be known. Dunn was buried near the town of Senafe, where his grave, after laying untended for several years, is now maintained and inspected regularly. In 1894, Dunn's VC and other medals were purchased by the Canadian Government and are now on display at his old school, Upper Canada College, in Toronto.

Dunn was the first of six Canadians to earn the VC on Imperial service before a Canadian serving in a unit of the Dominion of Canada received one. Interestingly, three of these initial six were doctors. Assistant Surgeon Herbert Reade and Able Seaman William Hall, who both earned their VCs during the Indian Mutiny of 1857–1858, followed Dunn. As a Nova Scotian, Hall's exploits are recounted in Chapter 1. Assistant Surgeon Campbell Douglas was next, for actions during the Andaman Islands Expedition of 1867, an extremely rare instance of the VC being awarded for bravery not in the presence of the enemy.

Lieutenant Raymond de Montmorency earned his VC during the Sudan Campaign in 1898. Although born in Montreal, for some reason he is not recognized as Canadian by Canadian authorities. Finally, Lieutenant William Nickerson gained his VC during the Boer War for attending a wounded soldier under fire. Nickerson was born in New Brunswick, and his story is told in Chapter 2. Like de Montmorency, he also is not considered a Canadian by most Canadian references.

While for most of its existence the Victoria Cross could only be received for actions "in the presence of the enemy," an amendment in effect from 1858 to 1881 allowed for awards "under circumstances of extreme danger." On two occasions during this period, six soldiers earned the VC for actions other than against the enemy in time of war. Interestingly, both these incidents have strong Canadian connections.

On June 9, 1866, Private Timothy O'Hea of the 1st Battalion, The Rifle Brigade (Prince Consort's Own) became the only person ever to earn the VC on what would be Canadian soil just one year later. Serving with his battalion as part of the Imperial troops garrisoning British North America, O'Hea was a member of a detail escorting an ammunition train between

Quebec and Montreal when a fire broke out in one of the rail cars. The alarm was quickly given and the car was disconnected at Danville Railway Station. While the sergeant in charge considered what he should do, O'Hea grabbed the keys from his hand and rushed to the burning car, shouting for water and a ladder. Although he was badly burned while fighting the blaze, O'Hea's quick thinking and the example he set for the other soldiers resulted in the fire being suppressed and in the award of the VC.

The second incident occurred eleven months later, on May 7, 1867, off the Andaman Islands in the Bay of Bengal, involving the 2nd Battalion, 24th Regiment (later the South Wales Borderers of the defence of Rorke's Drift fame). Assistant Surgeon Campbell Mellis Douglas and four privates risked their lives in manning a boat and proceeding through dangerous surf during a violent storm to successfully rescue some of their comrades who

ASSISTANT SURGEON CAMPBELL MELLIS DOUGLAS WAS THE FOURTH CANADIAN RECIPIENT OF THE VICTORIA CROSS, ONE OF A HANDFUL AWARDED FOR BRAVERY NOT IN THE PRESENCE OF THE ENEMY.

had landed earlier on Little Andaman Island. The doctor and the privates were all awarded the VC for this feat.

Douglas was born in Quebec City in 1840 and joined the British Army Medical Service in 1862. He retired to set up private practice in his native land in 1882, but soon found himself involved with the military again. During the Northwest Rebellion by the Métis of Saskatchewan in 1885, Douglas commanded one of two field hospitals deployed for the operation, and was shortly appointed director of the Ambulance Corps. Under his guidance, the wounded were successfully evacuated from the battlefields of Fish Creek and Batoche to Winnipeg. After the Riel Rebellion was suppressed, Douglas retired to England, where he died in 1909.

The original Royal Warrant was amended in 1859 (backdated to cover the period of the Indian Mutiny) and later to permit civilians to receive the Victoria Cross, and this took place on five occasions during the nineteenth century. Four of these VCs were earned during the Indian Mutiny, three by members of the Bengal Civil Service and one by a volunteer of the Indian Naval Brigade (with the most unheroic name of "Chicken"). The fifth and last medal was awarded in 1879 to a minister of the Bengal Ecclesiastical Department for rescuing a number of trapped cavalrymen under fire during the Second Afghan War, 1878–80. No Canadian civilian has ever received the VC.

The Boer War saw the first instance of the deployment of Canadian units overseas. Beside Lieutenant William Nickerson, four other Canadians earned the VC in South Africa. The first was Sergeant Arthur Richardson, an ex-member of the Northwest Mounted Police. He joined Strathcona's Horse, a mounted unit raised privately in the west by Lord Strathcona, formerly Donald Smith, who was the Canadian High Commissioner in London at the time. On July 5, 1900, at Wolve Spruit, Richardson rescued one of his wounded comrades, who had become trapped under his fallen horse as the Boers closed in. Richardson's actions resulted in the first award of a VC to a member of a formed Canadian unit. Three members of the Royal Canadian Dragoons followed Richardson's feat at Leliefontein on November 7. In a unique achievement in the annals of the VC, Lieutenant Hampden Cockburn, Lieutenant Richard Turner and Sergeant Eddie Holland earned their VCs in the space of a few hours, while fighting a rearguard action to prevent the Boers from capturing two 12-pounder guns of E Battery, Royal Canadian Field Artillery.

It was not until 1902, after the Boer War, that King Edward VII formally approved posthumous awards. (Although VCs had been awarded on numerous occasions to men who had died between the act and the award, posthumous awards had never been officially announced as policy.) The exact meaning of a "posthumous" award has been subject to debate. Today, it is usually understood to mean an award to someone who was killed in the actual performance of the act that resulted in the award of the VC, and not one to someone who died subsequent to that act but before the medal could be announced or presented. Because of the differences of opinion over what constitutes a posthumous award, the number of posthumous VCs varies, although 299 (including the American Unknown Warrior) is a logical estimate. Thirty-six Canadians have received a posthumous VC. Until 1977, the VC was the only medal that could be awarded posthumously, along with the Mention-in-Dispatches.

The first Canadian-born recipient of a posthumous VC was Lance Corporal "Bud" Fisher of Montreal's 13th (Royal Highlanders) Battalion, who earned his VC during the First World War. He was both the first Canadian-born recipient of a VC during that war and the first member of a Canadian unit to earn the VC in the conflict. Fisher was a machine-gunner during the Second Battle of Ypres in April 1915, 1st Canadian Division's baptism of fire. Fisher and his section were instrumental in covering the successful withdrawal of two Canadian 18-pounder guns, which resulted in the death of four of his comrades. He went to the rear, got four replacements and was returning to the front when German fire killed or wounded the reinforcements. Fisher carried on and reached the front lines alone. He set up his Colt and began firing at the attacking enemy until, his finger still on the trigger, a bullet struck him in the chest and killed him instantly.

Sergeant Hugh Cairns of the 46th Battalion (Saskatchewan Dragoons) became the last Canadian to earn the VC in the First World War, for four separate acts of bravery on the same day. On November 1, a mere ten days before the signing of the Armistice, the platoon he was leading was held up by German machine-gun fire near Valenciennes on two occasions. He single-handedly charged the enemy positions, killing or capturing their crews. Later, although wounded, he outflanked and captured a field gun position. In his final act of the day, he assisted in the capture of sixty Germans, but was wounded three more times. He died of his wounds in hospital the next day.

SERGEANT HUGH CAIRNS OF THE 46TH BATTALION (SASKATCHEWAN DRAGOONS) WAS THE LAST OF SEVENTY-TWO CANADIANS TO EARN THE VICTORIA CROSS DURING THE FIRST WORLD WAR. HE WAS ALSO HONOURED WITH A STREET NAME: AVENUE DU SERGENT HUGH CAIRNS IN VALENCIENNES, FRANCE.

During the First World War, a total of seventy-two Canadians earned the VC, twenty-eight of them posthumously. Sixty-one served in the Canadian Expeditionary Force (CEF), seven in the British Army, three in the British flying services and one in the Royal Navy (RN). Eight of these recipients were born in Atlantic Canada and are the subjects of later chapters, as are five additional recipients from that war who are associated with the region.

The original Royal Warrant established that if a VC recipient were later convicted of treason, cowardice, felony or any infamous crime, he could forfeit the award, have his name erased from the official Register and his pension cancelled. Such forfeiture occurred on eight occasions, but never to a Canadian recipient. Since 1920, when King George V strongly stated his distaste for the practice, it has been extremely unlikely that forfeiture would be invoked. The names of all eight men have been restored to the Register.

The original Warrant also authorized formed units—such as a battalion, squadron or ship's company—to select VCs by ballot when all members are deemed equally brave and distinguished. Officers and NCOs are each permitted to select one from amongst them, while junior ranks can choose two. This awarding of VC by ballot has taken place on forty-seven occasions, including to two individuals closely associated with Atlantic Canada:

Assistant Surgeon Valentine McMaster and Lieutenant Ronald Stuart. Their stories are told in Chapters 1 and 2 respectively.

Only three men—two British and one New Zealander—have earned bars to their VCs, indicating a second award. No one has ever received the medal on more than two occasions. The first person to receive a second VC was Arthur Martin-Leake. He earned the VC during the Boer War as a surgeon-captain in the South African Constabulary on February 8, 1902, at Vlakfontein. While attending to the wounded, under heavy enemy fire, Martin-Leake was wounded himself. He went on to earn the bar as a lieutenant in the Royal Army Medical Corps during the First World War. On that occasion, he rescued a large number of wounded who were lying close to the German trenches near Zonnebeke, Belgium, over a period of several days between October 29 and November 8, 1914. Martin-Leake died in Hertfordshire, England in 1953, not far from the village in which he had been born seventy-nine years earlier.

The second recipient of two VCs was Noel Godfrey Chavasse, who earned both his VCs in less than a year during the First World War. Captain Chavasse, like Martin-Leake, was a doctor in the Royal Army Medical Corps, and was attached to the 1/10th Battalion, The King's (Liverpool) Regiment. The first act that earned him the medal occurred on August 9, 1916, at Guillemont, France. During an attack, he attended to and searched for the wounded all day under heavy fire. He continued his efforts into the next day and night, saving the lives of at least twenty men, and becoming wounded himself in the process. His bar to the VC covered the period from July 31 to August 2, 1917, while he served at Wieltje, Belgium. Although severely wounded, he stayed at his post to search for those in need of medical attention. He again saved the lives of many who would otherwise have died. However, two days later, Chavasse succumbed to his own wounds, three months short of his thirty-third birthday.

The third and final recipient of the VC and bar was Charles Hazlitt Upham, who earned his medals during the Second World War—the only combat soldier to be distinguished by the double award. As a second lieutenant in the 20th Battalion, 2nd New Zealand Expeditionary Force (The Canterbury Regiment), he was serving on Crete during the German invasion of the Mediterranean island. Between May 22 and 30, 1941, Upham displayed outstanding leadership and courage in close-quarter fighting, despite being wounded three times and suffering from a severe attack of dysentery. He carried a wounded man to safety and successfully beat off an enemy attack, killing twenty-two Germans in the process.

Just over a year later, Upham was a captain serving in the Western Desert. During July 14–15, 1942, although wounded twice, he led his company in a determined attack at El Ruweisat Ridge and captured his objective after fierce fighting, personally destroying a tank and several guns and vehicles with hand grenades. Upham was subsequently captured by the Germans and sent to recover in an Italian hospital, where he began a private war with his captors. As a result, he was transferred to Colditz Castle, the German prison for repeat escapees and other "dangerous" prisoners. Upham died in his hometown, Christchurch, New Zealand, on November 22, 1994, at eighty-six years of age.

Only eight men under eighteen have received the VC. The youngest recipients of the award were both fifteen years and three months old. Hospital Apprentice Arthur Fitzgibbon of the Indian Medical Establishment earned the VC at the Taku Forts in China on August 21, 1860, while Drummer Thomas Flinn gained his at Cawnpore (now Kanpur), India on November 28, 1857. The youngest Canadian was Private Thomas Ricketts of the Royal Newfoundland Regiment, whose heroism is detailed in Chapter 8. Ricketts was seventeen and a half years old when his actions earned him the Empire's highest medal for valour.

The oldest person ever to receive the VC was Lieutenant William Raynor of the Bengal Veteran Establishment. He earned his award at Delhi during the Indian Mutiny on May 11, 1857, when he was sixty-one years and ten months old. Raynor was one of only nine individuals over fifty to receive the medal. The oldest Canadian was Frederick Peters from Prince Edward Island, who was fifty-three when he earned his VC while serving in the Royal Navy. His story is told in Chapter 9. Coincidentally, both the youngest and oldest Canadian VC recipients were from Atlantic Canada.

In a number of cases, several Victoria Crosses have been earned within the same family. The list includes six sets of uncles and nephews (including one great uncle and nephew), four sets each of brothers and cousins, three sets each of fathers and sons and brothers-in-law, as well as a father-in-law/son-in-law combination. To complicate matters, some of these individuals are doubly related. For example, a VC recipient was the son of one awardee and the nephew of another, the latter two individuals being brothers. In another instance, a VC recipient was the uncle and the brother-in-law of two other recipients. Finally, two VCs were achieved by men for saving the lives of their brothers. In one case, the brother who was rescued had previously earned the VC himself.

Although there are no Canadian awardees among these family related Victoria Cross recipients, there is a unique relationship shared by three Canadians who earned the VC during the First World War. Leo Clarke, Fred Hall and Robert Shankland all lived on the same road in Winnipeg—Pine Street. In 1925, it was renamed Valour Road in their honour, a fact commemorated by a bronze plaque mounted on an ornamental lamp at the street's intersection with Portage Avenue.

Of the three, only Lieutenant Shankland, who earned his VC in October 1917 at Passchendaele in Belgium, survived the war. As an NCO before being commissioned, he had won the Distinguished Conduct Medal (DCM) and later served as a lieutenant-colonel during the Second World War at Canadian Military Headquarters in London, England. He passed away in 1968. Acting Corporal Clarke died of injuries received from an artillery explosion six weeks after the act that earned him the VC in September 1916, near Pozières, France. Company Sergeant-Major Hall was killed at the Second Battle of Ypres in Belgium in April 1915, during the deed that gained him the VC: rescuing a wounded soldier.

There have been fourteen VCs awarded to non-British Empire/Commonwealth soldiers—five Americans, three Danes and two Germans, plus a Belgian, a Swede, a Swiss and a Ukrainian. As might be expected, the majority of these "foreigners" were serving in colonial forces at the time, with only five in British units. Of the remaining nine, six served in the Canadian Expeditionary Force (including all but one of the Americans), two in the South African Forces and one in the Australian Army.

The six non-British subjects who served in the Canadian Army all received their VCs during the First World War. The presence of four Americans in this group testifies to the desire of many United States citizens to fight in that war before their country's entry in 1917. Often, the easiest way to do so was to slip across the border and join the CEF. American recruitment was even actively encouraged by Canada, with an "American Legion" of five battalions formed. Eventually over thirty-five thousand Americans served in the CEF, although none of the American Legion battalions made it to the front before being broken up for reinforcements.

THE ADJUTANT OF PRINCESS PATRICIA'S CANADIAN LIGHT INFANTRY CONGRATULATES SERGEANT GEORGE HARRY MULLIN ON BEING AWARDED THE VICTORIA CROSS. MULLIN WAS ONE OF FOUR AMERICANS SERVING IN THE CANADIAN EXPEDITIONARY FORCE DURING THE FIRST WORLD WAR TO EARN THE VICTORIA CROSS.

Sergeant George Harry Mullin came from Portland, Oregon, and settled with his family in Saskatchewan when he was two years old. He was serving with the Princess Patricia's Canadian Light Infantry (PPCLI) on October 30, 1917, at Passchendaele, when he single-handedly captured a German pillbox fortification that had been causing numerous casualties and holding up an attack. His clothes riddled with bullet holes, he stormed the stronghold, killing or capturing its occupants, in the process saving the day and the lives of many of his comrades. Mullin had earned the Military Medal (MM) earlier in the year, as a corporal at Vimy Ridge. In addition to the VC, his bravery at Passchendaele also resulted in his promotion to lieutenant. After the First World War, he served as a major in the Assiniboia Regiment and in the Veteran's Guard during the Second World War. Later, he was sergeant-at-arms in the Provincial Legislature of Saskatchewan for many years. Mullin died in 1963, when he was seventy-one years old.

Another American to win the VC was also a sergeant and an immigrant to Saskatchewan. Raphael Louis Zengel (incidentally, last in alphabetical order of all VC recipients) moved from Faribault, Minnesota, with his widowed mother to a homestead in that prairie province at an early age. On August 9, 1918, near Warvilliers, France, he was leading his platoon of the 5th Battalion (North Saskatchewan Regiment) in an advance when they came under enemy machine-gun fire that mowed down troops on his left flank. Zengel immediately charged ahead of his men and overran the gun, killing or dispersing its crew. Later that same day he was rendered temporarily unconscious by shellfire, but quickly recovered and continued to direct harassing fire onto the enemy. After the war ended, he lived in Alberta and British Columbia. Zengel re-enlisted during the Second World War, attaining the rank of regimental sergeant-major. He passed away at eighty-two in 1977.

The last two "American-Canadians" to earn the VC returned to the United States after the war. William Henry Metcalf was born in Waite Township, Maine, in 1894. He crossed into New Brunswick and joined the CEF, ending up in France as a lance corporal. On the morning of September 2, 1918, during an attack near Arras, he earned the VC for an exceptional display of courage in the face of concentrated enemy machine-gun fire. After the war, he returned to Maine, but continued to serve in the New Brunswick militia for several years. Because of this Atlantic Canadian connection, further details of Metcalf's life are recounted in Chapter 6.

CORPORAL FILIP KONOWAL (RIGHT) STANDS OUTSIDE BUCKINGHAM PALACE BEFORE RECEIVING HIS VICTORIA CROSS FROM KING GEORGE V. KONOWAL IS THE ONLY UKRANIAN RECIPIENT OF THE VICTORIA CROSS.

Bellenden Seymour Hutcheson earned his VC on the same day and in the same battle as Bill Metcalf. He was a doctor from Mount Carmel, Illinois, and joined the Canadian Army Medical Corps in 1915. In France, he became Medical Officer (MO) for the 75th Battalion (Toronto Scottish) as a captain. Two months before he gained the VC, he won the Military Cross (MC) for attending to nearly one hundred soldiers under heavy fire. He acted in the same way in the attack on the Drocourt-Quéant Line, remaining on the battlefield until he attended to every wounded man in his unit. He returned to Illinois when the war ended and married a Nova Scotian, Frances Young. When King George VI and Queen Elizabeth visited the United States in 1939, they invited Hutcheson to accompany them to Arlington National Cemetery and lay a wreath on the Tomb of the Unknown Soldier. He died in 1954 after a lengthy illness.

The remaining two non-British subjects who earned VCs while serving in the CEF came from the Ukraine (then part of Russia) and Denmark. Filip Konowal was born in the Ukrainian village of Kudkiv in 1886 and served as a bayonet instructor for five years in the Russian Army before he immigrated to Canada in 1913, and worked as a lumberjack near Ottawa. In July 1915, he joined the army and ended up in the 47th Battalion (British Columbia Regiment) overseas. During the period of August 22–24, 1917, Acting Corporal Konowal was commanding a section that had the difficult task of mopping up remaining German positions after the successful Canadian assault on Hill 70, near Lens, in France. Under his able direction, all resistance was overcome, with Konowal personally dispatching sixteen Germans, many of them by bayonet. Shortly afterwards, he was severely wounded in the head by a German sniper and later was evacuated to England. After returning to Canada in 1918, Konowal subsequently took part in the Canadian Siberian Expeditionary Force as a sergeant, coming home again in 1919.

On civvy street, Konowal had trouble adjusting to life after the war, also suffering from medical problems that may have been a result of his wounds. In July 1919, he killed a man in a fight who had punched and kicked a fellow veteran. He was arrested, tried and eventually sent to a mental institution in Montreal, where his VC was taken away from him. On his release in 1928, he drifted aimlessly around Ottawa. Eventually, another veteran took pity on him and brought him to see the sergeant-at-arms of the House of Commons, fellow VC winner Milton F. Gregg from New Brunswick, whose story is told in Chapter 7.

The Great Depression was on, and the best Gregg could do for Konowal was to get him a job scrubbing floors in the Hall of Fame on Parliament Hill. When Prime Minister Mackenzie King saw this, he had Konowal's VC returned to him and reassigned him to his own office, Room 16, today the Speaker's Reception Room. In 1956, when a reporter from the *Ottawa Citizen* asked him about his job, Konowal replied, "I mopped up overseas with a rifle, and here I must mop up with a mop." He also explained what really happened when he earned his VC: "I was so fed up standing in the trench with water to my waist that I said the hell with it and started after the German army. My Captain tried to shoot me because he figured I was deserting." Konowal worked in Room 16 until his death in 1959, a few months short of his seventy-second birthday. His VC was eventually acquired by the Canadian War Museum, the first one to be obtained by purchase.

Thomas Dinesen was born in Denmark and tried to enlist in the British, French and American armies, all of whom turned him down. In New York City, he walked into the recruiting office of the Royal Highlanders of Canada (The Black Watch), who accepted him as a private and sent him overseas with the 42nd Battalion. On August 12, 1918, at Parvillers, France, during the Battle of Amiens, he displayed conspicuous bravery during ten hours of hand-to-hand fighting that resulted in the capture of over a kilometre and a half of strongly defended enemy trenches. Dinesen charged the enemy lines alone, five times in succession, putting machine guns out of action, accounting for twelve enemy dead and inspiring his comrades.

Dinesen's deeds garnered him not only the VC but also the French *Croix de Guerre* and the Danish Order of Dennebrog. After the war, he farmed in Kenya before returning to Denmark, where he continued farming and wrote a number of books. In this he followed in the footsteps of his more famous sister, Karen Christence Dinesen, who—under the pseudonym Isak Dinesen—is best known as the author of *Out of Africa*, which recorded her experiences running a Kenyan coffee plantation and hunting big game with her husband. In 1985, her memoir was adapted into a film starring Meryl Streep (as Karen Christence Dinesen) and Robert Redford. Thomas Dinesen died in 1974 when he was eighty-five.

There is one other foreign Victoria Cross "recipient" who deserves mention. On November 11, 1921, on behalf of King George V, Admiral of the Fleet Lord Beatty bestowed the VC on the American Unknown Warrior who is buried at Arlington National Cemetery. The medal is inscribed "The

Unknown Warrior of the United States of America" and is dated October 28, 1921. It was the only time a VC was not gazetted by an entry in the *London Gazette*. In reciprocation, the US Government presented its highest award, the Medal of Honor, to the British Unknown Warrior buried in Westminster Abbey.

It was not until the Second World War that members of the Royal Canadian Navy (RCN) and Royal Canadian Air Force (RCAF) first received VCs. Although two Canadian sailors and three airmen had earned the medal previously, they were in Imperial service—all but one, William Hall, during the First World War. During the Second World War, another Canadian sailor and another airman earned VCs while serving in the RN and RAF respectively.

In addition to the Victoria Cross earned by a member of the RCN and the two medals that went to RCAF recipients, eleven Canadians serving in the army earned VCs during the Second World War, all but one of them in the Canadian Army. With a total of sixteen Canadian VCs for that conflict, half were awarded posthumously. Of the eleven army VCs, one was earned at Hong Kong, two at Dieppe, three in

COMPANY SERGEANT-MAJOR JOHN ROBERT OSBORN WAS THE FIRST CANADIAN TO EARN THE VICTORIA CROSS DURING THE SECOND WORLD WAR. OSBORN WAS A MEMBER OF THE WINNIPEG GRENADIERS, PART OF THE ILL-FATED C FORCE, SENT BY THE CANADIAN GOVERNMENT TO ASSIST IN THE DEFENCE OF HONG KONG DAYS BEFORE IT FELL. DURING THE JAPANESE ATTACK, HE WAS KILLED INSTANTLY WHEN THREW HIMSELF ON A GRENADE TO SAVE HIS MEN, YELLING, "DUCK, LADS!" HE HAS NO KNOWN GRAVE.

Italy and four in northwest Europe, with one more received by a Canadian serving in the British Army in Burma (now Myanmar). Thirteen of the sixteen were members of the Canadian armed forces, although one was attached to a British unit. Three had close associations with Atlantic Canada, and their stories are told in Chapters 9 and 10.

The first Canadian VC of the Second World War went to Company Sergeant-Major John Osborn of the Winnipeg Grenadiers. On December 19, 1941, during the Japanese attack on Hong Kong, Osborn selflessly threw himself on an enemy grenade to save his comrades, and was killed instantly. Although Osborn's action resulted in the first Canadian VC of the war, it was the last one to be known and the second last to be gazetted, on April 2, 1946, because the surviving witnesses were captured and imprisoned by the Japanese until the end of the war. Osborn's VC was finally presented to his widow in 1956 by Queen Elizabeth and is now held by the Canadian War Museum. The last VC of the Second World War, and the last Canadian VC awarded to date, was to Lieutenant Robert Hampton Gray of the Royal Canadian Naval Volunteer Reserve, whose story is told in Chapter 10.

Some 1,178 VCs, or eighty-seven percent of the total number awarded, were awarded for five wars: 111 during the Crimean War, 182 during the Indian Mutiny, 78 during the Boer War, 626 for the First World War and 181 for the Second World War. The Korean War resulted in only four VCs, while the British campaign to retake the Falkland Islands from Argentina in 1982 saw two VCs awarded, both posthumously. Interestingly, the Vietnam War marked the award of four VCs to Australians—perhaps the only war in which VCs were earned that did not have British participation. There were no VCs awarded for the First Gulf War of 1990–91, but the Second Gulf War resulted in the first award of a VC to a living recipient in forty years. The remaining 166 VCs earned outside of these nine conflicts were for Britain's many small wars and campaigns, most of them waged during Queen Victoria's long reign. Table 1 shows the various conflicts in which Canada's VC recipients earned their medals, broken down further by live or posthumous awards.

War/Campaign	Live Award	Posthumous Award	Total
Crimean War	1	0	1
Indian Mutiny	2	0	2
Adaman Campaign	1	0	1
Sudan Campaign	1	0	1
Boer War	5	0	5
World War I	44	28	72
World War II	8	8	16
Total	62	36	98

Table 1. Live and posthumous awards of Canadian VCs by war/campaign.

As might be expected, individuals serving in the British Forces have obtained the most VCs, some 989. Included in this total are other nationalities, as many "colonials" joined the British Forces, especially before their countries gained independence and created their own armed forces. The next largest number were earned by soldiers serving in the Indian Army (136), followed by those in the armed forces of Australia (91), Canada (81), South Africa (28) and New Zealand (22), and one each for the Fijian Army, King's African Rifles and the American Unknown Warrior, plus five civilians.

Depending on the particular reference consulted, the number of "Canadian" Victoria Crosses varies. Most authorities count ninety-four, and for many years that has been the standard number quoted, used by the Department of Veterans' Affairs, the Department of National Defence and the Royal Canadian Legion. In the past fifty years, four major books have been written on Canada's VC winners: George Machum's *Canada's VCs*, published on the occasion of the VC's centenary in 1956, lists ninety-four recipients; John Swettenham's 1973 *Valiant Men*, profiles only ninety-three; John Blatherwick in his 1991 work, *1,000 Brave Canadians*, also counts ninety-four; while Arthur Bishop (son of the famous First World War ace and VC winner Billy Bishop), who outlines the peacetime and wartime careers of our VC recipients in *Our Bravest and Our Best*, considers there to be ninety-five.

Of course, the main criterion for deciding if a VC recipient is Canadian is whether the awardee was born in Canada or in a territory that later became a part of Canada. If not born in Canada, then other criteria are: whether the individual served in the Canadian Forces when the VC was awarded and/or was a resident of Canada at the outbreak of the war.

By strict adherence to these criteria, the number of Canadian VC recipients rises to ninety-eight. The difficulty with deciding the nationality of a VC recipient is that most authorities disregard their own criteria. For example, some individuals who were born in Canada are overlooked by many references or, if they are mentioned, they are listed as "associated" with Canada. The list of ninety-four recipients normally credited as being Canadian does not include four men born in Canada of British (or mixed British-Canadian) parentage, who subsequently served in the British Forces.

Lieutenant the Honourable Raymond Harvey Lodge Joseph de Montmorency, born in Montreal in 1867, earned his VC with the 21st

CAPTAIN JOHN ALEXANDER SINTON EARNED HIS VICTORIA CROSS IN MESAPOTAMIA (MODERN IRAQ) FOR ATTENDING TO THE WOUNDED EVEN THOUGH HE HAD BEEN SHOT THREE TIMES.

Lancers (Empress of India's) during a cavalry charge at Khartoum in the Sudan Campaign of 1898 and was later killed in action during the Boer War in 1900. Coincidentally, the 21st Lancers are known today as the Queen's Royal Lancers and are allied to a Canadian regiment, Lord Strathcona's Horse (Royal Canadians), formed to fight in the very war that resulted in de Montmorency's death.

William Henry Snyder Nickerson, born in Dorchester, New Brunswick, in 1875, earned his VC as a lieutenant in the Royal Army Medical Corps, while attached as MO to a mounted infantry battalion during the Boer War in 1900. He tended to a wounded man under fire and later rose to the rank of major-general. Because he was born in Atlantic Canada, further details of Nickerson's life and career are contained in Chapter 2.

John Alexander Sinton, born in British Columbia in 1884, also earned his VC as an MO, while serving in Mesopotamia (modern Iraq) in 1916. Sinton joined the Indian Medical Service and, after being stationed on the North-West Frontier of India, was sent to Mesopotamia with an Indian cavalry regiment. Despite being shot through both arms and his side during an action, he refused to be evacuated and continued to attend to the wounded under very heavy fire. He had displayed similar bravery on three previous occasions. Sinton retired from the army in 1921 as a major, but re-enlisted during the Second World War. He retired again in 1945, as a brigadier, after service with the East African Forces, Middle East Forces and the War Office. Sinton died in 1956, at seventy-one years of age.

Private Robert Edward Cruickshank, born in Winnipeg in 1888, also earned his VC during the First World War in the Middle East. He was serving with the 2/4th Battalion (City of London) in Palestine in 1918, after previously fighting on the Western Front, where he had been wounded. During a vicious little action in the desert, most of Cruickshank's platoon, including the platoon commander and sergeant, were either killed or wounded, when the Manitoban volunteered to go back for reinforcements. He was wounded three times while gallantly attempting to do so, and was forced to lie all day out in the open under enemy fire, until he could be evacuated under cover of darkness. After the war he returned to civvy street, passing away in 1961 at seventy-three years of age.

For some reason, Machum's *Canada's VCs* does not list these four men as even associated with Canada, although they were all born here. He does list eight other non-Canadians however, as having lived (or, in 1956, when the book was published, still living) in Canada. Swettenham's list of ninety-three further omits Lieutenant Thomas Orde Lawder Wilkinson, relegating him to the status of a VC recipient associated with Canada, along with a dozen others, including Nickerson and Cruikshank. Blatherwick mentions all four as having Canadian connections, under the heading "Persons born in Canada but who did not grow up in Canada," but gives only the barest details of their lives. Besides these four and Private Timothy O'Hea, he also mentions ten others as having some form of association with Canada. Bishop gets to ninety-five by counting Nickerson and Cruickshank, although, confusingly, he does not include Wilkinson. He lists Canada's "VC Associates" as O'Hea and fifteen others, whom he lumps together incorrectly as having "won the medal as non-Canadians, but later made the Dominion their home." (In fact, this description only applies to twelve of his fifteen associates.) Bishop also names two other associated VC recipients who are not in any of the other authors' lists.

Table 2 shows the birthplaces of Canada's VC recipients, while Table 3 documents the country, service and, in the case of the army awardees, branch or corps in which they served.

Canada – Total 56

NF	NS	NB	PE	QC	ON	MB	SK	AB	BC
2	4	4	1	10	20	7	1	1	6

British Isles – Total 35

Eng	Sct	Ire
20	9	6

Other – Total 7

US	Den	Ukr	Ind
4	1	1	1

Total 98

Table 2. Birthplace of Canadian VC recipients.

	ARMY			AIR FORCE		NAVY	
	Canada	Britain	India	Canada	Britain	Canada	Britain
Infantry	65	5					
Armour	8	2					
Medical	2	3	1	2	4	1	3
Engineer	1						
Chaplain	1						
National Subtotal	77	10	1	2	4	1	3
Service Subtotal		88			6		4

Total   98

Table 3. Canadian VC recipients by country, service and army branch.

By mid-2005, there were only thirteen living recipients of the VC. The majority, nine, are from the Second World War, with one each from the Korean War, the Malaysia-Indonesia Confrontation, the Vietnam War and the Second Gulf War. Canada's last surviving VC recipient, Ernest Alvia "Smoky" Smith, died on August 3, 2005. Smith earned his VC during the Italian Campaign, as a private in the Seaforth Highlanders of Canada. On the night of October 21–22, 1944, 1st Canadian Corps attempted to cross the raging Savio River in northern Italy during a torrential downpour. The Seaforths had established a small bridgehead, when three German tanks, two self-propelled guns and about thirty infantrymen attacked. Smith led his small two-man, tank-hunting team, equipped with PIATs (Projector, Infantry, Anti-Tank), to a shallow ditch. He fired one PIAT, disabling a tank, and then took on ten accompanying infantrymen with his tommy gun at point-blank range. He killed four; the rest scattered. He forced a second tank and other enemy soldiers to withdraw before helping one of his men, wounded in the encounter, to cover and medical aid. Smith returned to his post to wait for further attacks, but none came, as the enemy was apparently unwilling to tackle this one-man army.

Fifty-seven awardees, or just over half of Canada's VC recipients, are buried in Canada. Ontario has the most with twenty-six, followed by British Columbia with sixteen. Quebec has six, Alberta four and New Brunswick two. Manitoba, Newfoundland, Nova Scotia and Saskatchewan all have one VC grave. Toronto is the city with the most VC burials, with twelve, followed by Vancouver with ten. Vancouver's Mountain View Cemetery and Crematorium is the cemetery with the most VC remains, containing five burials and two cremations.

On May 1, 1972, the Canadian Government created a new system of bravery awards—the Cross of Valour (CV), Star of Courage (SC) and Medal of Bravery (MB)—with the first awards being made on July 20 of that year. A later decision on the adoption of this system upset literally millions of Canadians: the Victoria Cross and other British medals would no longer be considered a part of the Canadian honours system and would be replaced by the new awards. Led by the Royal Canadian Legion, a concerted campaign was launched to convince the politicians of the error of their ways in dropping the VC.

Ultimately, the fight was successful and, in 1993, the government announced the VC would remain as the highest gallantry award for Canadians, but with a difference. Although it still requires royal assent from the sovereign to be awarded, in its "Canadianized" version the VC's inscription "For Valour" has been amended to the Latin "*Pro Valore*," in line with the country's official bilingualism policy. The VC can only be awarded for "the most conspicuous bravery, a daring or pre-eminent act of valour or self-sacrifice or extreme devotion to duty in the presence of the enemy." To date, no Canadianized VC has been awarded.

The Cross of Valour, Star of Courage and Medal of Bravery have been retained in the Canadian honours system, with both civilians and members of the military eligible for them. They are not administered by the Canadian Forces, but by the Chancery at Rideau Hall. As of mid-2005, nineteen CVs, as well 398 SCs and 2,177 MBs have been awarded, a number of them posthumously.

The Canadian Forces subsequently instituted two additional gallantry awards in 1993: the Star of Military Valour (SMV) and the Medal of Military Valour (MMV). The SMV can be awarded for "distinguished and valiant service in the presence of the enemy," while the MMV can be awarded for "an act of valour or devotion to duty in the presence of the enemy." Roughly, this would make the SMV the equivalent of the Distinguished Service Order (for officers) and the Distinguished Conduct Medal (for other ranks), when these were awarded for gallantry. The MMV would then be the equivalent of the Military Cross (for officers and warrant officers) and the Military Medal (for other ranks). Both medals bear the same inscription as the VC, "*Pro Valore*." All three Canadian gallantry medals can also be awarded to "a member of an allied armed force that is serving with or in conjunction with the Canadian Forces." As with the Victoria Cross, no awards of the Star of Military Valour or the Medal of Military Valour have taken place as of mid-2005.

On October 21, 2004, to honour the 150th anniversary of the Victoria Cross, as well as its first Canadian recipient, Lieutenant Alexander Dunn, Canada Post issued a set of two forty-nine-cent postage stamps. One stamp is a photograph of an original VC, part of the Canadian War Museum's twenty-six-medal collection. The other is an illustration of the Canadian version, as approved by the queen and bearing her signature. As no "Canadian" VC has yet been created—because none have been awarded—a drawing had to suffice. The stamps were issued in a unique pane of sixteen stamps, which surrounds a centre panel inscribed with the names of the most commonly accepted ninety-four Canadian winners. The names are arranged alphabetically, by war. The stamp unveiling in Ottawa also coincided with the sixtieth anniversary of the action in which Canada's last living VC recipient, Smoky Smith, earned his medal during the Second World War. Smith, along with forty-four fellow veterans of that war, attended the unveiling ceremony at National Defence Headquarters.

The stories that follow recount the courageous deeds of twenty-one Victoria Cross heroes, all of whom were either born in or connected with Atlantic Canada in some way.

"I WILL TAKE THE CHANCE, SIR"

ASSISTANT SURGEON VALENTINE MUNBEE MCMASTER
78th Regiment of Foot, British Army
Lucknow, India, September 25, 1857

ABLE SEAMAN WILLIAM NEILSON HALL
HMS *Shannon* Naval Brigade, Royal Navy
Lucknow, India, November 16, 1857

"I will take the chance, sir." With these words to Captain William Peel, Able Seaman William Hall stepped forward to replace a wounded gunner during the Relief of Lucknow, the most famous battle of the Indian Mutiny of 1857. In doing so, he entered the history books as the first black man—plus the first Nova Scotian and the first Canadian sailor—to earn the Victoria Cross.

In March 1857, Hall's ship, HMS *Shannon*, sailed for the Far East under Captain Peel, carrying British troops to China. The Earl of Elgin, former governor general of British North America (BNA) from 1847 to 1854, also sailed aboard *Shannon*, en route to Peking (now Beijing) to serve as special commissioner to the Chinese government. While docked in Singapore on June 11, news reached *Shannon* of the mutiny of numerous sepoys, or native troops, in India. A number of British regiments immediately diverted to India, but *Shannon* continued to its original destination.

After the Earl of Elgin disembarked at Hong Kong, the navy dispatched *Shannon* to India. Arriving at Calcutta in August, Captain Peel received orders to send as many men and guns as possible overland to the besieged cities of Cawnpore and Lucknow. He quickly formed a Naval Brigade, a term denoting an armed naval force of any size working on land, either alone or in conjunction with the army. It contained 475 of his officers, sailors and marines, as well as six 68-pounder guns, eight 24-pounder howitzers, eight rocket tubes, two 8-inch howitzers and a pair of small field-pieces. On August 18, the Naval Brigade and its guns departed on a two-week journey, travelling thirteen hundred kilometres up the Ganges River to Allahabad, from which point the troops would begin their long trek overland.

By the mid-nineteenth century, the British firmly believed they had been chosen to spread the benefits of Western culture to the "uncivilized" parts of the world, whether these areas wanted them or not. Throughout Queen Victoria's long reign, a war was always being fought somewhere to overcome native opposition to British rule or suzerainty. Such colonial conflicts were popular with the British public, and the Indian Mutiny quickly became the most famous of all, assuming Homeric dimensions as the "thin red line" of Christian manhood battled the so-called heathen races. Today there is a debate among some historians over whether the mutiny was a simple mutiny or a popular uprising against British rule. Regardless of how one interprets the conflict, it was undeniably a horrific one, characterized by brutality and atrocities on both sides.

The immediate cause of the mutiny was a rumour circulating among the sepoys during the winter of 1856–57. According to the rumour, the British had greased the paper cartridges for the new Enfield rifles issued to Indian soldiers with a combination of pork and beef fat—the former unclean to Muslims and the latter holy to Hindus. There was some truth to the rumour. From sheer stupidity on the part of the War Office in London, some cartridges greased in this way had been sent to India, but had not been issued to the sepoys. Nevertheless, many Indians who heard the rumour took it as further evidence that the British were trying to impose Christianity, and some native regiments refused to handle the cartridges. When such units were punished with disbandment, some under humiliating conditions, other regiments mutinied. From there, the rebellion spread.

The British forces stationed in India at that time consisted mainly of the armed forces of the British East India Company, which effectively ruled the subcontinent from the eighteenth century until 1858. The officers in these armies were British, with a few British NCOs; most of the troops were Indians organized in numbered regiments and trained in British methods. In addition, there were also a few regiments of British infantry in India—known as Queen's regiments—on loan from the Crown to the East India Company. There was thus a large discrepancy between the numbers of British and native troops on the subcontinent, some 40,000 compared to 311,000, with the majority of the British spread thinly about. As a result, when word of the mutiny, which began at Meerut on May 10, became known, the British withdrew into hastily fortified compounds, such as Cawnpore and Lucknow, to await the next move by the mutineers.

At Cawnpore—an important military base on the Ganges River almost twelve hundred kilometres from Calcutta—about twelve hundred British and loyal native soldiers under Major-General Sir Hugh Wheeler defended the garrison, behind hastily erected and totally inadequate entrenchments, against three thousand rebels. This "stronghold" included about four hundred noncombatants, mostly English women and children. After holding out against numerous assaults and continuous cannon bombardment for three weeks, for the sake of the women and children Wheeler had no choice but to surrender to Nana Sahib, the mutiny's local leader, who solemnly promised safe conduct for the garrison to Allahabad, by river-boat.

On the morning of June 27, as British soldiers embarked in boats at the Ganges, Nana's men suddenly started firing grapeshot, an anti-personnel round, at point-blank range, joined immediately by musket fire. The thatched roofs of some of the boats caught fire from this fusillade, and many of the sick, wounded and helpless women and children burned to death. Some of the soldiers and noncombatants jumped into the water to escape, but the mutineers killed them. A few made it to shore, where Nana issued orders to kill the men and take the women and children back to Cawnpore. His men took the surviving 125 women and children prisoner and humiliated them in every way possible. Only one boat managed to escape; it carried four men to safety.

In early July, a relief column under Brigadier-General Sir Henry Havelock fought its way towards Cawnpore, covering two hundred kilometres in nine days in the sweltering heat of the Indian summer. On July 16, Havelock's thirteen hundred British and over seven thousand Sikhs assaulted and completely routed thirteen thousand mutineers from their entrenched positions about three kilometres from Cawnpore. The rebels evacuated Cawnpore that night, as the British camped outside the walls.

The next day the rescuers entered the city, but too late. The rebel leader had ordered the slaughter of all prisoners two days previous. In carrying out this heinous act, a group of rebels—including the town butchers, pressed into service by the mutineers—used every weapon available to them, from bayonets and knives to axes and clubs. They chopped off arms, legs, breasts and heads, beat or trampled women to death, tossed children into the air and impaled them on bayonets. The spectacle greeting Havelock's men horrified even the most battle-hardened. Two bloodstained huts contained shreds of women's clothing and other small personal items. One hut contained a row of women's shoes and, on the other side of the room, a row of children's shoes with their tiny owner's bloody feet still inside them, neatly lining the wall. Blood sloshed about freely in another room, while bits and pieces of bodies filled a nearby well.

When news of this slaughter reached Britain, it sent a shiver of revulsion through the nation. Victorian Britain placed women and children on a pedestal, and it was widely believed that they were entitled to special protection. All possible means were deemed appropriate to avenge the women and children massacred at Cawnpore, even if it meant committing similar atrocities against the Indians. The British wasted no time in taking terrible reprisals against anyone suspected of being involved in the butchery. They erected a gallows and several soldiers volunteered to act as hangmen, a task for which volunteers were ordinarily scarce. Before being hanged, the soldiers forced each mutineer to lick up a square foot of blood. Leaving a small force at Cawnpore, General Havelock marched off to relieve Lucknow, eighty-five kilometres to the northeast. However, he was forced to return to Cawnpore after three engagements with the mutineers.

At Lucknow, a twenty-five-kilometre square city of some half million people located on the Gumti River, Sir Henry Lawrence, the newly arrived District Chief Commissioner, commanded the garrison. Aware of sepoy unrest and learning of mutinies elsewhere, Lawrence had ordered his five hundred noncombatants into a compound on May 25 and started stockpiling supplies. The British were confined to the Lucknow Residency complex, a small fifteen-hectare collection of buildings. Inside this diamond-shaped compound, seventeen hundred British soldiers and civilians, including seven hundred loyal natives, manned a hastily erected defensive perimeter of some eighteen hundred metres—too long to be properly defended, but not large enough to comfortably hold the soldiers plus the noncombatant women and children. The Siege of Lucknow captured the imagination of the British public and soon took on mythic proportions, becoming perhaps the most famous episode in all of Britain's many nineteenth-century wars.

On July 2, a month after the siege commenced, an 8-inch shell seriously wounded Lawrence in the thigh, too high to amputate. Two days later he died. Command of the besieged residency fell to Lieutenant-Colonel John Inglis, forty-three, commanding the 32nd Regiment of Foot, the only British battalion in the garrison. His presence at Lucknow was yet another Nova Scotia connection. Inglis was born in 1814 in a house still standing on Barrington Street in Halifax, the grandson and son of the first and third Anglican bishops of eastern BNA. He attended King's College in Windsor, founded by his grandfather, and joined the 32nd Regiment as an ensign in 1832. He served in Canada and saw action in India, becoming commanding officer in 1855.

Six years before the Indian Mutiny, Inglis married seventeen-year-old Julia Thesiger who, like many British officers' wives at the time, accompanied her husband to India with their three children. Julia kept a detailed journal throughout the siege, lost when she was shipwrecked on her homeward journey. She salvaged her diary however, and in 1892 wrote a popular memoir based on it, entitled *The Siege of Lucknow: A Diary*. Inglis, holding the local rank of brigadier-general, was not a particularly inspiring commander, but his subordinates served him well and he listened to their advice. Within the compound, the defenders' numbers dropped daily from intense shelling, incessant musket fire, snipers, suicides by the despondent and the ravages of diseases. Julia herself was recovering from smallpox.

As the heat of the summer began to rise and rations ran short, non-stop fire from point-blank range reduced the walls of the small garrison to crumpled ruins. The pungent odours of death and excrement soon filled the air. Rats and mice ran over the wounded and noncombatants sheltering in the cellars. Then, at mid-morning on July 20, the mutineers launched their first attack. By mid-afternoon, the defenders had successfully repulsed it, at a cost of hundreds of sepoy casualties to only a handful of British ones. As the unceasing attacks and bombardment continued through the summer and into the fall, the heavy physical and mental toll they took on Inglis began to show. He experienced dizziness and headaches, while his hair turned prematurely grey.

The garrison expected help daily from Havelock's column, but it had returned to Cawnpore to wait for reinforcements, due to losses from enemy action and cholera. Then, Major-General Sir James Outram arrived with additional soldiers, bringing Havelock's force to about thirty-two hundred men, seventy-five percent of them British infantry. This reinforced column

THE SIEGE AND RELIEF OF LUCKNOW WAS THE MOST FAMOUS INCIDENT IN THE INDIAN MUTINY. THE SIEGE HAD AN AMAZING NUMBER OF NOVA SCOTIA CONNECTIONS: THE OFFICER DEFENDING THE GARRISON WAS FROM THE PROVINCE; THE GENERAL COMMAND-ING THE RELIEF FORCE HAD BEEN THE COLONY'S LIEUTENANT-GOVERNOR; A NOVA SCOTIAN FROM A SHIP NAMED AFTER A FAMOUS ONE THAT SERVED IN THE PROVINCE DURING THE WAR OF 1812 EARNED THE VICTORIA CROSS THERE, ALONG WITH AN OFFI-CER WHO WOULD LATER SERVE IN HALIFAX. THE DEFENDERS OF LUCKNOW ARE SHOWN UNDER FIRE FROM CLOSE-RANGE REBEL ARTILLERY.

set off on September 18, skirmishing and fighting the whole way. At Lucknow, the rebels redoubled their efforts to capture the residency before relief arrived. Finally, on September 24, the defenders could hear the sound of distant guns; the column had reached the outskirts of Lucknow where it halted for twenty-four hours before fighting its way through the final five kilometres to the shambles of the residency. The sorely tried defenders were overjoyed. Their fighting strength had been reduced by nearly fifty percent over the past eighty-seven days. Salvation had finally arrived.

The 78th Regiment of Foot, a British highland battalion hurriedly sent to India when the mutiny broke out, accompanied Havelock's force. Joseph Jee served as the unit's surgeon, with Valentine Munbee McMaster, who would later serve in Halifax with the 78th, as his assistant surgeon. McMaster actually carried the Queen's Colour at one point, when the colour party had been shot, and helped lead an attack during the final stages of the advance towards the besieged British. After three hours of des-

ASSISTANT SURGEON VALENTINE MUMBEE MCMASTER EARNED HIS VICTORIA CROSS DURING THE INDIAN MUTINY UNDER THE RARELY USED RULE 13, SELECTED BY BALLOT BY HIS REGIMENT FOR THE HONOUR.

perate fighting, the relief force broke into the Lucknow Residency on September 25. For the wounded, their only hope of survival was to be carried on litters by bearers and remain with the column's rearguard. However, part of the rearguard was cut off as they advanced towards the residency, trapped along Lucknow's narrow streets with a number of wounded Highlanders. Jee and McMaster kept the bearers together and, with the help of an escort, succeeded in moving them to a safer place, the Moti Mahal, a building about fifteen hundred metres from the residency, where they were besieged.

The two doctors risked their lives in looking after the wounded, taxing their own skill, courage and energy to the limit. The soldiers were grateful for McMaster's bravery, as he saw to their wounds while the mutineers' bullets whizzed about his head. The next day, Jee and McMaster succeeded in getting the wounded to the residency through a murderous crossfire. Subsequently, McMaster was wounded in a dangerous nighttime raid against the mutineers.

For their gallantry, the 78th received two VCs, one for Jee as an individual, and the other to the regiment as a whole for "its gallant advance to the Residency at Lucknow." In the case of the other VC, the Highlanders were instructed to vote on who should wear it, under a rarely used VC regulation known as Rule 13. Based on the "universal acclamation of the men and officers of the regiment by whom he was esteemed with a fervour amounting to devotion," McMaster received the regiment's VC. The *London Gazette* announced his award on June 18, 1858, "for the intrepidity with which he exposed himself to the fire of the enemy, in bringing in and attending to the wounded on September 25th."

Valentine McMaster was born in Trichinopoly, Madras, India—the country where he would eventually earn his VC—on May 16, 1834, of Scottish parentage. He joined the British Army in March 1855 as assistant surgeon with the 78th Regiment (later the Seaforth Highlanders, now The Highlanders) and qualified with the Royal College of Surgeons in Edinburgh in 1860. He served with the Highlanders throughout the Persian Campaign of 1856–57, fought at the battles of Kooshab and Mohumra and received the campaign medal and clasp. He accompanied his unit to India on the outbreak of the mutiny and served with them until the army finally put it down. The regiment returned home in 1859, to much popular acclaim for its service in India.

After the Indian Mutiny, McMaster served with the 6th Inniskilling Dragoons from 1860 to 1864, followed by a tour with the 18th Hussars, until 1869. During that time, he was promoted to surgeon in March 1868 and rejoined the 78th a year later. As part of the British army's rotation of its infantry battalions through the Empire, on May 14, 1869, McMaster and the 78th sailed into Halifax Harbour on the troopship *Crocodile* under the command of Lieutenant-Colonel Alexander Mackenzie to begin a two-and-a-half-year tour in the small outpost.

MCMASTER SERVED AS REGIMENTAL SURGEON WITH THE 78TH HIGHLANDERS IN HALIFAX FROM 1869 TO 1871. THIS PHOTOGRAPH WAS PROBABLY TAKEN AT THE TIME OF HIS MARRIAGE TO ELANOR ANNIE BURMESTER AT ST. PAUL'S CHURCH ON JUNE 23, 1870. HE WEARS HIS VICTORIA CROSS FLANKED BY THE PERSIAN CAMPAIGN MEDAL AND CLASP AND THE INDIAN MUTINY MEDAL AND TWO CLASPS. AT THE TIME, THE VICTORIA CROSS WAS WORN IN THE ORDER IN WHICH IT WAS RECEIVED, AND NOT BEFORE ALL OTHER MEDALS AS IT IS WORN TODAY.

Although it only had a population of twenty-nine thousand, Halifax was the fourth largest city in BNA and was grandly classified as an "Imperial fortress." Nova Scotia had only reluctantly joined Confederation less than two years earlier, and resentment still smouldered below the surface in many quarters. Some of this ill will spilled over into the debate about whether or not the British military and naval presence in Halifax was a good thing. Regardless of popular opinion, there is no doubt that the British garrison at Halifax was a key factor in shaping the character of the city.

At the time, the army in Halifax was concentrated in two areas: around the Citadel (the fortifications on the hill overlooking the harbour) and farther north, along Gottingen Street at Wellington Barracks, the site of today's Stadacona in Canadian Forces

Base Halifax. Two seven-hundred-man-strong infantry battalions occupied each location, normally spending a year in each during their tour, changing places every May. Artillery, engineers, staff and various support elements made up the rest of the garrison. The 78th Regiment started their tour in the Citadel, moving in on May 22 once the incumbent 30th Regiment had departed. McMaster and the other officers lived and messed in twelve casemates in the redan, the large v-shaped projection pointing towards the harbour, while the men were quartered in the Cavalier Building. The regiment moved to Wellington Barracks on January 20, 1870, to be replaced by the newly arrived 84th Foot and replacing the 1/16th Foot, which left Halifax. The Highlanders remained in Wellington Barracks for fifteen months, until May 1, 1871, when they returned to the Citadel.

The regimental surgeon was one of the specialist officers in the unit, the others being the paymaster, quartermaster and assistant surgeon. As surgeon (equivalent in status to a captain), McMaster was responsible for all matters pertaining to the unit's health, with the aid of his assistant, Nugent Wade. Together, they looked after any Highlanders admitted to the garrison hospital, checked the health of those undergoing a sentence of incarceration, kept an eye on food being served to the soldiers and inspected the barracks. Once a week, usually on Saturday mornings, McMaster and Wade carried out a formal medical inspection of all the soldiers in their barrack rooms, with the men barefoot and short-sleeved.

For the majority of common soldiers in Halifax, much of their time was spent in the *demi-monde* of mid-Victorian life, a world of bars and brothels, booze and brawls. Not so for the officers. They not only entered into the city's high society—such as it was—their presence was eagerly sought and formed a large and important part of Halifax's upper-class activities. In particular, Highland-born brewing magnate Alexander Keith seems to have taken the officers of the 78th under his wing—perhaps because of their shared Scottish connection—and invited them to a number of events at his imposing Italianate residence on Hollis Street. He even held a grand farewell ball for them on November 14, 1871, a few days before the regiment left the city.

McMaster quickly joined the city's social world and became intimately involved with it. He met and married Eleanor Annie Burmester, fifteen years his junior, the daughter of Colonel John Burmester, Royal Engineers, and Eleanor (Cogswell) Burmester. Burmester had earlier served in Halifax from 1844 to 1850 and, like McMaster, found his wife in Halifax, the daughter of Henry H. Cogswell, one of the city's leading businessmen in the first half of the nineteenth century, and Isabella (Ellis) Cogswell. The joyful event took place in St. Paul's Church on June 23, 1870. Six brides-maids attended the bride, while officers of the 78th in full dress accompanied McMaster. The *Acadian Recorder* noted, "The ancient edifice was crowned with the beauty and fashion of the city to witness the ceremony." Almost a year later, on May 11, 1871, a son, Bryce Belcher, was born to the McMasters.

Valentine McMaster left Halifax on the troopship *Orontes* on November 26, 1871, to accompany his unit to Belfast, Ireland. He died suddenly on January 22, 1872, shortly after arriving in Ireland, from long-standing valvular disease of the heart, only thirty-seven years old. One week after his death, the *Medical Times and Gazette* noted, "he has now terminated his brilliant and useful career among those who knew him and loved him most, and who now, with many a tear, will have the sad pleasure of placing his honoured remains, with regimental honours, in a soldier's grave." When word of his death reached Halifax, the *Acadian Recorder* observed, "He was well and favourably known in this community…and the intelligence of his demise will cast a gloom over a large circle of his friends in this city."

There are several memorials to McMaster in Northern Ireland. In Belfast City Cemetery, where he is buried, his widow erected a cross over his grave. The officers, NCOs and privates of the 78th placed a marble tablet in Londonderry's St. Columbus Cathedral "to mark their appreciation of the many good qualities which he evinced in the discharge of his duties both in the field and in quarters," and his name is on the Derry War Memorial. Valentine McMaster's VC is displayed at the National War Museum of Scotland, in Edinburgh Castle. The memory of his unit is perpetuated in the Halifax Citadel by the 78th Highlanders Association, whose members sponsor historical re-enactors dressed in the regiment's full highland regalia, to perform period drill and firepower displays every summer.

At Lucknow, in late September 1857, the sense of salvation felt in the residency after the arrival of General Havelock's relief column was unfortunately short lived: It soon became obvious his force was insufficient to push the rebels from the city. The siege would continue for another fifty-three days through the torrential monsoons. Towards the end of October, word reached the besieged garrison, by then surrounded by some sixty thousand rebels, that another relief force was on its way. This second column contained between five and six thousand men, including Peel's Naval Brigade with Able Seaman Hall in it. On the way up the Ganges, Hall had rescued a fellow sailor from drowning. He was a superb athlete, as one of his contemporaries noted: "He was always a man remarkable for his steady good conduct and his athletic frame, at a foot race in camp he had distanced by far all competitors, and I have never seen his superior as swimmer or diver."

After disembarking at Allahabad in early September, the Naval Brigade was joined by 280 additional sailors, bringing the total strength of Peel's Brigade to 755 officers and men. On October 28, the sailors, known as "bluejackets" for their dress, moved off cross-country towards Cawnpore. Amazingly, there was yet another Nova Scotia connection with this force: At its head was General Sir Colin Campbell, sixty-five, appointed Commander-in-Chief of all British forces in India on the outbreak of the mutiny. A veteran of the Napoleonic Wars with some forty-nine years of military experience, Campbell had been lieutenant-governor of Nova Scotia between 1834 and 1840. He followed Havelock's first relief with a

WILLIAM NEILSON HALL WAS THE FIRST BLACK MAN, THE FIRST NOVA SCOTIAN AND THE THIRD CANADIAN TO RECEIVE THE VICTORIA CROSS. HALL WAS SERVING IN THE ROYAL NAVY AS A MEMBER OF HMS SHANNON'S NAVAL BRIGADE WHEN HE EARNED THE VICTORIA CROSS DURING THE RELIEF OF LUCKNOW. HE CONTINUED TO LOAD AND FIRE HIS HEAVY NAVAL CANNON IN THE FACE OF CONCENTRATED FIRE BY THE REBELS.

force of thirty-four hundred British and native soldiers, plus irregulars, marines and sailors.

As Hall and the Naval Brigade moved towards Cawnpore, another Canadian was earning the VC nearby. Staff Surgeon Herbert Taylor Reade, from Perth, Upper Canada, served with the 61st Foot. On September 14, during the Siege of Delhi, Reade was attending to the wounded when they were fired upon by a party of rebels. The doctor immediately drew his sword and, with a few British soldiers, drove them away. Two days later, he took part in the Assault on Delhi and was one of the first through a breach, spiking a gun along with a sergeant. These two acts earned Reade, nicknamed the "Fighting Surgeon," Canada's second VC.

While on the march to Cawnpore, the seamen attempted to capture some mutineer-occupied ruins surrounded by a high stone wall. After considerable loss of life, one crew succeeded in dragging their gun to a commanding position to cover the movement of their comrades. As the mutineers concentrated their fire on this gun, its crew began to fall. Hall, serving another gun, rushed forward to help. The officer in charge of the gun, Lieutenant Nowell Salmon, cried out, "Ah! Hall! You're a man!" Three other sailors joined Hall and this new crew succeeded in forcing the sepoys back.

When the Naval Brigade arrived at the Cawnpore massacre site in November, Hall later remarked, "the blood of the helpless women was still upon the walls" of the rooms where the natives slaughtered them. After having witnessed the results of the atrocities committed at Cawnpore, the British eagerly anticipated the fight ahead, prepared to die if necessary to spare the women and children in the Lucknow Residency from a similar fate.

Campbell's force, now grown to five thousand, set out on November 9 for Lucknow, where the exhausted remaining defenders waited desperately for relief. With detachments left behind and losses due to sickness and enemy action, Peel's Brigade mustered only 250 men with eight heavy guns and howitzers, plus two rocket tubes. As Campbell approached Lucknow, he obtained inside information on the city's layout from a civilian clerk who made his way through enemy lines (and for which he would later receive the first civilian VC).

This information enabled Campbell to make a flanking attack and avoid much of the street fighting Havelock's force had endured. On November 16, Campbell attacked the Sikander Bagh, a high-walled, castle-like fortification with towers at the corners and loopholes all around it. The attack began with a bombardment of the fortress by the Royal Artillery and the Naval Brigade, who suffered heavy losses in their exposed gun positions. The guns made a small breach in the thick masonry walls and soldiers rushed forward, each man wanting to be the first through, even though it meant certain death. By late afternoon, after a violent and bloody hand-to-hand struggle, the Sikander Bagh finally fell. Despite the late hour, Campbell now turned towards the enemy's next strong point.

The Shah Nujjiff was a heavily fortified mosque surrounded by a high loopholed wall, even more formidable than the Sikander Bagh. Campbell immediately ordered its bombardment, which commenced about 4:00 P.M. The sailors dragged their 24-pounders forward again, this time to within four hundred metres range, and the gunners fired shell after shell at the walls. But the domed mosque's stout two-metre thick walls held. Captain Peel continued to work his guns, in Campbell's words, "very much as if he had been laying the *Shannon* alongside an enemy's frigate." The British bombardment continued for three hours, all the time under a murderous double crossfire, which eventually forced Peel to withdraw the crew of one piece and lessen the fire of others. As his sailors fell, the naval officer became increasingly concerned.

Then Campbell ordered an assault. The sailors doubled their efforts shelling the walls, an artillery battery galloped forward to begin pouring grapeshot into the fortress from pistol range and the soldiers advanced, bayonets fixed. But they did not carry scaling ladders and the high walls remained unbreached. As the infantry desperately searched for a way in, they dropped like flies from well-aimed musket fire. The critical point of the battle had been reached. Peel, realizing the danger, ordered two of his 24-pounder guns nearer to the mosque's walls in a final attempt to make a breach. One of the gun crews was short a man and Hall stepped forward to replace him.

Peel turned to Hall and said, "You had better not, it means almost certain death."

But Hall went anyway. He and his courageous companions dragged the two guns to within a few metres of the mosque and began firing. Each time they fired, a cloud of smoke and dust enveloped them. Hall later said, "After firing each round we ran the gun forward until finally the crew were in danger of being hit by splinters of brick and stone torn from the wall by the round shot." Lieutenant Thomas Young, in charge of the two guns, went from crew to crew, encouraging them amid a hail of bullets. Soon all of one crew was dead and Hall's crew was being rapidly depleted. He continued to work his piece until he alone remained. Young stepped in and together the two sponged, loaded and fired the 24-pounder, sending round after round smashing into the wall. On many occasions, they double-shotted the gun to increase its impact. With his tremendous strength, Hall could push the heavy gun forward after each recoil, the two men carrying out drills normally done by half a dozen.

As the artillery onslaught continued without a breach being made, a rocket battery opened up and fired over the walls into the mosque. At the same time, an infantry sergeant found a crack in the wall just wide enough for one man at a time to squeeze through. A few soldiers got inside only to find the mutineers had fled through the back gate. The Shah Nujjiff had fallen at last. Hall later said, "We would have liked to go in with the soldiers, but the guns' crews had to stay with the guns."

The next day, the sailors brought their guns into action again as two more strong points fell, the last between the relievers and the besieged. With the way to the Lucknow Residency now clear, its defenders were relieved for a second time. Under the cover of darkness and a bombardment by the Naval Brigade, the British quietly withdrew, evacuating everyone on the night of November 22–23. Three months of living hell were over. The party reached Cawnpore on the evening of November 28, and Campbell sent the women and children on to Allahabad, while he continued with his task of putting down the remaining rebels.

For their courage and steadfastness while the enemy killed or wounded all those about them, Captain Peel recommended Hall and Young for the VC. The *London Gazette* announced their awards together on February 1, 1859. Campbell called the deeds of those involved "an action almost unexampled in war." Nowell Salmon, whom Hall had assisted when capturing the mutineer-occupied ruins, also earned the VC at Lucknow for climbing a tree under fire and spotting for the artillery. He later rose to command the RN and said of Hall: "He was a fine powerful man and as steady as a rock under fire." Of the 182 VCs awarded during the Indian Mutiny, sixty-six were earned at Lucknow. The British Army received sixty-one, the Royal Navy four and the civilian clerk the remaining one. Twenty-four were gained on November 16 (the day Hall earned his), which is a record for the most VCs earned in a single day.

But the Indian Mutiny was not yet over, and there was much more hard marching and fighting still to come. A few days later, the Naval Brigade again saw action at Cawnpore, as Campbell's force cleared the area. The Commander-in-Chief spoke highly of Peel and his gallant sailors: "their guns have been constantly in advance throughout our late operations, from the relief of Lucknow till now, as if they were light field-pieces, and the service rendered by them in clearing out our front has been incalculable." With the recapture of Cawnpore, the turning point of the mutiny was reached.

In March 1858, the Naval Brigade, as well as the 78th Highlanders and Valentine McMaster, attacked Lucknow for the third time, thirty-one thousand of Campbell's men against one hundred thousand sepoys. Storming fortifications he had taken the previous fall, Campbell recaptured Lucknow on March 21. However, before the ultimate victory, a musket-ball seriously wounded Peel. After surgery to extract it, he made a slow but steady recovery. With the capture of Lucknow, his Naval Brigade's work was finished. Known as "Peel's Jacks," the sailors and marines performed yeoman service during the mutiny. Enduring many hardships of heat, thirst, lack of adequate food, disease and fatigue, they handled their heavy naval guns like light field artillery, providing valuable direct fire support to the army's operations and contributing in large measure to its final success.

On April 1, the sailors folded up their tents and started back to Calcutta. The government decided to give Peel and his brigade a public reception there, to recognize their sterling services. On March 2, Peel's elevation to a Knight Commander of the Order of the Bath (KCB) was announced in London. After arriving safely in Cawnpore, Peel was struck by smallpox on April 20. In his already weakened state he succumbed to the disease one week later, only thirty-three years old. The news of his knighthood never reached him.

Both the public at large and Peel's men expressed universal grief over the loss of such an inspiring leader, one who could have achieved the highest ranks in the navy. *The Times* of London stated, "No seaman of this time appeared to inherit in so large a proportion the calculated daring and the felicitous enthusiasm which gave Nelson the instinct of victory. If his contempt of danger was excessive, he never overlooked the minutest detail which could tend to the safety or success of his undertakings." One of his officers wrote: "What a sad loss we all feel this to be, and how deeply his death is felt and regretted by every officer and man; the mainspring that worked the machinery is gone. We never felt ourselves to be the *Shannon*'s

Naval Brigade, or even the *Admiralty* Naval Brigade, but always *Peel's* Naval Brigade." Such was the respect accorded the man who recommended Hall for the VC.

As the British routed out and destroyed the last pockets of mutineers around the country, *Shannon's* crew could at last leave India. On September 15, the ship sailed for home, with Leading Seaman Hall—he had been promoted in February—safely on board. In addition to earning the VC, Hall was also awarded the Indian Mutiny Medal, 1857–58, with two bars—Relief of Lucknow and Battle of Lucknow.

John Inglis also received high honours. For his heroic defence of the Residency he was promoted major-general and made a KCB. Inglis's citation referred to "his enduring fortitude and persevering gallantry in the defence of the residency at Lucknow for eighty-seven days against overwhelming forces of the enemy." His native province also recognized him: The Nova Scotia Legislature presented him with a sword of honour, and a full-length oil painting of him hangs in the magnificent Palladian Red Chamber of Nova Scotia's Province House. His hometown of Halifax named a street in his honour, but as an Inglis Street already existed in memory of his illustrious grandfather, the street recognizing the grandson became Lucknow Street. Fittingly, the two streets intersect in south end Halifax.

Inglis became commander of the garrison at Cawnpore, but did not live long to enjoy his life as Major-General Sir John. While traveling in 1862, he died of a fever in Hamburg. Most people believed the strain of the Lucknow experience severely damaged his health. He was only forty-seven. His wife Julia lived much longer, writing a book on her experiences and becoming an honorary housekeeper at Saint James Palace in London. With a pension as a result of her husband's heroism, she lived comfortably until she passed away in 1904.

The Relief of Lucknow was only one of many actions in which William Hall fought during his naval career. His first experience with battle occurred during the Crimean War. Conflict among the Great Powers (Austria-Hungary, France, Great Britain, Prussia/Germany and Russia) was common during the nineteenth century and could be set off by any number of reasons. In the case of the Crimean War, it was Russia's longtime desire to acquire naval power in, and access to, the Mediterranean Sea which instigated hostilities. In Czar Nicholas's eyes, Turkey—"the sick man of

Europe"—did not deserve to live any longer. In July 1853, Nicholas found the excuse he had long been seeking and marched his armies into Turkish territory.

Although Britain stayed neutral initially, she was fearful of a Russian challenge to her naval supremacy in the Mediterranean. In September the British and French fleets, including HMS *Rodney* with Able Seaman Hall on board, arrived in Constantinople (now Istanbul) as a precautionary measure. On October 4, the Turks advanced into the territory occupied by Russia, defeating the czar's forces in early November. However, the Russians turned the tables later that month, when their fleet defeated an outgunned and outnumbered Turkish flotilla in the Black Sea.

In January 1854, the British and French fleets entered the Black Sea and allied themselves with Turkey, declaring war on Russia in March. While an Anglo-French expedition sailed to help repel the Russian invasion, the Russians fired on the frigate HMS *Furious*, which was trying to enter Odessa under a flag of truce. In retaliation, an allied squadron, including *Rodney*, bombarded the Russian shore batteries and inflicted heavy damage on them. Hall later said of the incident, "We chastised the Russians for not recognizing the flag of truce."

The Allies invaded Russia in September 1854, intending to destroy her main naval base, Sebastopol (now Sevastopol), on the Crimean Peninsula. In response to the Allied army's request for assistance, on October 1 over two thousand sailors and Royal Marines formed a Naval Brigade. At Balaclava the brigade hauled 32- and 68-pounder cannons, plus Lancaster guns, up the hill from the harbour and constructed and manned two gun batteries facing Sebastopol. The Allied bombardment of the Russian fortress began on October 17. The siege of Sebastopol, which would last eleven months, was to be the major operation of the war.

Hall commanded a Lancaster gun, a 68-pounder that fired a round weighing thirty-nine kilograms a distance of over five kilometres. Hall's battery of two guns, known as the Right Lancaster Battery, was under Acting Mate William Hewett. When the Russians threatened the battery, Hewett's superiors ordered him to spike his gun and retreat. Disregarding the order, he shouted, "Retire? Retire be damned! Fire!" and poured a devastating barrage onto the advancing Russians, forcing them back. For this deed and his later actions at the Battle of Inkerman, Hewett received the VC. With Hall serving at close quarters to this conspicuous bravery, it could only have inspired the Nova Scotian sailor.

Also present at the siege was one of the most remarkable men ever to serve in the RN—another VC recipient, who would figure prominently in Hall's future and recommend him for his VC. William Peel was the son of British Prime Minister Sir Robert Peel. After service in several ships in a number of locations, including the west coast of Canada, he made captain in 1849. At twenty-five, he was the youngest to hold that rank in the Royal Navy. During the Crimean War, Peel, commanding the twenty-eight-gun frigate HMS *Diamond*, earned his VC for three separate acts of bravery.

Eventually, the British and French forced the Russians out of Sebastopol and occupied the port. With Russia's main fortress captured, the war gradually petered out and a peace treaty was signed in March 1856. Losses on both sides totaled more than half a million men, with over sixty percent lost to disease. Hall survived and received two campaign medals, one British and one Turkish. His British Crimean War medal bears two bars, attesting to his participation at the battles of Inkerman and Sebastopol.

Nothing in William Neilson Hall's early years indicated he would lead a life filled with adventure and receive the highest military award possible. Hall was born on April 25, 1829, probably at Horton Bluff, King's County, Nova Scotia, about three kilometres east of Avonport, on the banks of the Avon River. His parents, Jacob and Lucinda, former slaves who came to the province from Maryland during the War of 1812, had sought refuge with British warships harrying the east coast of the United States in the summer of 1814. When the British fleet withdrew for the winter on October 14, they brought a number of slaves with them to Halifax—some of the sixteen hundred blacks who came to Nova Scotia during that war. In their new home, Jacob and Lucinda met and married after processing at a depot established on Melville Island in Halifax's Northwest Arm to handle the influx of black refugees.

Jacob and his new wife moved to the Avon River area, where Jacob worked in a shipbuilding yard owned by Abraham Cunard, father of Sir Samuel Cunard, and Peter Hall, a Windsor merchant. Jacob took his surname from his employer, a common practice among blacks at the time. Later he worked in shipbuilding yards at Hantsport, as a rigger and caulker. In yards like these, Nova Scotians built wooden ships that established a world-famous tradition of excellence. It's likely that the younger Hall was familiar with this environment from his early years. The idea of a sailor's life may first have entered his mind here as he watched ships sailing in and out of Minas Basin. As a poor, young, black boy in an era without free education, he would have had very little formal schooling and had little choice but to enter the workforce at an early age.

Hall first went to sea in 1845, at sixteen, in the barque *Kent*, carrying a load of lumber to London, then a cargo to Boston. But other events soon interrupted his career as a merchant seaman. Although Hall remained at sea, it was in another capacity. In the spring of 1848 he enlisted in the United States Navy (USN) in Boston, under the name William Harvey, and served in the guard ship USS *Franklin* until February 1849, when the navy transferred him to the frigate USS *Savannah*. He sailed around Cape Horn to San Francisco in the *Savannah*, arriving there in the summer of 1849. That fall he joined the battleship USS *Ohio* and served until May 1850, when he was paid off and returned to the life of a merchant sailor.

After his discharge from the USN, Hall served in ships trading out of Boston and arrived in Liverpool, England, in the clipper ship *Tam O'Shanter* in 1852. But naval life must have held greater appeal and, on February 10, he walked into the naval recruiting office in Red Cross Street and came out an ordinary seaman in the RN. Hall's first posting was to a battleship named after a man with Canadian connections, including a Nova Scotian affiliation—the first of many such coincidences linking Hall's time in the RN with his native province. When Hall joined *Rodney*, it lay at anchor at Portsmouth; at ninety guns, it was one of the Royal Navy's biggest and mightiest warships. It was named for Admiral George Rodney, who served as Governor and Commander-in-Chief of Newfoundland for two years and participated in the capture of Fortress Louisbourg on Cape Breton Island from the French in 1758.

In mid-nineteenth century, the RN was the largest and most powerful navy in the world. It was, in considerable measure, responsible for putting the "Great" in Great Britain. The British Empire reached its apex in the nineteenth century, making Britain the leading industrial and trading nation in the world. The ships of Her Majesty's Navy linked together and protected Britain's far-flung empire—which comprised one quarter of the land surface of the globe. "Britannia Rules the Waves" was not just a jingoistic song; it was a statement of fact.

At Portsmouth, while awaiting *Rodney*'s return to duty, the navy billeted Hall and his fellow recruits in Admiral Horatio Nelson's flagship *Victory*, where they received their training. In honour of Nelson's defeat of the combined French and Spanish fleets at Trafalgar in 1805, *Victory* had never been paid off and remained in commission as a British warship, a tradition continuing to this day. At twenty-three, Hall must have been in awe at the thought of the brave men and the daring deeds that were *Victory*'s legacy. Little did he know he would soon join that pantheon of heroes. Following training, Hall served in *Rodney* for two years, guarding the English Channel and during the Crimean War.

After *Rodney*'s decommissioning in January 1856, Hall rejoined *Victory*, serving as an able seaman from January 31 to March 12. For some reason, he then deserted (euphemistically known as "French leave") and on March 12 his name was entered in the ship's books with an "R" for "Run." Hall soon rejoined the navy and all must have been forgiven, as he was almost immediately back to his previous rank of able seaman. On October 29, he joined *Shannon*, a new, experimental, fifty-one-gun, ironclad steam frigate only commissioned that fall. His commanding officer was none other than Captain William Peel.

After his exploits during the Indian Mutiny, Hall's career continued to advance. In England, on July 1, 1858, he was made captain of the mast, and later that same month captain of the foretop. In June of the next year, he was posted to the battleship *Donegal*, attached to the Channel Fleet. He was presented with his VC at a special parade held in *Donegal* at Queenstown, Ireland on October 28, 1859. *Donegal*'s officers and men paraded on the quarterdeck, while the Commander-in-Chief at Cork called Hall forward and delivered a short address. He then gave Hall a copy of the *London Gazette* entry for his award, the regulations entitling him to £10 a year and the General Order on the subject. After he pinned the medal on Hall's chest a band struck up "God Save the Queen." Besides being only the third Canadian VC ever, there are other unique aspects to Hall's medal. His is the only one ever awarded to a Canadian with a blue ribbon, denoting the naval award of the medal, and the only pre-Confederation VC awarded to a native of the Atlantic region.

Hall next served in the warship *Hero*. He was with *Hero* in 1860 when it brought the eighteen-year-old Prince of Wales (the future King Edward VII) on the first-ever royal visit to British North America, including Hall's home province of Nova Scotia. One of the ship's officers wrote of the crew, "We had one Victoria Cross man amongst them; curious to say, he was a Negro, by name William Hall. VCs were not so plentiful as they are now."

In November 1862, Hall joined *Kangsoo*, part of the Imperial Chinese

Squadron, but fitted out in England with the full sanction of the British government and manned by RN personnel. In *Kangsoo*, Hall saw hard service in Chinese waters for two years. He then returned to the RN, serving in many ships around the world. He was with *Canopus* in 1866 when a controversy arose over his date of birth. Hall wanted to sign on for ten years continuous service, but his certificate of service gave his date of birth as April 28, 1821, making him over forty and ineligible for ten more years of continuous service. His captain referred the whole matter to the Admiralty for a ruling.

Hall then left *Canopus*, where he served only a short time, before moving to his next ship, *Bellerophon*, where he was quartermaster. The Admiralty eventually decided his year of birth was 1828, and in February 1869 Hall signed up for the continuous service he wanted, with the engagement backdated to 1866. He was in *Bellerophon* until September 30, 1870, followed by service in *Impregnable*, *Petrel* and *Royal Adelaide*, his last ship. Along the way, he was promoted to petty officer first class. On July 4, 1876, Hall was paid off and discharged with a good conduct certificate after a long naval career.

Local tradition in Nova Scotia has it the British Government offered Hall a sinecure in Whitehall, where he could have lived a retirement in relative ease. However, he refused, saying, "I want to spend my days in the old place, the land of my birth." And that is just what he did. Hall settled on a small farm along the Bluff Road about seven kilometers from Hantsport, where he lived quietly with two of his sisters, Mary and Rachel, who kept house for their bachelor brother. His farmhouse overlooked Minas Basin, protected from the region's heavy winds by a border of spruce trees. He stocked the farm well with cattle and poultry and had a large orchard just under a hectare in size.

The outbreak of the Boer War aroused Nova Scotians' interest in the exploits of the province's native sons in other wars. A reporter visited Hall in September 1900 for an interview. After some polite small talk, the newspaperman came right to the point: "By the way," he asked, "Haven't you served in the Royal Navy?" to which Hall replied he "served a good many years in the navy." The reporter eventually coaxed Hall to tell him how he earned the VC and to show it to him. The old sailor led him into a neatly furnished room with pictures of British warships on the walls, where he took down a small cardboard box from the mantel and emptied its contents out on the table. The VC, its blue ribbon missing, lay among them, fastened by wire to a heavy watch chain, along with Hall's three other medals. Hall remarked, "It's nothing to have a Cross now; they're as thick as peas. It isn't worth very much to a man after all, only £10 a year. If it wasn't for my regular navy pension of £40 a year besides I don't know how we'd get along here. The farm is small, and my two sisters live with me, you know."

In 1901, the Duke and Duchess of York (later to rule as King George V and Queen Mary) visited Halifax. The Royal British Veterans' Association invited Hall to participate in a ceremony at which the Duke would unveil a memorial at Province House to Nova Scotians who fought in the Boer War. As Hall stood on parade with a number of other veterans, the Duke passed by and, noticing Hall's VC pinned to his chest, stopped to shake his hand and talk with him, inviting him to join in the Royal Procession. A carriage was provided and Hall drove through city streets lined with cheering crowds. However, this was a rare intrusion into his quiet life: Hall told the compilers of a biographical dictionary his chief recreation was "shooting crows."

On August 25, 1904 "Ol' Bill," as he was known locally, died of paralysis at his home at seventy-five and was buried without honours in the little hillside cemetery of the Stony Hill Baptist Church, Lockhartville. One month after his death, on September 27, a crowd gathered at Hall's church, the Brooklyn Baptist Church. In a memorial address, the Reverend B. D. Knott said, "He was a peaceable God-fearing citizen. He was honoured and respected by all who knew him. He was ever humble." Hall left his two sisters with a $500 debt on the little farm. To cover it, they sold his VC and other medals.

Eventually, Hall's medals ended up in Britain at the RN Barracks in Portsmouth. During Centennial Year, in 1967, they were displayed at the Atlantic Provinces' Pavilion at Expo 67. Looking to obtain them permanently, the Nova Scotia Government purchased another RN VC that came up for sale, and traded it for Hall's in 1967. Hall's medals are now in the possession of the Nova Scotia Museum in Halifax.

Over the years, the tiny cemetery where the war hero was put to rest became neglected and his grave fell into disrepair. In 1945, his remains were disinterred and reburied in the Hantsport Baptist Church Cemetery, in a plot deeded to the Hants County Branch of the Royal Canadian Legion and adopted by the town for perpetual care. Two years later, the same Legion branch, assisted by donations from the William Hall, VC, Branch in Halifax and twenty-four other branches, erected a memorial

HALL'S FUNERAL PROCESSION WENDS ITS WAY TO THE STONY HILL BAPTIST CHURCH CEMETERY, LOCKHARTVILLE, KINGS COUNTY. HE WAS BURIED THERE WITHOUT HONOURS IN AUGUST 1904.

cairn at the grave, containing a large replica of the VC, cast in bronze. It was unveiled in a ceremony on November 9, 1947, in the presence of Hall's relatives. Based on information known at the time, it incorrectly shows his middle name as Edward and his date of birth as April 28, 1821. Members of the local Lucknow Branch of the Royal Canadian Legion, named after the site of Hall's valour, place a wreath on it annually on November 11. The town of Hansport maintains the memorial and last refitted it in 1994, on the occasion of the town's centennial.

Today, Hall's heroism is commemorated in many different forms. In Montreal, the DaCosta-Hall Education Programme for black students shares his name. In his home province, the gymnasium at Canadian Forces Base Cornwallis bore his name when it was in operation, as does the William Hall Block in Halifax's Windsor Park, a naval establishment. A plaque on the Cornwallis Street United Baptist Church in Halifax commemorates his memory, and the Hantsport Sea Cadet Corps is named after him. At the world famous Nova Scotia International Tattoo, held annually in Halifax during the first week of July, one of the most popular events is often the naval gun run. In a competition testing teamwork, strength, endurance, agility, speed and dexterity, teams disassemble a heavy naval cannon, hoist the component parts onto a sling, carry them in relays across a gap and reassemble the gun on the far side before firing it. Appropriately, the teams compete for the William Hall, VC Trophy, displaying some of the skills exhibited by the war hero so many years ago in a faraway land.

CHAPTER 2

ON IMPERIAL SERVICE

The first few of the twenty-one Victoria Cross recipients born in or associated with Atlantic Canada served in the British, or Imperial, Forces. Like William Hall and Valentine McMaster—who earned their VCs during the Indian Mutiny, in the Royal Navy and British Army, respectively—the next group of awardees also received their VCs while serving in the Royal Navy or British Army. They, however, fought in a variety of wars spanning a sixty-four-year period. These recipients include three Royal Navy sailors associated with the region—one who fought in the Crimean War and two who fought in the First World War—and a soldier who was born in the region and served in the British Army during the Boer War. Although these men fought in three different wars, they are linked together by their connections to Atlantic Canada and their time fighting for the Crown on Imperial service.

Commander John Edmund Commerell
HMS *Weser*, Royal Navy
Putrid Sea, Russia, October 11, 1855

John Edmund Commerell was the last officer to receive the Victoria Cross in the first group of VCs—those awarded for heroism during the Crimean War. Commerell commanded the six-gun steam gunboat HMS *Weser*, part of Britain's Black Sea Fleet, and led a daring commando-type raid against

Russian buildings and stores along the shores of the unappealingly named Putrid Sea. At about 2:30 on the morning of October 11, 1855, Commerell

ADMIRAL SIR JOHN EDMUND COMMERELL WAS A COMMANDER WHEN HE EARNED HIS VICTORIA CROSS DURING THE CRIMEAN WAR. FROM 1882 TO 1885, HE WAS COMMANDER-IN-CHIEF OF THE ROYAL NAVY'S NORTH ATLANTIC AND WEST INDIES STATION, IN WHICH CAPACITY HE WAS HEAD-QUARTERED AT HALIFAX FROM MAY TO OCTOBER EVERY YEAR.

and four sailors set off in one of *Weser*'s boats, heading for the shores of the Sea of Azov. They landed on the Spit of Arabat and dragged their boat across two to three hundred metres of dry land before relaunching it in the Putrid Sea, where they rowed across to the inland shore.

Commerell landed around 4:30 A.M. and, leaving two sailors behind to look after the boat, led the other two inland for about three kilometres, where they hid while waiting for dawn. Once visibility improved, they could see their objective about a kilometre and a half away—a fodder store containing some 350 tonnes of corn. Beside it stood a large red building and a Cossack guard station and signal post.

Commerell and his companions headed towards the storehouse, wading through two neck-deep canals on the way. On arrival, they set fire to the fodder magazine, but could not get the red building to burn. While Commerell continued attempting to light it, Cossack guards came running out of their post and started to chase the British raiders. In the confusion caused by the fire, the sailors managed to gain a significant lead on their pursuers. However, after Commerell and his two men fled across the first canal, one of the sailors was so exhausted he asked to be left behind.

Refusing to do so, Commerell and Quartermaster William Rickard removed the winded man's boots, swam across the second canal with him and half-carried him to the boat, running as best they could with their live burden.

They made the boat safely, under covering fire from the two sailors left behind. As they shoved off, the nearest Cossacks were only fifty or so metres away and Commerell killed the closest horseman with a pistol shot. When they reached their ship, lookouts watching from *Weser*'s mast reported the fodder store had burned to the ground. Both Commerell and Rickard received the VC for their actions, with Rickard earning his based on Commerell's personal recommendation: "I must bring to your notice the excellent conduct of the small party who accompanied me, more especially that of William Rickard, Quartermaster, who, though much fatigued himself, remained to assist the other seaman who from exhaustion had fallen in the mud and was unable to extricate himself."

John Edmund Commerell knew no other life but a sailor's, serving a total of fifty-seven years before retirement, fifty of them during Queen Victoria's long reign. In this time, he achieved many awards and honours and reached the pinnacle of his profession. He was born on Park Street, near London's Grosvenor Square on January 13, 1829, and joined the RN as volunteer first class in 1842. He served in China in *Cornwallis*, followed by the steam frigate *Firebrand*, under Captain James Hope. It was in *Firebrand* that Commerell saw his first real action, in 1845, during the struggle between Argentina and Uruguay, in which England, France and Brazil intervened.

In 1848, Commerell passed for mate and was commissioned lieutenant at the end of that year. He commanded the six-gun gunboat *Vulture* in the Baltic Sea from February 1854 until he was promoted commander and took over *Weser* a year later. In April, *Weser* sailed for the Black Sea and the Crimean War, but misfortune struck when the ship caught fire, struck a rock and had to beach at the entrance to the Dardanelles. Commerell eventually refloated *Weser*, but the vessel had to be towed to Constantinople by another RN warship. After his exploits against the Russians in the Putrid Sea, Commerell remained in *Weser* until 1856, when he went on to command *Snake* in the Mediterranean Sea.

Although Commerell was awarded the VC in the first *London Gazette* list of February 24, 1857, he missed the first investiture in London's Hyde Park conducted by Queen Victoria on June 26, 1857. At the time, he was proceeding to China to command the six-gun steam vessel *Fury*. On the China

Station, during the Second Opium War (1856–1860), Commerell again served under Hope, now Admiral Sir James. A few years later, Hope went on to command the North American and West Indies Station at Halifax during the American Civil War, a post Commerell also eventually achieved.

The Treaties of Tientsin, signed between China and England, France, the United States and Russia in June 1858, were supposed to end the war, with China agreeing, among other provisions, to open more ports to foreigners and admit foreign diplomats to Peking. However, China soon abrogated many of these concessions, in particular refusing to let diplomats into the capital. In retaliation, on June 25, 1859, Admiral Hope's squadron bombarded the Taku Forts guarding the mouth of the Hai River below Tientsin.

Commerell led a Naval Brigade ashore against the forts, which the Chinese garrison repulsed with significant losses to the British—64 killed and 252 wounded. Commodore Josiah Tattnall, commanding the American Asiatic Squadron, assisted the British—with whom the Americans were not allied—to withdraw and uttered his famous phrase to justify his decidedly partisan action: "Blood is thicker than water." Tattnall, like Hope and Commerell, would also come to know Halifax.

A Southerner by birth, Tattnall had seen action in the War of 1812, fought pirates in North Africa and the West Indies, and was wounded during the Mexican War. He resigned his USN commission in February 1861, as southern states seceded from the Union, and became an officer in the Confederate States Navy, commanding the pioneer ironclad *Virginia* after her famous battles. With the defeat of the Confederacy in 1865, Tattnall made his way to Halifax where he joined a group of about thirty other "un-Reconstructed" rebels (in Thomas H. Raddall's phrase). He lived in Canada for four years before returning to his home state of Georgia, where he died in 1871.

Despite the defeat of the British landing force against the Taku Forts by the Chinese, Commerell received great praise for his part in the operation. He collected a Mention-in-Dispatches and received an illuminated address of thanks from both Houses of Parliament. A month after the attack, he was promoted captain and given command of the paddle-steamer *Magicienne*, remaining on the China Station. In contrast to many other Victorian-era VCs, Commerell did not retire at a low rank or die of wounds or illness. Furthermore, he managed to do something interesting or noteworthy during most of his postings.

In 1865, Commerell commanded the new ironclad *Scorpion*, equipped with innovative gun batteries shaped like cupolas. The next year found him in command of the twenty-one-gun steam vessel *Terrible*, which assisted in laying the transatlantic cable—for which he received a civil Companion of the Order of the Bath (CB). While in command of the ironclad turret war-ship *Monarch*, he carried the body of American philanthropist George Peabody across the Atlantic for burial in the United States in December 1869.

By 1871, Commerell was a commodore and senior officer on the West Coast of Africa. Here, he participated in the Second Ashanti War (1873–1874). In August 1873, he was seriously wounded by a musket ball in the lungs while reconnoitering the Prah River and had to be sent to England. He recovered, was elevated to Knight Commander of the Order of the Bath on March 31, 1874, became an aide-de-camp to the queen and was promoted rear admiral on November 12, 1876. The next year Commerell became second-in-command of the Mediterranean Fleet under Admiral Sir Geoffrey Phipps Hornby and flew his flag in the five-masted ironclad *Agincourt* during the Russo-Turkish War (1877–1878). Hornby maintained his fleet in the eastern Mediterranean and the Dardanelles for more than two years as a stabilizing influence in the region.

Many regarded Hornby as the finest seaman of his day, and he in turn thought highly of Commerell. When Hornby was knighted in 1878, four years after his subordinate, Commerell, he wrote to his wife, "It will give me no pleasure to be called 'Sir Geoffrey'; but I certainly am pleased and proud to know that the best men in the service—I mean such as Commerell, Hewett [who served with Hall during the Crimean War], Salmon [who served with Hall during the Indian Mutiny], Baird &c—are glad to serve under me." When Commerell nearly drowned in a sailing acci-dent a few days later, Hornby noted, "The country would indeed have suf-fered a grievous loss if Commerell had been drowned the other day."

As he entered his last twenty years of service, Commerell received addi-tional promotions and honours. He became the Junior Naval Lord of the Admiralty in 1879 and was promoted vice admiral on January 19, 1881. Later that year, he assumed Hope's role and became Commander-in-Chief of the North American and West Indies Station in November, with head-quarters at Halifax and Bermuda, a post he retained from 1882 to 1885. Just before he took up the appointment, the famous English magazine, *Vanity Fair*, published a print of him in its "Men of the Day" series in

December 1881. It showed Commerell in a civilian suit under the title "A Jingo." The original watercolour from which the print was made is now a part of the collection of the National Portrait Gallery, London.

In the early nineteenth century, Halifax had been the sole headquarters for the North American Station. Admiralty House, a stately Georgian stone mansion, was built high on a hill on Gottingen Street overlooking the dock-yard, during the period 1814–18, to serve as the official residence for the Commander-in-Chief. Then, in 1819, the Naval Board abruptly moved the headquarters to Bermuda. Although Halifax and Bermuda each had various geographical, political, economic, social and other advantages and disadvantages, it has never been clear why the Naval Board ordered the move, given that, all things considered, Bermuda was probably marginally inferior to Halifax as a location for the naval headquarters.

Although the real reason for the change of headquarters will likely never be known, a humorous story has grown up around the move. Apparently, the admiral commanding at the time raised Berkshire pigs in his back garden and permitted them to roam freely, a practice that upset his civilian neighbours. They asked him to get rid of the pigs, he refused and, so the story goes, in fit of pique, moved his headquarters to Bermuda.

The admiral and the fleet returned to Halifax each May, however, and remained for the summer before sailing to Bermuda in October. The admiral took up residence in Admiralty House whenever he was in Halifax, hosting garden parties in the house's spacious grounds, as well as receptions and other functions as part of his social responsibilities. A new wing was added on the north side of Admiralty House just before Commerell arrived.

After the War of 1812, the duties of the North American and West Indies Station changed very little through the nineteenth century, until the Royal Navy left Canada for good in 1905. The navy's main role was to show the flag, patrol the fishing grounds and keep a suspicious eye on the United States as it continued its western expansion driven by the concept of Manifest Destiny. In 1870, Imperial troops were withdrawn from Canada, except for the garrisons at Halifax and Esquimalt, British Columbia, and the headquarters of the Commander-in-Chief was transferred from Quebec to Halifax. Now, at least for part of the year, the British naval and army commanders in Canada were co-located.

The number of ships on the North American and West Indies Station after Confederation varied from ten to twenty, usually averaging twelve. Halifax profited greatly from the continued naval and military presence in the city, with merchants, tradespeople and farmers reaping the benefits of catering to this market. Haligonians were also very conscious of the cosmopolitan look that the large numbers of sailors and soldiers gave the city, which many felt "elevated and refined the tone of Halifax society." They were delighted when visitors from Britain compared their city to a small English garrison town. On the other hand, the large number of taverns and brothels, as well as incidents of public drunkenness and brawling, displeased many. Some felt the city had been hurt more than helped by being a garrison town, but others tacitly accepted this status as part of the cost of maintaining Halifax's prosperity.

When Commerell returned to England in 1885, he ran for Parliament and served as an MP for three years. He was promoted full admiral on April 12, 1886, and the next year his KCB was advanced to a Knight Grand Cross (GCB) in honour of the queen's Golden Jubilee. In 1888, he became Commander-in-Chief at Portsmouth, the RN's major station. While there, he was the navy's host for the visit of Victoria's cousin, Kaiser Wilhelm II, to a naval review in 1889. The kaiser wanted to present Commerell with a decoration, but was prevented from doing so by protocol, so instead gave him a beautifully jewelled sword. The same year, *Vanity Fair* published another print of Commerell, wearing naval evening dress.

More honours followed. In 1891, Commerell became Groom in Waiting to the Queen and reached the pinnacle of his career on February 14, 1892, when he was promoted Admiral of the Fleet. Commerell retired in 1899, but did not live very long to enjoy it. He died at his home at 45 Rutland Gate, near Hyde Park in London, on May 21, 1901, just four months after the long-reigning queen, whom he had served so well for so long. He was buried in the Cheriton Road Cemetery, Folkestone, close to Dover, overlooking the waters of the English Channel. Representatives of the newly-crowned King Edward VII (Victoria's son), the kaiser and several nobles, as well as a host of serving and retired naval officers attended his memorial service in London. Commerell's wife, Matillda Maria, whom he had married in 1853, survived him, and went on to live to a very great age, before she died in 1930. His name is on his wife's memorial in Holy Trinity Church, Brompton, in southwest London; there is also a plaque in his memory in St. Ann's Church in the Portsmouth Naval Dockyard, Hampshire. Commerell had a daughter, Ella, who died in 1887, two years after she married Captain Alexander Russell. Commerell's VC is privately held and not on public display.

Lieutenant William Henry Snyder Nickerson
Royal Army Medical Corps,
attached Mounted Infantry, British Army
Wakkerstroom, South Africa, April 20, 1900

William Henry Snyder Nickerson was the first Canadian and the only soldier from Atlantic Canada to be awarded the Victoria Cross for service in the Boer War, where he served in the British Army. However, he is rarely, if ever, recognized as Canadian. Many references on Canadian VC recipients do not even record him, or, if they do, he is listed as someone "associated" with Canada. Yet he was the first person born in New Brunswick to earn the VC, as well as the first of only two junior officers from the region to achieve this high distinction. He was also the only regional VC recipient from the army not to earn his VC as a member of the infantry, serving instead in the Royal Army Medical Corps. Finally, he was the only Atlantic Canadian to make the military a full-time career. Although others served for many years and in more than one war, Nickerson was the only one to serve continuously throughout his working life (although William Hall comes close).

Nickerson joined the army just in time to participate in the last of Queen Victoria's "little wars"—the Boer or South African War of 1899–1902. The war was fought against the descendants of the original Dutch farmers who first settled in the southern tip of Africa in 1652. When Britain acquired the region in 1815, the Boers remained fiercely independent and did not take kindly to outsiders meddling in their affairs, especially the British, the world's inveterate meddlers at the time.

In frustration, the Boers made what is called The Great Trek northwards from 1835 over a period of several years. With this exodus, the Boers established two independent states, the South African Republic, or Transvaal, and the Orange Free State, far inland and away from the interfering British—or so they thought. The discovery of diamonds and gold in Transvaal brought in so-called *Uitlanders* (outsiders) bent on making their fortune. As the large foreign population grew it soon outnumbered the Boers and *Uitlanders* began demanding the same rights as Boer citizens, and in this they received British backing.

Matters came to a head in 1898, when Britain attempted to force Transvaal to permit *Uitlanders* to vote. When negotiations failed, both sides began preparations for war. Transvaal then issued an ultimatum: Britain had to withdraw its troops from the borders of Transvaal and recall those who had landed in South Africa since June or were on the way by ship. The British refused, and in the early morning hours of October 12, 1899, troops of the Boer's citizen militia advanced into the British territories of Cape Colony and Natal. The South African War had begun.

At the time, no one in authority expected a handful of mere farmers to hold off—and defeat on several occasions—the most experienced regular army in the world for three years. However, the Boers had several advantages. They were a rugged people, exceptional marksmen and horsemen who were fighting on familiar terrain and were used to living off the land. They also possessed a strong belief in being God's chosen people and in the righteousness of their cause. In the end, it took nearly half a million of the Empire's soldiers to finally subdue perhaps forty thousand Boers.

Lieutenant Nickerson arrived in South Africa in August, 1899, one of five thousand soldiers sent from Britain that summer to reinforce the seven-thousand-man garrison in Cape Colony and Natal. The Boer offensive soon ran out of steam. By the end of the year, the Boers had bogged down in sieges of British forces at Ladysmith, Kimberley and Mafeking. When the British attempted to relieve the first two towns, they suffered defeats at the battles of Magersfontein, Stormberg and Colenso during the second week of December 1899, which soon became known as "Black Week." The British Army and the British public, accustomed to their soldiers triumphing repeatedly over poorly armed natives, were stunned. The British changed generals.

Organized loosely as mounted infantry into groups called commandos, the Boers were exceptionally mobile on horseback, skilled in the bushcraft of the veldt and expert marksmen equipped with modern, high-powered rifles. Fortunately for the British, the Boers ignored their advantages and resorted to static warfare, the worst possible course of action for them. It gave the British generals time to build up and organize their forces. The new British commander, Field Marshal Lord Roberts, took a page from the Boers' book of warfare and adopted their principle of mobility. Using cavalry and mounted infantry, he quickly outflanked the Boers, relieved Kimberley and trapped a large Boer army under "General" Piet Cronje at Paardeberg Drift, a ford across the Modder River. The desperate fight that followed marked Canada's first overseas battle.

The Canadian contingent, a one-thousand-man composite infantry unit of militia volunteers, designated the 2nd (Special Service) Battalion, Royal

Canadian Regiment (RCR), was part of the British 19th Infantry Brigade. The brigade was itself part of a larger force of four divisions which encircled the Boers at Paardeberg Drift, who were skillfully dug into the banks of the Modder. The Canadians first fight occurred on February 18, 1900. After hours under fire in the scorching sun—and a brief, icy cold rainstorm—they joined a British battalion in a suicidal frontal assault against the well-protected Boers. It ended in failure. Twenty-one Canadians were killed and another sixty wounded in the regiment's bloodiest engagement of the war, a day that came to be called "Bloody Sunday." The Canadian battalion's chance to redeem itself came a few days later, on February 27, against a new position the Boers had withdrawn to about three kilometres away.

The Canadians attacked in the early pre-dawn hours, bayonets fixed, only to run into withering Boer fire less than a hundred metres from the enemy trenches. Someone yelled "Retire!" but the two companies from the Maritimes—G from New Brunswick and Prince Edward Island and H from Nova Scotia—either did not hear the order or chose to ignore it and tenaciously hung on. They dug in, maintained their position and kept up a steady close-range fire on the Boers. Shortly after dawn, a white flag fluttered above the enemy trenches and the Boers, forty-one hundred strong— nearly ten percent of their army—surrendered at Paardeberg. At a cost of another thirteen dead and thirty-six wounded, the Royal Canadian Regiment won Canada's first overseas battle and earned their country's first foreign battle honour. Canada and the Empire heaped praise on the Royal Canadians. Paardeberg became known as "The Dawn of Majuba Day" for avenging a British defeat by the Boers at Majuba Hill, nineteen years earlier to the day. It was the first significant victory of the war, hailed as the beginning of the reversal of British fortunes. The RCR still celebrates Paardeberg Day annually.

Meanwhile, Nickerson had been attached to the Mounted Infantry as their medical doctor. On April 20, 1900, his unit attacked a feature known as Bwab's Hill, while the infantry of the Worcestershire Regiment at nearby Wakkerstroom advanced in support of his unit. A Worcestershire soldier, who was severely wounded in the stomach and had his innards protruding, lay exposed in the open where he fell. Due to heavy, concentrated fire from the Boers, designed to hold back British reinforcements, stretcher-bearers were unable to reach him.

That evening, as the infantry launched their attack in support of the mounted troops, Nickerson moved forward to the wounded man. Under

WILLIAM HENRY SNYDER NICKERSON WAS THE FIRST NEW BRUNSWICK–BORN RECIPI-
ENT OF THE VICTORIA CROSS. A DOCTOR AND CAREER ARMY MAN, HE EARNED HIS
MEDAL ON APRIL 20, 1900, DURING THE BOER WAR.

intense rifle and shell fire, he saw to his injuries, stitching up his stomach
and remaining with him until he could be moved to safety. This bravery
under fire earned Nickerson his VC. The citation was published in the
London Gazette on February 12, 1901.

Nickerson was an outstanding army doctor. Among the entries in his
personnel records for his time in South Africa are such comments as "good
work performed after the Battle of Stormberg [one of the British defeats of
Black Week]" and "repeatedly brought to my notice for the excellent work
he has done under fire." Yet, most of his work was not with the wounded;
far more soldiers died of disease during the Boer War than of any other
cause. Only six thousand of twenty thousand deaths during the conflict
were battle casualties. Heat, dust and flies contributed to much of the illness, but the main cause was drinking water from polluted sources, which
led to the ubiquitous "enteric fever" (as typhoid was then called) and
dysentery.

When Nickerson did look after wounded soldiers, their wounds were usually "remarkably benign," the result of the high-velocity, small-calibre Mauser rifles used by the Boers, intended to kill cleanly. The steel-plated Mauser bullets caused less tissue destruction than the large calibre lead bullets normally used by armies, and did not ricochet and damage other areas of the body as much, or introduce foreign matter into the wound, causing infection. They usually passed straight through the body. Soldiers described Mauser wounds as being painless at first, feeling like "being pushed, or tapped with a hammer." One war correspondent even noted, "Death from a Mauser bullet is less painful than the drawing of a tooth. Such at least appears to be the case, speaking generally from apparent evidence, without having the opportunity of collecting the opinions of those who have actually died."

Since the medical disasters of the Crimean War, the Army Medical Department had been undergoing continuous improvement, resulting in the creation of the Royal Army Medical Corps in 1898. During the Boer War, medical attention was rapid and efficient, benefiting from recent major advances in surgery, sterilization, anaesthesia and x-rays. The system was geared to initial treatment by unit doctors on the battlefield or at nearby dressing stations, followed where necessary by evacuation to mobile field ambulances, where primary surgical care was given, and on to stationary hospitals and base hospitals. An added bonus of the dry South African heat was it speeded up the healing process without infection. Except for serious chest and abdominal injuries, most wounds were well treated.

After the victory of the Royal Canadian Regiment at Paardeberg, Field Marshal Lord Roberts continued his relentless advance against the Boers and entered Bloemfontein, the Orange Free State capital, in March 1900, and Pretoria, the Transvaal capital, in June. The British thought the war was over, but somebody forgot to tell the Boers, who resorted to guerilla tactics, a form of warfare that suited their highly mobile commandos. The war dragged on, forcing the British to introduce some of the innovations of modern warfare: a scorched earth policy to deny supplies to the Boers, fortified strong points, wire fence barriers, mobile flying columns and, much to their discredit, the first use of concentration camps, in which they interred Boer women and children.

Later that year, on November 29, Nickerson became a captain, "specially promoted for services in S. Africa." In April 1901, a year after the act that earned him the VC, he received a Mention-in-Dispatches. Nickerson remained in South Africa throughout the war, and did not return to England until September 1902, several months after the signing of the Treaty of Vereeniging on 31 May, at which the Boers finally accepted British rule.

Nickerson was born in Dorchester on March 27, 1875, the son of the Reverend David Robert Nickerson, a retired Royal Navy chaplain, and Catherine, the daughter of the late Reverend W. H. Snyder. His father was born in St. Thomas, Upper Canada and his mother was also born in Canada. He was educated at Portsmouth and Manchester Grammar Schools in England, followed by medical training at Owens College at Manchester University. Upon qualifying as a doctor in 1896, he followed in his father's footsteps and joined the British Army, enlisting in the newly formed Royal Army Medical Corps on July 27, 1898, as a lieutenant. As the senior subaltern in the initial group of officers gazetted into the corps, he was, in a sense, the very first officer of the corps.

An older brother, George, born in Shelburne, Nova Scotia, on May 19, 1873, also joined the army at the same time and was commissioned on the same date. George was seconded to the Egyptian Army and served in Egypt until he retired in 1907, having received a Mention-in-Dispatches in 1900, promotion to captain in 1901 and the Imperial Ottoman Order of the Osmanieh, 4th Class, in 1907. George Nickerson died in Egypt two years after he left the army.

After the war, Captain William Nickerson returned to England briefly, then served overseas in Egypt from November 1902 to August 1904, then in Sierra Leone from November 1905 to December 1906. This was followed by a long period of home service until early 1911, during which time he became a major, in July 1909. He also pursued his professional studies, qualifying as a specialist in bacteriology in 1905 and obtaining a Diploma in Public Health in 1907 from Victoria University, Manchester. Nickerson was then posted to India, where he served until May 1914. During the First World War, he was with the cavalry of the British Expeditionary Force (BEF) during the Retreat from Antwerp in 1914, and was at the First and Second Battles of Ypres as well as at the Battle of Neuve Chapelle and on the Somme in 1915. On the Western Front, "His idea of a pleasant afternoon ride was to view the countryside and canter out to whatever spot seemed to be the centre of enemy activity." On one such occasion, he rode out to a dressing station where "a young corporal was putting up a fine show under very sticky conditions." On returning to headquarters, Nickerson asked who the corporal was and, on being told his name, said, "He must get a MM." True to Nickerson's words, the young corporal subsequently received the Military Medal.

Nickerson was promoted lieutenant-colonel in March 1915 and temporary colonel in July 1916. He left France in November 1915, having been Mentioned-in-Dispatches twice, to serve on the Salonika Front in Greece, a little-known, almost ignored, campaign. Although almost all of the Canadian war effort was on the Western Front in France and Flanders, in that out-of-the-way corner of the war, Nickerson served with Canadian medical personnel first as assistant, and then deputy, director of medical services in British divisions.

Allied operations came about on the Salonika Front because of the threat of a renewed attack by the Central Powers on Serbia in mid-1915, with Serbia requesting Greece's assistance. In response, a French and a British division began landing at Salonika in northeastern Greece, in October. Then armies from Germany, Austria and Bulgaria (the latter a recent entry to the war), overran Serbia in November. Greece promptly declared her neutrality, leaving a threat to the Allied rear throughout the campaign. The French and British forces, reinforced by the remnants of the Serbian army, grew to more than a quarter of a million men entrenched in a fortified position around Salonika known as the "Bird Cage." The German press had another name for it, contemptuously referring to the Allied position as their "largest internment camp."

Unfortunately, Allied planning for the administrative side of the campaign appeared to be almost non-existent and their ranks were soon decimated by sickness due to a lack of medical personnel and equipment. With their medical resources already severely overstretched, the British called on the Canadians for help. In response, Canada sent three Army Medical Corps units to the Salonika Front, to be attached to the XVI British Corps. The first to arrive was No. 4 General Hospital, which disembarked in Salonika in early November and set up a tented hospital six kilometres north of the city in a record forty-eight hours. Among its ranks was a young orderly from Toronto who worked as a clerk in the bacteriological department—Private Pearson, Lester B. By the end of the month, more than a thousand patients graced its tented wards. No. 5 General Hospital followed in mid-December and set up to the east of the city, while the third and final unit, No. 1 Stationary Hospital, did not arrive until early March 1916. It took over a New Zealand tented hospital about five kilometres northeast of the city. Nursing sisters served with all three units.

Initially, the majority of hospital patients were suffering from diseases, such as typhoid and paratyphoid, enteritis, dysentery and malaria, or injuries from accidents. That changed in September, with the first Allied counteroffensive, which petered out after ten weeks, leaving fifty thousand casualties, ten percent of them British. The weather added to the numerous problems the hospitals and their patients already experienced in a remote, hostile region at the end of a tenuous supply line. The winters were bitterly cold, while by June temperatures inside the tents soared to 38° Celsius. Lice and fleas pestered medical staff and their charges alike. Warmer weather brought out the anopheles mosquito and, by early summer 1917, the hospitals began to fill with malaria patients. They stayed full. Because many soldiers required treatment for the disease more than once, by the end of the war 110 percent of the British Army on the front had been treated for it, including large numbers of medical staff.

All three Canadian hospitals left Salonika in mid-August 1917. Nickerson was not so lucky. As in South Africa, he remained long after the war ended, only leaving Greece in September 1919, almost a full year after the Armistice. During that period, he was deputy director of medical services for the Allied Corps in Constantinople, administering the complicated return of wounded British and Indian soldiers, Turkish prisoners and Russian refugees. For his distinguished services he was Mentioned-in-Dispatches four more times.

Nickerson was a stern disciplinarian with a fearless, upright character. A rugged, bronzed, wiry figure, spartan in his personal habits, his dress in the field consisted of one khaki uniform and a change of underclothes. Even high in the Balkan mountains, he took a cold-water bath in a small canvas tub outside his tent every morning. Although it took a while to get to know him, he was universally liked and respected by all ranks. He would often be found "chatting reassuringly to small groups of men undergoing stress and strain in forward areas and never as the VIP stalking impressively through avenues of whitewash followed by a dejected and apprehensive procession."

Nickerson seems not to have known the meaning of the word fear. When any part of the division was being shelled, he would ride straight out to the area to ensure casualties were being evacuated promptly. On one such occasion, he noticed a medical officer and a stretcher party coming from the front towards a bridge that was being shelled heavily, carrying a wounded officer. Nickerson directed the stretcher-bearers to stay where they were, while he calmly sat nearby and watched the MO "render rather difficult and urgent assistance to the patients under fire." He wrote out a recommendation for the immediate award of an MC for the officer. Another time, after just returning from leave, he wandered off before dawn to check on new positions his units had occupied during his absence. As British infantry advanced to attack that morning, they spotted a lone figure under a tree in No Man's Land. It was Nickerson, having wandered slightly astray.

After the war, Nickerson married Nancy Waller in 1919; together they had a daughter and a son. From 1922–25, he served in Egypt, confirmed in rank as a colonel. Nickerson returned to England in March 1925 on promotion to major-general (having skipped the rank of brigadier) and was appointed deputy director of medical services for Eastern Command, headquartered in London, as well as Honorary Surgeon to King George V. In 1929, he became director of medical services in India, a position he held until 1933, when he came home for the last time, on retirement.

Though retired, Nickerson did not stop working. Four months later he was appointed Colonel Commandant of the Royal Army Medical Corps, an honorary position he held until the end of the Second World War. During that conflict, he did his bit for the war effort, serving as a ship's doctor in an Atlantic convoy in 1940, and in the Port of London Authority Emergency Service in 1941. He then joined the Home Guard, in which he served until the war ended.

Nickerson received many honours during his lifetime, including Commander of the Order of St. Michael and St. George (CMG), Companion of the Order of the Bath (CB) and the British Medical Association's Gold Medal. He died on April 10, 1954, aged seventy-nine, almost the last of the surviving medical corps VCs. At his memorial service in the chapel of London's Queen Alexandra Military Hospital "could be seen several elderly gentlemen, some of them 'rather feeble of foot and rheumatic of shoulder,'" veterans of the First World War, who forty years ago had been young NCOs and privates in one of Nickerson's units. After so many years, these veterans "had come back to pay their last respects to their beloved chief." Nickerson is buried on the grounds of his home in Cour, on the Kintyre Peninsula in Argyll, Scotland. His Victoria Cross is privately held.

Lieutenant Ronald Neil Stuart

HMS *Pargust*, Royal Naval Reserve
The North Atlantic Ocean, June 7, 1917

During the First World War, the German use of a new type of weapon, the submarine, brought Britain nearly to starvation and the Allies to the brink of defeat. Almost too late, it was learned that the convoy system was the best defence against unrestricted submarine warfare, but the Admiralty did not introduce it until the end of April 1917. In the meantime, various expedients were tried against the submarines. One of these, the Q-ship, was introduced in 1915 and was initially successful until the Germans cottoned on to the new tactic.

Q-ships, or mystery ships, were civilian vessels—tramp steamers, colliers (or coal transports), sailing ships—that appeared to be easy prey for German submarines, but once a U-boat came within range the Q-ship would suddenly reveal its true nature: it was heavily armed with guns, torpedoes and depth-charges. A Q-ship used many strategies to lure the enemy to within range: its crew might wear civilian clothes, sometimes the ship's appearance would be altered, the captain's "wife" might be present on the bridge, and—once the submarine had made itself known—there would be a hasty and clumsy abandonment of the ship by a "panic party" while the captain and the remainder of the crew stayed concealed on board. At the appropriate moment, once the U-boat was at the closest possible range, the White Ensign was run up, camouflage screens dropped and the ship's guns opened fire. By the end of 1916, Q-ships had sunk six U-boats.

Q-SHIPS, OR MYSTERY SHIPS, WERE PART OF BRITAIN'S ANSWER TO THE GERMAN U-BOAT MENACE. DISGUISED AS CIVILIAN SHIPS, THEIR EXTENSIVE ARMAMENT AND GUN CREWS REMAINED HIDDEN UNTIL AN UNSUSPECTING U-BOAT SURFACED. HMS DUNRAVEN IS PICTURED ON FIRE IN 1917.

In 1917, Ronald Stuart was first lieutenant in *Q.5*, the ex-collier *Loderer*, which had been converted with all the normal devices of a Q-ship. *Q.5* was armed with a 12-pounder gun in a fake steering house aft, two more hidden behind hinged partitions on the main deck and a further two in dummy cabins on the upper deck. In addition, she carried a hidden 6-pounder at each end of the bridge and a Maxim gun in a "chicken coop" amidships. On February 17, *Q.5* was sailing off the west coast of Ireland when a torpedo track was sighted heading for the ship at about 9:45 A.M. In accordance with standard practice, her captain, Commander Gordon Campbell, altered her speed and course, allowing the torpedo to strike his ship in the area of the engine room bulkhead. The panic party got away immediately in their boats while the ship began to settle by her stern. Meanwhile, the captain and the gun crews remained hidden as *U-83* approached closer, still submerged.

The German submarine surfaced at 10:05, on the port bow, about 275 metres away, where none of *Q.5*'s guns could be brought to bear. The U-boat then began to pass down the port side, headed for the panic party's boats. She was fully surfaced as she passed abeam when the captain ordered the guns to open fire at ninety metres range. Almost all of the forty-five shells that were fired hit their mark, sinking *U-83* with all hands, except for an officer and a sailor.

By this time, *Q.5* was so low in the water that she was in danger of sinking as well. Campbell sent off a signal: "*Q.5* slowly sinking respectively wishes you goodbye." Fortunately, two RN warships arrived in time to take her in tow and safely beach her. Among the decorations awarded to the crew were a VC for Campbell, who had earlier received the Distinguished Service Order (DSO), and a DSO for Stuart. When awarded for gallantry, especially to a junior officer, as Stuart's was, the DSO is considered second only to the VC.

Virtually all of the ship's company, including Stuart, followed Campbell to his next command, *Pargust*, the three thousand-ton converted collier *Vittoria*. Amongst her armaments were one 4-inch and four 12-pounder guns, two 14-inch torpedo tubes and depth charges. In addition, Campbell had overseen her conversion to include improved radio equipment and better and quicker acting gun concealment.

At 8:00 A.M. on June 7, 1917, *Pargust* was well out into the Atlantic when a torpedo fired from close range struck her starboard side. The panic party duly departed and at 8:15 a submarine's periscope was spotted on the port bow. The U-boat circled the ship before surfacing on the starboard beam, stopped about forty-five metres away, and her captain came out onto the bridge. Campbell immediately gave the order to fire, most of the thirty-eight rounds fired hitting their target. As the submarine *UC-29*, a minelayer, tried to get under way it blew up and sank. Again, there were only two survivors. *Pargust* was immobilized, and had to be towed back to Queenstown, Ireland.

In a rare gesture, King George V awarded the Victoria Cross to the whole ship. Under Rule 13 of the Royal Warrant of January 29, 1856, the crew was allowed to select one officer and one seaman among them by ballot to receive the VC on behalf of them all. Lieutenant Stuart and Seaman William Williams were the two chosen. The king presented them with their medals in the forecourt of Buckingham Palace on July 21, 1917, only one day after they had been announced. Campbell got a bar to his DSO, as well as promotion to captain, ahead of five hundred others on the list. The citation for Stuart's VC, published along with Seaman Williams's in the *London Gazette* on July 20, 1917, did not divulge their roles as members of a Q-ship's company, or any details of the award, because of the secrecy surrounding the Q-ships

Stuart left *Q.5* to command his own vessel, the Q-sloop *Tamarisk*. While he was captain of *Tamarisk*, he stood by USS *Cassin* after a submarine torpedoed it on October 15, 1917 (believed to be the first hit scored by the Germans against an American destroyer). *Cassin*'s stern was blown off, making it impossible to steer

KING GEORGE V PRESENTED RONALD NEIL STUART WITH HIS VICTORIA CROSS AT BUCKINGHAM PALACE ON JULY 21, 1917. BECAUSE OF THE SECRECY SURROUNDING Q-SHIPS, THE DETAILS OF HIS CITATION WERE DELIBERATELY VAGUE.

it, while one sailor was killed and five more injured. With great difficulty, and at very great risk to his own ship, Stuart got a line on *Cassin* and towed it safely back to port. For this action he was awarded the United States Navy Cross. The next year he was promoted lieutenant-commander and subsequently awarded the French *Croix de Guerre avec Palmes*. He also commanded one of the first destroyers, the 250-tonne, twenty-seven-knot *Opossum*, which was armed with a 12-pounder and two torpedo tubes.

Ronald Neil Stuart had the sea in his blood. He was a professional seaman, carrying on the seafaring traditions of at least five generations of his forebears. He had a double connection to Canada, through his family and his vocation. Although Stuart was born at 31 Kelvin Grove, Toxteth Park, in Liverpool, England, on August 26, 1886, his grandfather had settled in Prince Edward Island and his father, a master mariner who sailed clipper ships from England to Australia, was born there.

Stuart received his education at Shaw Street College in Liverpool and went to sea at fifteen, as an apprentice in the barque *Kirkhill*, in 1902. He soon learned of the dangers of the sea. On one occasion, in his third year as an apprentice, *Kirkhill* spent forty-two days trying to round Cape Horn, eventually foundering off the Falkland Islands. Stuart and the rest of the crew spent quite a few days in lifeboats before they made landfall. Another incident from the days of sail, an accident involving a cargo of sugar, left him with scarred fingertips for the rest of his life.

Stuart was a typical bluff sailor: blond, ruddy and powerful. He was known as a hard man and a hard taskmaster. After *Kirkhill*, he joined the Allan Line steamship company and served in various ships around the world. In 1915, the Canadian Pacific Railway (CPR) acquired the Allan Line, and Stuart remained with them for the rest of his working life. Shortly after the outbreak of the First World War, he joined the Royal Naval Reserve (RNR), becoming a probationary sub-lieutenant in October 1914, confirmed in rank in May 1915 and promoted lieutenant in September 1916.

When the war ended, Stuart resumed his pre-war career with Canadian Pacific and remained in the RNR. In the spring of 1919, he married Evelyn Wright. By a special Ensign Warrant of May 14, 1927 he was authorized to fly the Blue Ensign from any ship he commanded. He maintained his naval qualifications, becoming commander on June 30, 1928 and captain on July 1, 1935. He also became honorary president of the Sea Urchins, the Royal Naval Reserve Officers' Club.

His career in the CPR paralleled that in the RNR. He was staff captain in the RMS *Empress of France* (from 1924 to 1926), master of *Minnesota* (1926 to 1929) and captain of the RMS *Duchess of York* (1929 to 1934). In this latter capacity, he brought a group of Canadian VC recipients to the Victoria Cross Dinner in the Guildhall, London, in November 1929. In 1934, he achieved the top rank of his profession when he was appointed captain of the 38,550-tonne liner *Empress of Britain* and commodore of the entire CPR fleet. Stuart remained in this position until 1936, when he finally came ashore for good. First, he was general superintendent for CP Steamships in Montreal, followed in 1938 by general manager for the company in London. While there, he was appointed naval aide-de-camp to King George VI in 1941. He remained as the general manager in Great Britain until his retirement in 1951.

He and his wife, Evelyn, had three sons and two daughters. Two of their sons carried on the Stuart family tradition of going to sea by serving in the RN and RCN. Stuart was predeceased by Evelyn in 1930, and spent his retirement years living with his three sisters in Charing, Kent. Ronald Stuart died there at his home, Beryl Lodge, on February 8, 1954, at the age of sixty-seven and is buried in the Charing Cemetery, under a commemoration headstone. British newspaper obituaries at the time referred to him as "Anglo-Canadian." Stuart's VC and other medals are on display at the National Maritime Museum in Greenwich, England. A road, Stuart Close, in Lee-on-Solent, Hampshire, England, is named after him.

Commander Claude Congreve Dobson
CMB.31, Royal Navy
Kronstadt, Russia, August 18, 1919

Claude Dobson had an interesting connection to Nova Scotia—he met his wife there while on official duty for the RN. Dobson and a subordinate, Gordon Steele, were the last two VCs awarded for what was ostensibly the First World War, although the raid in question occurred nine months after the guns fell silent on November 11, 1918. In fact, Dobson and Steele were gazetted for their VCs on November 11, 1919, the first anniversary of Armistice Day.

While the First World War may have ended in 1918 for the vast majority of fighting men, for several thousand others it lasted well into the next year. After the Bolshevik Revolution took Russia out of the war, the Allies dispatched an intervention force to Russia, which fought in Siberia, the Far East and other parts of that vast country. Several nations contributed to this force, including Canada. The Canadian Siberian Expeditionary Force, made up of five thousand veterans from the Western Front, landed at Murmansk and Archangel and distinguished themselves on the Dvina Front. Other Canadians served in the Far East, at Vladivostok, or in the south, on the Persian border. At last, by the fall of 1919, all Canadians were withdrawn.

On the British side, an expeditionary force protected large stocks of Allied supplies sitting at Murmansk and Archangel, which had been originally intended for Imperial Russian troops while they still fought Germany. At the same time, an RN squadron under Rear Admiral Sir Walter Cowan blockaded the huge naval base at Kronstadt, which guarded the entrance of the channel leading to St. Petersburg in the Gulf of Finland. It operated from a base established at Bjorko Sound, on the Finnish side, about fifty kilometres west of Kronstadt, and eventually consisted of some eighty ships.

Britain's instructions to Cowan were not clear; although he had to blockade two Russian battleships at Kronstadt, he was not allowed to take action with motor boats or aircraft. Such inactivity did not please Cowan. anxious to get into action. He realized, however, that his flotilla of light cruisers and destroyers was insufficient to force an action or stop the larger Russian ships should they decide to break out. As he considered ways to immobilize the Russians, Lieutenant Augustine Agar, in two shallow draught, twelve-metre, thirty-five-knot coastal motor boats, *CMB.4* and *CMB.7*, was carrying out operations clandestinely, ferrying secret agents and information out of Kronstadt Harbour. When an anti-Bolshevik insurrection broke out in Kronstadt in mid-June, Agar undertook a daring raid into the harbour and torpedoed the 5,950-tonne cruiser *Oleg* in the face of murderous fire, for which he received the VC.

After Agar showed what could be done with CMBs, the Admiralty lifted the ban on offensive action in July, and eight eighteen-metre craft, armed with Lewis machine guns and one or two 18-inch torpedoes, joined Cowan's Baltic squadron. The idea of striking a heavier blow with CMBs appealed to Cowan, and he discussed the possibilities with Agar. The result was another operation in the RN's great tradition of raiding and cutting-out parties. Although officially named "Operation RK" (after Admiral Roger Keyes, who conceived the great Zeebrugge, Belgium, raid of 1918), it became known as "The Scooter Raid." It would draw on Agar's experience to successfully navigate the attackers through a chain of forts guarding the North Channel, connected by a submerged seawall.

On August 17, at 8:15 P.M., the eight CMBs left the RN base at Bjorko Sound in two designated groups under command of Commander Claude Congreve Dobson in *CMB.31*, heading for Kronstadt, on the south side of Kotlin Island across the bay. Two officers, an engine-room artificer and a Finn with knowledge of the local waters manned each CMB. Although Dobson was a relative newcomer to CMBs, his selection to command the raid was a popular one and he had already proven his bravery and skill after four long war years in submarines.

In July 1915, while in command of *C.27*, Dobson attacked and sank the German sub *U-23* in the Atlantic. However, the submarine service took its toll on Dobson. In August 1918, he was diagnosed with neurasthenia, a condition variously known as combat fatigue or combat stress—the post-traumatic stress disorder of today. He was posted to a shore billet with the Admiralty in London and, eight months later, after being declared fit for service at sea, was sent to the CMB depot at Osea Island in Essex, probably for further recovery. Ten weeks later, he was on his way to Finland to join Cowan's squadron.

Dobson's small force reached the north side of Kotlin Island about 12:30 A.M., ten minutes before a diversionary bombing attack by eight aircraft. The air attack aimed to assist the CMBs in crossing the submerged seawall and slipping by the forts guarding the harbour's entrance to northeast of the island. At the time, Kronstadt was the most heavily defended naval port in the world, although its overall effectiveness had been reduced somewhat by the Bolsheviks removal of many of its guns and most experienced personnel. The forts were supposed to be armed with large-calibre 11-inch, 9-inch and 6-inch guns, but some of them were equipped with only rifles and machine guns. The aerial bombing distraction worked and the gun crews were caught off guard. Even when the CMBs reached the inner harbour, some of the heavy gun crews did not fire, either because they thought they might hit each other or they could not depress their guns sufficiently to hit the small craft.

In addition to the two groups of three CMBs, two other motorboats were to act independently. One was to attack the guard ship anchored off the narrow entrance to the inner basin, while the second, commanded by Agar, was a small reserve, ready for the unexpected. The first group, which included Dobson, started its attack at 1:40 A.M. *CMB.79* led the way into the inner basin and scored a direct hit on a submarine depot ship, alerting any Russians who still might be asleep to the attack. As the defenders scrambled to man machine guns and searchlights, Dobson's craft and the third craft of his group swung in a wide arc to port, to line themselves up on two battleships moored against the seawall. Dobson's attack was picture perfect and he released both his torpedoes within a few hundred metres of *Andrei Pervosvanni*. His "tin fish" ran true and achieved direct hits on the battleship, as his craft moved alongside the seawall to await the attack of the third boat of his group, *CMB.88*.

But things were not going well in *CMB.88*. As she started her turn inside the basin, her commander, Lieutenant "Mossy" Dayrell-Reed, slumped over the wheel, shot in the head. Lieutenant Gordon Steele, the second officer aboard the CMB, immediately left the Lewis gun he had been firing, dragged his wounded captain from the controls and took over. He brought the boat back on course, pressed home his attack through the smoke coming from Dobson's target and fired his torpedoes at less than two hundred metres. One of them hit *Petropavlovsk*'s mooring cable, but the other blasted a gaping hole in the ship's port bow. Steele then joined the other two CMBs waiting nearby and headed for home, with *CMB.88* leading because of his injured captain. They made it safely to Admiral Cowan's waiting flagship, where Dayrell-Reed was transferred to her sickbay. He lived long enough for the Admiral to congratulate him.

While the first attack was still underway, the second group of three CMBs began their run. At the entrance to the inner basin, one of them collided with a CMB from the first group that was making its way out of the basin, and damaged it sufficiently that its commander had to blow it up. Then the CMB that rammed the other was hit by shell fire from the Russian guardship, blowing her out of the water and killing the crew. Agar, standing off the entrance, successfully fired his torpedoes into a group of auxiliary vessels. He waited until the surviving CMBs made it out of the harbour and followed them, bringing up the rear.

The results of the attack were impressive. The British lost three CMBs with eight men killed and nine taken prisoner. In exchange, two battleships and a submarine depot ship were sunk. Virtually everyone involved in the raid received an award. Dobson and Steele were awarded the VC, and were gazetted together on November 11, 1919. Six officers received the DSO and another eight the Distinguished Service Cross (DSC). All fifteen sailors who survived the raid received Distinguished Service Medals, while three collected a Mention-in-Dispatches. A handful of brave men in flimsy little boats had scored an impressive victory. Unfortunately, the raid came at an inopportune time, just as the British government's attitude towards the Bolsheviks started to change. It had also commenced delicate negotiations for the withdrawal of British land forces from Archangel.

Claude Congreve "Tommy" Dobson was born at Barton Regis, Bristol, Somerset (now Avon and Somerset), on January 1, 1885, the son of Nelson Congreve Dobson and Louise Pierce. The elder Dobson was house surgeon at Bristol General Hospital from 1867 to 1871, and later practiced medicine in Clifton from 1871 to 1898. Dobson went to Clifton Preparatory School, followed by Clifton College, then to the RN cadet training ship Britannia at Dartmouth Naval College in 1899, before joining the fleet in 1901. Interestingly, his two first ships each had a Canadian connection. The first was the battleship *Magnificent*, her name later reincarnated as Canada's first aircraft carrier in 1948. (Canadians had manned two RN escort carriers, *Puncher* and *Nabob* during the Second World War, and later "borrowed" the light fleet carrier *Warrior* for a year before returning it to the RN.) Dobson's second ship was the cruiser *Niobe*, later sold to the fledgling RCN in 1910, along with *Rainbow*, as Canada's first naval ships.

After service in the Channel, the Mediterranean and China, Dobson was promoted lieutenant in 1906, having achieved five "firsts" in his examinations. He commenced training for the new and rapidly expanding submarine service in early 1907 and commanded his first sub, *A.7*, in mid-1909. He was commanding *C.27* when the First World War started, and served on submarines for the rest of the war. On July 20, 1915, while Dobson's submarine was dived and under tow of the armed trawler *Princess Louise* (another British ruse, similar to the Q-ships, to lure enemy submarines into attacking a seemingly vulnerable target), he attacked and sank the German U-boat, *U-23*. For this action, Dobson received the DSO, which was gazetted on September 13, 1915.

After four very hard years in submarines Dobson was diagnosed with neurasthenia, put in Cowan's squadron and given command of the Kronstadt Raid. He continued in command of a CMB flotilla after the war and in 1920 was chosen for a mission to Canada. In July of that year, he travelled to Baddeck on Cape Breton Island with two other RN officers, one an engine expert and the other experienced in small craft design. Their mission was to inspect and witness demonstrations of *HD-4*, a high-speed hydrofoil built by Alexander Graham Bell and Casey Baldwin.

Bell and Baldwin had been working on hydrofoils since 1908, originally as a means of assisting an aircraft in taking off. They soon began experimenting with hydrofoils for their own sake and built several. Their experiments culminated with the HD series, which stood for "hydrodrome," Bell's term for a hydrofoil. On September 9, 1919, *HD-4* set the world speed record for watercraft. It sped across the water like a dragonfly skimming the surface of a pond and attained 114.01 kilometres per hour, a record unbroken for another ten years. After *HD-4*'s incredible performance, Bell sent further details to the RCN and British Admiralty.

Such speeds were of obvious interest to the Admiralty for the adoption of hydrofoils to their CMB fleet, and Dobson, with his background and experience, was an obvious choice to lead the British team. The British witnessed nine hydrofoil trials from July 7 to 31, including one with Dobson at the wheel, under various weather and loading conditions and were impressed with what they saw, reporting favourably upon it. Dobson

LESS THAN A YEAR AFTER RECEIVING THE VICTORIA CROSS, CLAUDE CONGREVE DOBSON (SECOND FROM LEFT) WENT TO CAPE BRETON ISLAND TO WITNESS TRIALS OF A RECORD-BREAKING HYDROFOIL BUILT BY ALEXANDER GRAHAM BELL AND CASEY BALDWIN.

believed that Bell and Baldwin's hydrofoil would make an excellent gun platform, significantly better than a CMB. He was also impressed with Edith "Polly" MacMechan, who had been Mabel Bell's secretary at the Bell estate, *Beinn Bhreagh*, since 1917.

Polly was the daughter of Nova Scotian scholar and writer, Professor Archibald MacMechan of Dalhousie University, author of such provincial histories as *Red Snow on Grand Pré*, *Sagas of the Sea*, *Old Province Tales* and *There Go the Ships*, among others. Although Dobson did not leave with a commitment to purchase *HD-4*, he did leave with something else. During his time at *Beinn Bhreagh* he saw Polly at the top of a staircase in the Bell house and said to himself, "That's the girl I'm going to marry!" And so he did. Two days after the British left, Bell recorded in his notebooks, "On Tuesday Commander Dobson paid me a little visit in my study and instead of talking about the trials of the *HD-4*, he startled me with the announcement of his engagement to Miss MacMechan."

Dobson and Polly were married in England three months later at the father of the groom's home in Bristol. Bell gave the bride away. Although the RN never purchased Bell's hydrofoil, Polly noted, "My husband thought *HD-4* could be successful, and he was very disappointed that the Admiralty didn't take it on." She continued, "Mr. Bell was indeed surprised by my engagement. The romance proceeded quite quickly…the Admiralty Commission was only here three weeks! But I think he was pleased it took place under his roof. I think he was a romantic and in a way a sentimentalist in spite of being such a scientist."

The same year he was married, Dobson began to suffer from vision problems and was eventually diagnosed with having a corneal ulcer in his right eye in 1922, which was operated on in 1924. From this time onwards, he suffered from gradually deteriorating vision, but continued to serve in the RN in a variety of command, staff and training appointments. Although he was promoted captain in 1926, his vision forced his premature, but voluntary, retirement in 1935. The next year he was honoured with promotion to rear admiral in retirement. Dobson died in the Royal Naval Hospital, Chatham, Kent, on June 26, 1940, at fifty-five years of age. Eight RN chief petty officers carried his coffin to the graveside in nearby Woodlands Cemetery, Gillingham. In 1990, after Polly's death, Dobson's VC, DSO and other medals were donated to the National Maritime Museum in Greenwich.

CHAPTER 3

SLAUGHTER ON THE SOMME

Private John Chipman Kerr
49th Battalion, Canadian Expeditionary Force
Courcelette, France, September 16, 1916

John Chipman Kerr was the first Nova Scotian and the first Atlantic Canadian to earn the VC in the First World War. He was also the only one of his home province's VC recipients from that war to survive it; the other three Nova Scotians were killed in the actions that earned them their VCs. It was during this "war to end all wars" that the majority of Atlantic Canadian awardees—eight out of eleven—earned their VCs.

Kerr was born on January 11, 1887, in Fox River, Cumberland County, a small village a few miles west of Parrsboro, on the shores of Minas Basin. The communities along this shore were important shipbuilding centres from the late nineteenth century to the 1920s. During this time, more than sixty three- and four-masted schooners were launched from their shipyards. Kerr attended the local Fox River School, walking over three kilometres each way, and went on to study at the Saint John Commercial School. After completing his education, he worked in the lumber business with his brothers Gesner, Roland and Ernest.

Kerr went out west with Roland in 1906, working as lumberjacks in the interior of British Columbia in the Kootenay area. They eventually moved to the Spirit River region of northern Alberta in 1912 to farm a sixty-five-hectare homestead they bought. One day in 1915, Kerr turned to his brother and said, "I am sick of these bloody bulls. I am going to join up." Roland replied, "And leave me with them? I am going too…" Together, the two brothers trudged eighty kilometres south, to the railhead, to get the train to Edmonton. There, they enlisted in the army on November 1, joining a dozen relatives in uniform. On the door of their cabin they left a note reading, "War is hell, but what is homesteading?"

They enlisted in the 66th Battalion, Canadian Expeditionary Force (CEF), which was sent to England in May 1916 for further training. The 66th, like the other CEF battalions, was formed out of the confusion caused by Colonel Sam Hughes, the Minister of Militia and Defence. Instead of using existing mobilization plans based on actual militia units to structure the Canadian contingents for overseas service, he ignored them and created entirely new units designated by a nondescript—and soulless—numbering system. Eventually, there would be 260 battalions in the infantry alone. These new units soon started embellishing their titles with geographic locations and other modifiers to set them apart from the rest of the CEF.

In England, Private "Chip" Kerr was transferred as part of a draft to the 49th (Edmonton) Battalion, in need of reinforcements after the Battle of Sanctuary Wood. The battalion was one of four in 7th Brigade of 3rd Canadian Infantry Division that had been formed at the end

JOHN CHIPMAN KERR FROM FOX RIVER, NOVA SCOTIA, WAS THE FIRST OF EIGHT ATLANTIC CANADIANS TO EARN THE VICTORIA CROSS DURING THE FIRST WORLD WAR. HE HAD THIS PHOTOGRAPH TAKEN IN HASTINGS, ENGLAND, IN 1916, SHORTLY BEFORE HE WAS SENT TO FRANCE AS PART OF A REINFORCEMENT DRAFT.

of 1915 and the beginning of 1916. The other battalions in the brigade were the Royal Canadian Regiment (RCR), Canada's only Permanent Force infantry regiment; the Princess Patricia's Canadian Light Infantry (PPCLI), formed originally from veteran soldiers and the first Canadian unit to reach France; and the 42nd Battalion (Royal Highlanders of Canada), the Canadian Black Watch.

The 7th Brigade began its front line duties in January 1916, replacing 1st Brigade from 1st Division on the Flanders Front in the Canadian sector, between Ypres in the north and Armentières in the south, an area known as the Ypres Salient. It was here that the soldiers of the 49th Battalion were first "bloodied," gaining their initial experience of battle; and it was here that Kerr joined them in June 1916, shortly before his gallant act.

Today, the poppy-covered, gently rolling fields of the Somme belie the slaughter that took place there in 1916. While generations have passed, the expression "the first day on the Somme" is still a potent reminder of the cost of the Allied High Command's failure to break the stalemate of trench warfare on the Western Front. In the Somme area, the Germans were firmly established in their extensive trench and bunker system, occupied since October 1914, behind masses of barbed wire and with their machine guns and artillery dominating No Man's Land. The only response from General Sir Douglas Haig, Commander-in-Chief of the British Expeditionary Force (BEF), of which the Canadian Corps was a part, was a succession of direct, frontal assaults with ever increasing numbers of soldiers—and ever increasing numbers of wounded, maimed, missing, captive and killed.

Plans for a great Anglo-French offensive had been developing since February 1916—an offensive that was to be the decisive knock-out blow to the Germans. However, while these plans were being finalized, the Germans struck first, at the great French fortress-city of Verdun, in February. Verdun soon turned into a symbolic battle for the French, where defeat there was equated with defeat of the entire nation. By the time the battle ended in December 1916, the French had recaptured all the territory they lost earlier to the Germans, but at the cost of 377,000 casualties. For their part, the Germans suffered losses totaling 337,000.

As the French were engaged in what they viewed as a battle for their very survival, it limited their participation in the planned Allied offensive on the Somme farther north. French numbers were curtailed drastically and the British were forced to assume the main burden for the offensive, using divisions from their so-called "New Armies," inexperienced troops raised since the outbreak of the war to replace earlier casualties and hurried into battle with a minimum of training.

At 7:30 A.M. on July 1, 1916—the first day on the Somme—after a five-day preliminary bombardment by 1,537 guns, thirteen British divisions of some one hundred thousand men climbed out of their trenches along a thirty-two-kilometre front. They calmly walked towards the German lines at a stipulated pace of ninety metres per minute, each man struggling forward under an equipment burden of thirty kilograms. The operational planners had expected the intensive British artillery fire to cut the barbed wire, destroy the trenches, kill the enemy and neutralize their machine guns and artillery. However, it soon became clear that this procedure was disastrously unsuccessful. Instead, the Germans scrambled from the protection of their deep shelters as soon as the bombardment ceased, cutting down the British infantry in droves as they struggled across No Man's Land, trying to find gaps in the still largely uncut wire.

As the war progressed, the Germans had learned to counter the massed artillery barrage of the Allies, through a system of defence in depth. The earlier single trench line became a thick fortified belt, with two more similar belts in the rear. Each belt was sufficiently behind the one in front of it to require the Allied artillery to move forward in order to bombard it. All three belts were strongly wired, contained deep dugouts and were linked by a series of strong points, fortified woods and villages. Once their own artillery lifted, the Allies had to get into the German front line before the Germans got out of their dugouts, and then repeat this two more times, each time waiting for their artillery to deploy forward to bombard the next line. Until this problem was solved, the war became one of attrition—reduced to the simple, cold mathematical problem of which side had the most lives to sacrifice.

In that first fateful day on the Somme, the British Army suffered the greatest one-day losses in its history—thirty thousand casualties in the first hour and a total of sixty thousand by nightfall, of which nineteen thousand were fatal. There was nothing to show for these unprecedented injuries and loss of life, except for the smallest of territorial gains, some one thousand metres on a flank, which had no tactical advantage whatsoever. Mercifully, no Canadian units were a part of the massacre. But a unit from a colony that would become part of Canada in another thirty-three years was virtually wiped out near the little village of Beaumont Hamel. More than ninety percent of the Newfoundland Regiment that went into action that day became casualties (see Chapter 8).

Instead of cutting his losses, General Haig persisted in carrying on with the battle over the following days, weeks and months. Ostensibly, he was trying to relieve pressure on the French forces, which were still being bled to death by the Germans at Verdun, a battle already in its 132nd day when the British marched towards the enemy lines on July 1. Unfortunately, the Allies were facing a German Army at the apex of its effectiveness and combat power, dug in behind an enormously strong defensive system.

Over the next two months, two hundred thousand British and seventy thousand French soldiers were lost in this war of attrition, as the cost for an Allied advance of six thousand metres. Haig needed fresh troops to continue, and he called upon the Canadian Corps, commanded by British Lieutenant-General Julian Byng. The Corps started to pull out of its positions in the Ypres Salient in mid-August to training areas at Saint-Omer near the English Channel. Here they were put through their paces in advanced training for the attack, using new tactics based on the lessons learned during the early fighting on the Somme, tactics largely concerned with improving direction-keeping, employing knowledge of leading troops' positions and battlefield control. New orders were also being put into effect concerning offensive operations: thirty percent of a unit's strength would be sent to the rear, to reconstitute it in case of massive casualties; and, from now on, a commander and his deputy at all levels could not be in the same battle. Something was brewing.

The Canadian Corps left its training grounds on August 27 and marched to the Somme, taking over a three thousand-metre section of the front on September 3, along the Pozières Ridge. There, they came under heavy shelling and frequent small attacks. In one of them, Corporal Leo Clarke of the 2nd Battalion earned the VC for single-handedly beating off an attack by over twenty Germans, killing two officers and sixteen soldiers, despite being wounded himself. He never lived to receive his award; he was killed in action three weeks later. His was the first of two VCs earned in the Battle of Courcelette. The first Atlantic Canadian and first Nova Scotian to receive the VC in the war—John Kerr of Edmonton's 49th Battalion—would receive the second.

The various actions along the Pozières Ridge were preliminaries to the next big British push in which the Canadians were about to play their part. This attack would see the introduction of two innovations designed to cut down on the appalling loss of life: the tank, to assist the infantry in breaking through the enemy's trench lines, and the rolling barrage, which enabled the infantry to move forward immediately behind their advancing artillery fire and forced the enemy to stay down in their dugouts until the infantry were upon them. The forgotten principle of fire and movement was about to be reintroduced to the static battlefields of the Western Front.

By September 15, General Haig was ready to begin another major assault. The Canadian Corps, now consisting of three strong divisions, made two attacks on that day. On the right, 4th and 6th brigades of 2nd Division supported by six tanks and preceded by a rolling barrage, attacked towards the village of Courcelette at 6:20 A.M.; their objective was to capture two German trench lines, Sugar and Candy trenches, running roughly at right angles to each other about 800 metres in front of the village. By 7:30, after some stiff fighting, both enemy trenches were firmly in Canadian hands. A follow-on attack, which saw ferocious hand-to-hand combat, commenced early that evening and advanced the division to the far side of Courcelette. Taking part in this attack and the clearing of Courcelette were

NO MAN'S LAND IN FRONT OF THE VILLAGE OF COURCELETTE, THE CANADIAN CORPS'S FIRST OBJECTIVE ON THE SOMME. BY THE TIME THE CANADIANS ARRIVED THERE IN SEPTEMBER 1916, A FIERCE BATTLE HAD BEEN RAGING FOR TWO MONTHS, DEVASTATING THE COUNTRYSIDE.

two units from the Maritimes: the 25th (Nova Scotia Rifles) Battalion and the 26th (New Brunswick) Battalion. Both had entered the trenches for the first time in the Ypres Salient on a wet September evening in 1915, only ten months earlier.

During the First World War, twenty-one infantry battalions were raised in Nova Scotia and New Brunswick for service overseas, eleven in the former province and ten in the latter. All but three of these were broken up to provide reinforcements to other units—the majority after they arrived in England—and were the only infantry units from the Maritime Provinces to serve on the Western Front.

The 25th was organized in Halifax in October and November 1914—the province's first attempt at providing a full battalion for overseas service—from men who enlisted at recruiting centres established across Nova Scotia. Volunteers poured in from several militia units. The 26th was formed in Saint John in November 1914 of men recruited from New Brunswick and Prince Edward Island, many with previous militia service.

The 25th sailed from Halifax on May 20, 1915, while the 26th departed Saint John on June 12. In England, the 25th and 26th were concentrated on the south coast, in the Shorncliffe area, near Folkestone. There they joined the other units of the recently formed 2nd Canadian Division—including the French Canadian 22nd Battalion—as part of 5th Brigade, with whom they remained throughout the war.

In mid-September, the battalions crossed the English Channel and moved off to training areas close behind the front lines in Flanders. In the distance, the low rumble of artillery barrages drove home the point that the war was close at hand. Before the end of the month, the two units entered the trenches near Kemmel, south of Ypres, in the first of many front-line trench tours. A stay in the trenches was governed by a routine developed over time. At dawn and dusk, known in the army as "first light" and "last light" respectively, all soldiers "stood to," weapons at the ready, in case the enemy took advantage of favourable conditions offered by the dim light to launch an attack.

After the morning stand to, soldiers cleaned their rifles, rubbed their feet with whale oil to prevent trench foot and washed and shaved. Breakfast was next, normally consisting of bacon, bread, jam and tea. With breakfast over and the trenches cleaned, those who were not on sentry duty went to sleep. Dinner, the main meal of the day was next, usually a hearty stew or bully beef accompanied by more bread, jam and tea. Rest or various jobs needing to be done followed in the afternoon. Supper arrived after dark, about 10:00 P.M., often consisting of soup, bread and cheese, washed down with the ubiquitous tea.

After dark, it was easier to move about freely and the real work began: reliefs took place; dugouts, machine-gun posts and trenches were dug or repaired; wire was laid; rations, ammunition and other supplies were brought up from the rear; night sentry and listening posts were manned and patrols ventured out into No Man's Land. The trenches were shared with huge rats, far too many to eliminate, attracted by the decaying bodies of men and horses, either unburied or disinterred by artillery fire.

When the battalions' first trench tours ended after a week, each unit had the same number of casualties—five men wounded and one dead. As the Maritimers marched out of the trenches in their mud-spattered uniforms they felt like veterans for the first time. The battalions were to see several more trench tours during the war, as well as many of the other tasks com-

COURCELETTE WAS SUBJECTED TO RELENTLESS ARTILLERY BOMBARDMENT, WHICH OBLITERATED THE TOWN. HUNDREDS OF GERMANS REMAINED HIDDEN IN THE RUBBLE, AND HAD TO BE MOPPED UP BY THE 26TH (NEW BRUNSWICK) BATTALION.

mon to all infantry units—reserve, support, raids, attacks, defence and working parties, to name but a few.

Courcelette was the first major attack for the 25th and 26th battalions. By now, the men of both units were battle-hardened veterans of almost a year in the trenches of the Ypres Salient—the New Brunswickers and Nova Scotians had already earned the respective nicknames "The Fighting 25th" and "The Fighting 26th"—and they were about to start a new phase of warfare on the Somme.

Once 4th and 6th brigades captured Candy and Sugar trenches, the orders from 5th Brigade Headquarters for the follow-up attack against the Germans entrenched in the village of Courcelette spelled out its tasks. As the 22nd and 25th battalions advanced on a 1,150-metre front, 26th would follow close on their heels, mopping up the village and collecting prisoners.

At 5:00 P.M. on Friday, September 15, the three battalions started their advance. The soldiers of the 25th moved forward as if on parade, personally led by their commanding officer, Lieutenant-Colonel E. Hillam. Some 140 metres behind them, the 26th was spread out in two long lines, each 140 metres apart. In addition to his normal equipment, each advancing soldier carried 250 rounds of ammunition, two Mills bombs, three sandbags, two days supply of water and rations, as well as his iron or hard ration to be used in an emergency.

The attacking force had to first advance some 2,750 metres towards a crest, then cross over seven hundred metres of open plateau before reaching the area from which the attack was to be launched, still some nine hundred metres short of Courcelette. As they advanced, a concentrated enemy artillery barrage opened up on them. Soldiers were knocked over, dead or wounded, or blown apart. Others were flung up into the air, some in pieces, or buried under falling earth. With strict orders not to stop to help their wounded comrades, the line pressed resolutely forward.

Under the severe and sustained enemy barrage, the Canadians reached their start line for the attack, deployed into open formation and carried on without the normal brief stop before attacking. The open country and deadly German fire, now heavier due to the addition of machine guns and rifles, prevented such a pause. The 22nd and 25th battalions reached the village and quickly attacked through it, with the French Canadians clearing one half of Courcelette and the Nova Scotians the other, divided by the main street running through the centre of the village. They attained most of their objectives within thirty minutes, after some difficult hand-to-hand fighting, and consolidated their positions to the east of Courcelette. Behind them, the task of mopping up the entire village and the collection of prisoners was left in the capable hands of the 26th Battalion.

Mopping up was the difficult yet essential chore of ensuring no enemy were left behind after the leading troops had passed through, enemy who could suddenly appear from the rear and the flanks and ruin the advance. First, the Germans had to be found and ordered to surrender. If they refused, they had to be attacked and rooted out. Any prisoners taken then had to be escorted to the rear. It was slow, tedious and dangerous work in which soldiers were liable to be fired at by enemy machine guns or snipers at any moment. The New Brunswickers went about their job in a detailed and systematic manner, thoroughly searching the ruins in what proved to be a long, strenuous and costly operation, which took all night and the next day to accomplish. In the end about six hundred prisoners were captured.

Once the Germans realized they had lost Courcelette, they commenced a heavy bombardment that reduced the village to rubble. Under continuous enemy shell and machine-gun fire, casualties continued to mount and sporadic German counterattacks took their toll on the three Canadian battalions. Amongst the ruins, there were many acts of heroism.

After three days, the units of 5th Brigade were relieved. In the darkness of the pre-dawn hours, the remnants of the battalions slowly made their way to the reserve area, eight kilometres to the rear. Moving in small groups to avoid further casualties, they passed the bodies of the dead still lying about on the battlefield. Courcelette was the first of about 250 villages, towns and cities to be captured or liberated by the Canadians during the First World War. The Nova Scotia Rifles and the New Brunswick Battalion had played their parts; the 25th and the 22nd were the first Canadian units to capture an enemy town, while the 26th was the first to mop up a captured village.

Lieutenant-Colonel Hillam concluded his report on the battle to the brigade commander with the words, "General, I have the honour of commanding the finest body of men I have ever seen." The division commander, Major-General Turner, told the New Brunswickers on parade that "if it had not been for the good work of the 26th, the Canadians could not have held Courcelette." The corps commander, Lieutenant-General Byng, later Canada's governor general, complimented the men on the "conduct displayed during the attack and holding of Courcelette."

But the honours and praise had come at a price, with few survivors reaching the reserve area. Although future battles would bring more deaths, the fighting at Courcelette resulted in the largest number of total casualties for the three battalions in any one engagement during the war. The 25th's casualties numbered 304, with thirty-six killed, while the 26th lost 325, including eighty killed. The commanding officer of the 22nd noted in his War Diary, "If Hell is anything like I saw in Courcelette, I would not want my worst enemy to go there." Such was the ferocity of the fighting that a large percentage of the dead were never found. Their names are commemorated on the Canadian National Memorial at Vimy Ridge.

Meanwhile, on the Corps' left flank, 3rd Division had an even more difficult task than 2nd Division. Their objective was a major German trench line to the west of Courcelette, the Fabeck Graben, only a few hundred metres from the Canadian trenches. With 7th and 8th brigades leading the assault, the attacking battalions advanced under determined machine-gun and artillery fire across No Man's Land. They first captured several separate sections of the German line, and by nightfall, 3rd Division's battalions had linked up and were in control of all but the final 250 metres of the Fabeck Graben.

On the next day, September 16, the objective of Private John Kerr's C Company, 49th Battalion, was this last section of German trench. During a bombing attack that afternoon, Kerr was first bayonet man leading twelve men against the trench. The new tactic of "bombing" assumed greater and greater importance as the war continued. "Bombs" were, in fact, early versions of what today are called grenades. Used extensively by infantry during the seventeenth and eighteenth centuries by men known as grenadiers, their use had practically ceased by the end of the eighteenth century.

Grenades were reintroduced during the First World War, especially in trench warfare. The first type of bomb, in use since the end of 1914, was the "jam pot": a crude homemade device constructed from an empty jam tin, filled with shredded gun cotton and tenpenny nails mixed together, into which a detonator attached to a short length of fuse was stuck, and the open top filled with clay to prevent the insides from falling out. When the time came to use it, the fuse was lit and, as official instructions to the bombers stated, thrown "for all you are worth." These early missiles could explode at any moment, and the men who used them were called the Suicide Club. In 1915, Sir William Mills invented the fragmentation grenade that bears his name, and the Mills bomb (officially the No. 5 Mark

1), which resembled the well-known pineapple grenade of the Second World War, became the grenade most widely used by British and Empire forces. Although safer than the rudimentary jam pots because of its built-in four-second delay, Mills bombs still posed a certain danger to their users, and many men were killed or injured while learning to throw them.

The bombers soon became unit specialists, employed centrally under the direction of a battalion bombing officer, usually a junior subaltern. Eventually, this arrangement proved to be entirely unsatisfactory, because of a turf war that emerged between the companies manning the trenches and the bombers, over control of the front lines. The power struggle was only resolved when additional bombers were trained from the companies, with the battalion bombers likewise absorbed into the companies.

During the 49th's bombing attack on September 16, Private Kerr advanced well ahead of the rest of his group, jumped into one end of the enemy trench and began slowly moving along it. He had advanced less than thirty metres when a German sentry threw a bomb at him. Kerr reacted instinctively and put up his arm to protect himself from the blast, but the explosion blew off part of his right forefinger and slightly wounded his right side. By this time, Kerr's buddies had caught up with him, but he remained at the scene rather than report to an aid post. As the fight became a stationary bomb-throwing match over and around a corner of the trench, with a dwindling supply of grenades, Kerr took the initiative. He climbed out of the trench and ran along the parados (the mound at the back of a trench), until he spotted the enemy below him.

Despite loss of blood, Kerr tossed his two remaining bombs down at the Germans and opened fire with his rifle. When his bolt jammed, he continued to direct the bomb-throwing efforts of his comrades by voice and gesture, forcing the enemy back. He then jumped into the trench, discovered a dugout and went in alone, his fellow soldiers close behind him. The Germans were so dispirited by Kerr's tenacity they surrendered. Sixty-two prisoners and the final section of trench were captured. Under continuing enemy fire, Kerr escorted the Germans to Allied lines before reporting for duty. He was immediately sent to an aid post to have his wounds dressed. For this brave act, Kerr was awarded the VC, one of four earned by Canadians on the Somme. He was the ninth Canadian to earn the VC in the war; sixty-three more were to follow. Kerr's VC citation was published in the *London Gazette* on October 26, 1916. In a ceremony at Buckingham Palace on February 5, 1917, King George V pinned the medal on Kerr's chest.

Kerr survived the war to return to his homestead in Alberta. His brother did not; Roland was killed at Ypres in 1917. When Kerr arrived in Edmonton in August 1918, he was given a hero's welcome. Crowds blocked the streets leading to the CPR station as they waited for him and his English bride, Gertrude, to arrive. Mayor Harry Evans and the city's aldermen greeted them and a procession through Edmonton's flag- and bunting-decorated streets followed, as ten thousand spectators cheered and bands played. The parade ended at the Legislative Building where Lieutenant-Governor Robert Brett, Premier Charles Stewart, cabinet ministers and members of the legislature met the Kerrs. In an address, the premier stated, "you have brought an honour that could not be bought and it is the highest honour a soldier can win." He then presented the couple with $700 in gold.

The Kerrs were overawed. Kerr responded to the premier's praise: "We don't go in for heroics at the front. If a man is chosen for the job, he does it and that is all there is to it unless someone sees him doing his duty and rewards him for it. Nobody thinks of gaining distinction. If a man saves his hide, he thinks himself well off."

Kerr took up farming again on his property, but grew tired of it. He sold the Spirit River homestead six years later and went to work in the oil fields at Turner Valley, a few miles south of Calgary. Later, he returned once more to Spirit River, patrolling the Peace River as a forest ranger and running the government ferry at Dunvegan. On the outbreak of the Second World War, Kerr, now fifty-three-years old, re-enlisted in the army. Hoping to improve his chances of being sent overseas, he transferred to the RCAF. He remained in Western Canada however, serving as an RCAF policeman and sergeant of the guard at Sea Island in British Columbia.

At the end of the war, Kerr retired to Port Moody, BC, and was involved in the salmon fishery for a while. A. Y. Jackson, a member of the famous Group of Seven landscape painters, was also a war artist. He painted an official portrait of Kerr, the first Canadian VC recipient to be so recognized by the Canadian Government. In 1951, 2,560-metre high Mount Kerr in Jasper National Park's Victoria Cross Range was named after him, one of five mountains in the seventeen-peak range named after VC recipients. Kerr attended a reception for VC recipients hosted by Queen Elizabeth in 1956, and three years later was presented to the Queen and Prince Philip in New Westminster during a royal tour of Canada. He died in Port Moody on February 19, 1963, aged seventy-six, and was buried in the Veterans' Division of Mountain View Cemetery on Prince Edward Avenue in

Vancouver. Like so many true heroes, and like so many of the surviving veterans of the First World War, Kerr was reluctant to talk about the war or the actions that earned him the VC.

A memorial plaque was placed near the ferry he ran at Dunvegan, Alberta. In 1975, Kerr's widow donated his VC to the Canadian War Museum. It is on loan to and displayed in the Royal Alberta Museum in Edmonton. In July 2001, Nova Scotia Lieutenant-Governor Myra Freeman dedicated a memorial in Port Greville, near Kerr's home village of Fox River, in his memory, as well as to 156 other men and women from the area who served in both world wars and Korea. In his own self-effacing way, Chip Kerr would be proud his efforts, and those of his neighbours, have been so recognized.

Private Robert Edward Ryder
12th (Service) Battalion, The Middlesex Regiment
(Duke of Cambridge's Own), British Army
Thiepval, France, September 26, 1916

A few days after John Kerr's conspicuous bravery at the Fabeck Graben, and only a few hundred metres away, a British soldier who would later have a connection with Atlantic Canada was about to earn his VC. Almost due west of Courcelette stands the village of Thiepval, then dominated by its now-gone chateau to the southwest. Over a twenty-month period, the Germans had turned the village itself into a fortress, with redoubts, blockhouses and concrete shelters, linked by trenches bristling with machine-gun pillboxes. The Germans regarded Thiepval as the key to the defence of the whole area. Attacks on July 1 and afterwards had failed to dislodge the Germans and, by the end of the month, the village itself was totally destroyed. Later attacks were no more successful, until the Allied assault was renewed on September 26.

The 12th Middlesex—part of 54th Brigade, 18th (Eastern) Division—had the task of capturing Thiepval. Many of the German dugouts were still intact despite the constant shelling; they were deep and immensely strong, especially around the chateau. The British attacked at 12:35 P.M. after a three-day bombardment. The Middlesex cleared several trenches until they reached the chateau, where machine-gun fire stopped them. However, a tank rolled up and dealt with the machine guns, enabling the lead company to pass around to the flanks of the chateau.

During the advance, Private Bob Ryder's company was held up by heavy rifle fire coming from a German trench, which killed or wounded all his company's officers. Without leadership, the attack had begun to wane when Ryder stepped into the breach. Disregarding his own safety, he stormed the enemy trench alone and succeeded in clearing it by the skilful handling of his Lewis gun. His bravery inspired his comrades to continue the advance, making a potential failure into a success. For this act, he was awarded the VC, one of five earned by soldiers serving in the Middlesex Regiment (known as the "Die Hards") during the war, including another earned in the same battle on the same day.

Ryder later described what happened, in a report submitted to the War Office:

Next we were at Thiepval, which had been taken and lost several times. At midday, September 26, 1916, we went over the top to attack. At the first check I volunteered to take my gun on and take the trench that was holding up the battalion. I succeeded in getting to the parapet of the German trench, which was two hundred yards from the English lines, and enfiladed it with fire.

The trench was taken and it was reported to my Colonel that I had killed from 100 to 120 Germans. Of my section I had lost the other five. After this trench was captured I went on to the next, about forty yards further on. Halfway we had to take cover and await the tanks. Then, having run out of ammunition, I abandoned the guns and collected the bombs from the dead and wounded and started to bomb the second trench when I was wounded in the hand and leg.

I was then ordered back by an officer of the Northampton Regiment. On my way back I met two German prisoners whom I made bind me up and go back with me. For this I was again recommended, the third time since being in France. I was sent home to England and went to Norwich Military hospital for about two months and was then sent on seven days sick leave, my first leave since leaving England early in 1915.

The citation for Ryder's VC was published in the *London Gazette* on November 26, 1916, and King George V presented Ryder with his medal in December at Buckingham Palace.

Robert Edward Ryder was born in the old workhouse in Harefield, Middlesex, on the outskirts of London, England, on December 17, 1895,

ROBERT EDWARD RYDER POSES WITH HIS PARENTS AND SISTERS, PROUDLY WEARING THE VICTORIA CROSS PRESENTED TO HIM BY KING GEORGE V IN DECEMBER 1916. HIS FIRST WIFE, BESSIE, WHO LATER DIED FROM ILLNESS CAUSED BY WORKING WITH ASBESTOS IN A GAS MASK FACTORY, STANDS TO HIS RIGHT.

the youngest of thirteen children. He started school when he was only three years old, for which his parents paid a penny a week. By the time he was fifteen, he was driving a hay cart into London, a job that started at midnight and ended at 7:00 P.M. the next day. He married his first wife, Bessie, in 1913, when he was eighteen, and worked in construction, eventually becoming a bricklayer. When the First World War broke out, Ryder joined his county regiment, the Middlesex, on September 3, 1914, and went to Colchester for training, and afterwards was posted to the 12th Battalion, The Middlesex Regiment (Duke of Cambridge's Own). In all, the Middlesex (now the Prince of Wales Royal Regiment) raised forty-six battalions for the war, some with such unusual titles as the 16th (Public Schools), the 17th (1st Football) and the 18th (1st Public Works Pioneers) battalions.

Ryder went to France in early 1915, directly into the fighting lines. His battalion occupied trenches along the Somme, where it remained for some time. Ryder recalled, "I expected to be killed...in the winter of 1915. I was up to my waist in water. We used to tie pieces of rope round our middles and secure them to our bayonets so that we didn't fall asleep in the mud. I never thought I would ever get out of that. I was prepared to die." Somehow, like many others, Ryder survived the hell of trench warfare, in the process becoming an automaton: "It was blind obedience. Everything our colonel asked us to do, we did. From the time you go over [the top] you don't have [the] chance to be afraid. You have nothing else on your mind but getting there [on the objective]."

The fact that Ryder was tough may also have helped him survive. He was muscular and strong, able to dive into the water carrying two children on his back. He was also an amateur boxer, and once went fifteen rounds with the great featherweight Jimmy Wilde. "Though he was getting on a bit," Ryder recalled, "and he did hit me six times for every punch I gave him. He never put me down though."

One of his early actions was in the protracted fighting for Trônes Wood, where Ryder was No. 1 (the gunner) on a Lewis machine-gun team. When the soldiers of a fellow battalion, the Royal West Kents, were cut off, they sent a message asking for a machine-gun section to help them. Ryder volunteered, but he and his men were driven back by the Germans and suffered four wounded. Although his actions were commended, he did not receive any award. Subsequently, he rescued three wounded soldiers under heavy fire and was again commended for his action, again without tangible recognition. But that changed very dramatically at Thiepval, where Ryder earned his country's supreme award for courage.

When the fighting on the Somme petered out in mid-November, as winter rains prevented the exhausted men from dragging themselves through the daily deepening mud, the Allies had advanced just under thirteen kilometres on a thirty-two-kilometre front. Casualties were unbelievable, totaling 420,000 for the British, 195,000 for the French and 650,000 for the Germans. The bankruptcy of the British High Command under Haig was complete. Men who had once followed their leaders unquestioningly now began to doubt them and even lose faith in the cause for which they fought. Only one loyalty remained—to their comrades who stood beside them in that living hell.

By Christmas 1916, Ryder was back at the front. According to him, "They wanted to put me on the [parade] square [as an instructor], but I wouldn't have it. I wanted to be back with my pals. When I got there, I didn't know anyone. They'd all been killed." The army promoted Ryder sergeant, "the youngest in the British Army at the time," he claimed. He was only twenty-one years old.

By this time, Bessie Ryder had died of tuberculosis, brought on by asbestos dust from the factory where she worked making gas masks. She left her husband with three small children. After the war, Ryder had only been out of the army and back in Harefield, Middlesex, for a few days when he again displayed the bravery that earned him the VC. He had borrowed his brother's bike to go to nearby Uxbridge to buy some clothes for work, when he saw two runaway horses galloping down the main street, just as children were coming out of school at lunchtime. He managed to grab the reins and somehow stop the horses. The Uxbridge local council promised him a medal for his bravery, but when it learned he wasn't from Uxbridge, the matter was dropped. During the Second World War, Ryder served as a training sergeant at various army installations around the country. Although well into his forties at the time, he could still outrun the much younger men he was training. He was also awarded the Italian Bronze Medal for Military Valour.

After the war, Ryder immigrated to Canada along with his second wife, Rose (Fairbrother), and daughter, Brenda. Rose's oldest daughter from her first marriage had married a Canadian soldier from Hartland, New Brunswick, during the war and, on this basis, Rose decided Canada was the place to go. The family embarked on *Queen Elizabeth* on Boxing Day 1946, disembarked in New York on New Year's Day and took a train to Hartland, arriving on January 3. They stayed with Rose's family initially and Ryder got a job in a lumber mill that first winter. He bought a hundred-acre mixed farm in the spring at Avondale, about twenty-two kilometres from Woodstock, New Brunswick.

Ryder's old shrapnel wound bothered his hip and leg, a condition aggravated by working the farm. After living in Canada for over six years—and although he loved farming—he and Rose sold the farm and returned to England in 1953, where they settled in Hucknall, Nottinghamshire, Rose's home village. Not long after, Ryder had one of the earliest hip replacement operations in the country. But Ryder and Rose never got along very well and, two years after returning to England, he divorced Rose and married

Edna Thornley. Rose returned to Woodstock, where Brenda, now married, had remained. In 1964, Edna embroidered a tablecloth with the names of all VC recipients up till then—some 1,346. In the centre of the tablecloth, she incorporated the VC and the Middlesex regimental badge. Through his later years, in addition to his hip problem, Ryder also suffered from emphysema.

Ryder died at his home in Hucknall, Nottinghamshire, on December 1, 1978, just seventeen days short of his eighty-third birthday. He was buried on December 11 in his home village of Harefield, in the churchyard of St. Mary the Virgin; a Commonwealth War Graves Commission headstone was erected later over his grave. He is honoured with a plaque inside the

Middlesex Guildhall in Westminster and he also served as the model for the full figure of the soldier on the fine First World War memorial there. In accordance with his last wishes, Ryder's VC and ten other medals were presented to the Imperial War Museum, London, in February 1979, where they are on display in the museum's Victoria Cross and George Cross Room. Some of his descendants remained in the Woodstock area, where they still reside.

RYDER POSED AS THE MODEL FOR THE FULL FIGURE OF THE SOLDIER ON THE FINE FIRST WORLD WAR MEMORIAL IN THE MIDDLESEX GUILDHALL IN WESTMINSTER, LONDON. HE IS ALSO HONOURED WITH A PLAQUE INSIDE THE GUILDHALL.

CHAPTER 4

"THE GREATEST MARTYRDOM OF THE WAR"

Temporary Lieutenant-Colonel Philip Eric Bent
9th (Service) Battalion, The Leicester Regiment, British Army
Polygon Wood, Belgium, October 1, 1917

Siegfried Sassoon, one of the greatest British soldier-poets of the First World War, brilliantly encapsulates one of the most horrific battles of the war in his poem "Memorial Tablet (GREAT WAR)":

...I died in hell—
(They called it Passchendaele). My wound was slight,
And I was hobbling back; and then a shell
Burst slick upon the duck-boards: so I fell
Into the bottomless mud, and lost the light.

Equally telling of the horror that was Passchendaele was the reaction of a British general to the muddy quagmire. It was a month after the battle that Lieutenant-General Sir Launcelot Kiggell, who was chief of staff for the recently promoted Field Marshal Haig, paid a rare senior staff officer's visit to the Ypres Front, his first to that combat zone. As he proceeded in his staff car from the town of Ypres through the former battlefield, he surveyed the devastation around him, becoming more and more agitated. Finally, Kiggell burst out crying, "Good God, did we really send men to fight in that?" The officer who was escorting him, a veteran of the battle, replied quietly, "It's worse farther up."

At 3:50 A.M. on July 31, 1917, Haig mounted an offensive in Flanders intended to dislodge the Germans from the high ground east of Ypres. Known to the British as the Third Battle of Ypres, the Canadians called it Passchendaele, after the nearby village. Haig had a number of reasons for launching an offensive in Flanders. In the first place, he had always wanted to fight the Germans here, closest to the British supply ports of Le Havre and Calais. Secondly, he wanted to capture the German submarine bases on the Belgian coast, as the Admiralty believed U-boats were about to sever Britain's Atlantic lifeline. Finally, the operation had another purpose, which the British Commander-in-Chief did not even communicate to his own government. Mutiny, mass desertions and refusals to obey orders had broken out in as many as sixty French divisions, and the French Army was incapable of withstanding a major attack, or launching a major offensive, for some time. In the meantime, the British would have to keep the Germans occupied until the French Army was once again in a fit state to fight.

Initially the British attacks met with little resistance and achieved some degree of success. In the northern half of the Ypres Salient, the advancing British quickly captured the villages of Pilkem, Langemarck and Saint-Julien, the latter the scene of the courageous stand by 1st Canadian Division during the Second Battle of Ypres in 1915, when chlorine gas was first used. In the southern portion, the British experienced similar early successes, capturing the village of Hooge and Bellewaerde Ridge. When the Germans did react, they managed to halt the British advance, and even pushed them back in the north.

Then, another key adversary entered the picture—the weather. Three days of torrential downpour followed the initial attacks, turning the low-lying Flanders Plain surrounding Ypres into a sea of mud. Previous artillery barrages had already destroyed the region's normal drainage system and the water had no place to go. Mingling with soil and clay, it created a gooey, clinging, waist-deep mass that slowed down all movement and dragged hundreds of heavily laden or wounded soldiers to their deaths as they struggled across the stinking ooze. Unusually high levels of rain and the results of millions of exploding shells ensured the mud remained.

Throughout August, the British attacks continued, retaking the ruined villages of Langemarck and Saint-Julien in mid-month, and advancing slowly against determined German opposition. But by the end of the month the expected breakthrough had still not occurred and the British had suffered 70,800 casualties. It was time to regroup and refit before going on the offensive again. On September 20, British and Australian troops resumed the attack, moving in an easterly direction towards the village of Zonnebeke, driving back the Germans over the next few days. On September 26, the Australians captured Polygon Wood, a key position south of Zonnebeke, and the remains of Zonnebeke itself, but at great cost. Then, on the night of September 30, 110th Brigade, made up of four Leicestershire units, joined the battle to relieve the Australians, marching up to Polygon Wood along wooden duckboards, the only safe means of traversing the battlefield.

While the 8th Battalion of the Leicestershire Regiment took over the left hand side of the brigade frontage inside the wood (by this point almost completely denuded of trees), the 9th Battalion under Lieutenant-Colonel Philip Bent occupied the right, with both units facing roughly southeast. One of the soldiers in Bent's battalion headquarters, D. A. Bacon, recalled that night:

Though we had fully prepared for a rough night, the first hours passed quietly enough and we began to hope that after all, the Ypres bark might be worse than its bite. The ordinary precautions of a battlefront were observed; patrols were pushed out to reconnoitre the ground and to give alarm in case of sudden attack. At headquarters, as soon as the relief was reported complete and the Australians had cleared, and orders as to dispositions and instructions in case of alarm had been given, it was decided to try to obtain a night's rest. I use the word 'try' because we were mud-wallowing in the open air, it was bitterly cold and no blankets could have been brought, and we were on the edge of a volcano that might and as a matter of fact did, belch forth at any moment. Firstly, we dug ourselves in as well as possible, in front of the headquarter Mebus [an abandoned German pillbox], and with the aid of some old wood planks lying about, contrived to make a little shelter and firing position. At midnight, we lay down in the mud with the idea of sleeping, each taking one turn at sentry.

In these miserable surroundings and depressing circumstances, Lieutenant-Colonel Bent spent his last night on earth. Shortly after the relief of the Australians was complete on the early morning of October 1, the Germans launched a strong counter-attack from the southeast against the 8th and 9th Battalions in an attempt to retake Polygon Wood. It began about 4:40 A.M. with a terrific artillery barrage that included smoke to cover the movement of the German troops as they formed up for the attack. Again, in Bacon's words:

> *At 5:30 A.M., the enemy launched a determined infantry assault against our positions, through the smoke screen. The first wave of attackers was beaten off by 'A' Company using Lewis gun and rifle fire. The second wave was also successfully driven off on the* [battalion's] *Front, but penetrated somewhat into the lines of the battalion on our left flank. By this time the SOS was being sent up all along the Front—several were discharged at Head Qrs, both night and daylight rockets—and the situation looked threatening; Brigade Headquarters was called upon for immediate help. Under the determined pressure of the enemy 'A' Company commenced and continued to fall back. Lieut Col PE Bent DSO commanding the 9th Leicesters, decided to make a counter-attack, with such forces as were available, as no help could be expected from the troops in support for some hours, owing to the conditions of approach and the heavy and deep enemy barrage.*

With the situation so critical and confused, Bent took charge and formed a small force from his headquarters personnel, the reserve company and others. In a letter to Bent's mother, Sophy, one of his officers explained what happened next:

> *The Colonel immediately led a counter-attack.... Utterly regardless of his own safety he went ahead of the men, waving his revolver and shouting 'Forward the Tigers!' The attack was a brilliant success and the enemy definitively driven back, but at the moment of victory the Colonel was struck by a bullet and killed instantly.*
>
> *It was the finest act possible, and undoubtedly saved the day.... We feel the loss of our Colonel more than words can say, for he was beloved by all ranks. I am very proud to have had the privilege of knowing such a fine*

Christian gentleman, whose memory will live forever in the history of the Regiment.

For this final act of heroism, Bent was awarded the VC. His body was never found, being lost to the Ypres mud forever. He was one of twenty-six officers and 491 soldiers from his unit killed in the war. His name is inscribed on the Tyne Cot Memorial to the Missing eight kilometres north of Ypres, along with 34,888 others killed in the Ypres Salient who have no known grave, including three other VC recipients. The citation for Bent's VC was published in the *London Gazette* on January 11, 1918. His mother received her son's VC and the DSO he had been awarded earlier by the king at Buckingham Palace. His sword hangs in the Cathedral Church of All Saints in Halifax, while his VC is on display in the Royal Leicestershire Regimental Museum in England. His name is on the War Memorial outside St. Alban's Church, Hindhead, Surrey, and on a memorial at Ashby-de-la-Zouch Grammar School, which he had attended.

TYNE COT CEMETERY, A FEW KILOMETRES EAST OF YPRES, BELGIUM, WAS NAMED BY BRITISH SOLDIERS AFTER GERMAN BUNKERS IN THE AREA THAT REMINDED THEM OF THE SMALL COTTAGES ON THEIR NATIVE TYNESIDE IN NORTHERN ENGLAND. IT IS THE LARGEST COMMONWEALTH WAR GRAVES COMMISSION CEMETERY IN THE WORLD AND COMMEMORATES 47,000 DEAD AND MISSING SOLDIERS, INCLUDING 966 CANADIANS.

Philip Eric Bent, although he served in the British Army (as William Nickerson did) is always considered a Canadian. Bent was the only officer from Nova Scotia to earn the Victoria Cross, and was the first Atlantic Canadian to be awarded the VC posthumously. Bent was born in Halifax on January 3, 1891, and moved with his family to Leicestershire, England, where he attended Ashby Boys Grammar School in Ashby-de-la-Zouch. In 1910 he joined HMS *Conway*, a former RN two-decker moored in the

PHILIP BENT FROM HALIFAX BECAME COMMANDING OFFICER OF THE BRITISH ARMY'S 9TH BATTALION, THE LEICESTERSHIRE REGIMENT, AT THE AGE OF 25. HIS OFFICIAL RANK WAS "SECOND LIEUTENANT, TEMPORARY LIEUTENANT COLONEL." BENT'S SWORD HANGS IN THE CATHEDRAL CHURCH OF ALL SAINTS, HALIFAX.

River Mersey, near Birkenhead, and used as a training ship to turn out officers for Britain's huge merchant fleet. After graduation in 1912, Bent went to sea. When the war broke out he had his second mate's ticket and was a qualified Merchant Navy officer. Bent and a friend joined the Royal Scots on October 2, 1914, believing the war would be over by Christmas and wanting to see some action. (If the recruiters had known of his nautical qualifications, he would never have been allowed to join the army and would have been commissioned into the navy. He may well have survived the war as well, but it is highly unlikely he would have earned the VC.) The next month Bent was granted a temporary commission as a 2nd lieutenant in the Leicestershire Regiment, nicknamed "The Tigers."

The Leicestershire Regiment had been raised in London as the 17th Regiment of Foot in September 1688, during the last years of the reign of James II, at the time of the creation of the first true standing army in

Britain. Previously, colonels raised or disbanded regiments as the need arose. Prophetically, one of the unit's earliest campaigns was against France in Flanders, the cockpit of Europe, during the War of the League of Augsburg. The regiment earned its first battle honour, "Namur," there in 1695, the second oldest of all British battle honours.

The Seven Year's War (1756–1763) saw the beginning of the regiment's connection to Canada, when the 17th Foot served in North America as part of General James Wolfe's brigade. It took part in the capture of Fortress Louisbourg on Cape Breton Island in 1758, for which it was awarded its second battle honour, "Louisbourg," and the regiment's grenadier company participated in the Battle of the Plains of Abraham at the fall of Quebec. The 17th Foot's link with Leicester began a few years later, in 1782, when regiments were allocated separate recruiting districts across the country.

The regiment's nickname, "The Tigers," came about in 1825, when George IV recognized the unit's service in India by approving the figure of the "Royal Tiger" on its colours and appointments, with the word "Hindoostan" superscribed "as a lasting testimony to the exemplary conduct of the Corps during its period of service in India from 1804 to 1823." After the Crimean War, a second battalion was formed and, during the latter half of the nineteenth century, both battalions served in Canada, at Montreal and Quebec, as well as at Halifax. The 1st Battalion was stationed in Halifax from 1863 to 1865, while the 2nd Battalion was posted there from 1891 to 1893, making it one of the last Imperial units to be stationed in Canada before the final withdrawal of British troops in 1906. Coincidentally, its service in Halifax overlapped with Philip Bent's infancy there.

On the outbreak of the First World War, British Prime Minister Herbert Asquith appointed Field Marshal Lord Kitchener, the nation's greatest living soldier, as Secretary of State for War. Whatever his many failings, Kitchener clearly recognized one fact: the war would not be over by Christmas as almost everyone else believed, but would be a long war of three or more years. Accordingly, he gained cabinet approval to call for hundreds of thousands of volunteers. At the time, the Leicestershire Regiment consisted of two regular battalions, the 1st and 2nd; a reserve battalion, the 3rd; and two territorial battalions, the 4th and 5th. In short order, four more battalions—the 6th, 7th, 8th and 9th—were raised in August and September 1914 and termed "service" battalions, as they were created only for war service. However, perhaps uniquely, these latter four battalions were kept together and formed into the 110th Brigade at the end of April 1915, becoming known, not surprisingly, as The Leicestershire Brigade.

At Perlam Down on Salisbury Plain, the brigade, and Bent, underwent their final training, with Bent in command of Number 2 Platoon, A Company. Then, Bent was temporarily attached to the Bedfordshire Regiment, where he received his permanent commission in June 1915. Later that month, with Bent still away, King George V inspected the Leicestershire Brigade, a sure sign it would be proceeding overseas short-ly—but where? The Middle East and Gallipoli headed the list of possible soldier-speculated locations.

In the end, the brigade went to France, landing in the pre-dawn hours of July 30, 1915, and entering the front lines near Berles-au-Bois in northern France in September after a period of instruction from experienced troops. The 110th spent the winter of 1915–16 in the trenches, until transferred south in July to replace another brigade decimated in the opening days of Haig's great Somme offensive. Here, each battalion suffered about three hundred dead or wounded in taking Bazentin Wood. It took a few weeks for the news of the attack to filter through to the home front. When it did, "Across Leicester, in street after street, the blinds were being drawn as they had never been before up to this point in the war." Among the casualty replacements was one 2nd lieutenant who wrote home, "Have just received my orders to go up the line. I go at 7:40 tonight to the 9th Leicesters (some mouldy crowd I s'pose)."

Meanwhile, Bent had been made temporary captain with the Bedfordshires in April 1916, before he was transferred back to the Leicesters to help rebuild its depleted companies. He rejoined the 9th Battalion in time to take part in its next battle on the Somme, at Gueudecourt, on September 25. Attacking rather unusually in the middle of the day, at 12:35 P.M., instead of in the early morning, the 8th and 9th battalions led the brigade, followed by the 6th and 7th. The Leicesters man-aged to capture Goat Trench, the first of three German lines in front of the town, but according to the 9th Battalion's War Diary, "Advance hung up on account of MG fire and rifle fire. Enemy still occupying Grid Trench [the second German line]." With the help of a lone tank, the Leicesters eventual-ly succeeded in capturing Gueudecourt on the morning of September 26, but again with heavy losses. Once more a period of rebuilding was required before the men from Leicestershire would be able to rejoin the fight.

The spring of 1917 found Bent, as a twenty-six-year-old temporary lieutenant-colonel, in command of the 9th Battalion. From March through to June, the Leicesters were part of the concerted attempt to break through the Hindenburg Line, one of the strongest fortified positions ever constructed by the Germans. Bent's performance as CO during this period was recognized in June when he was awarded the DSO, given only to commissioned officers "for distinguished conduct and devotion to duty" who had been previously honourably mentioned in dispatches "for meritorious or distinguished service in the field, or before the enemy."

On June 16, as Bent led his battalion forward up the communication trenches in support of another brigade's attack on the Hindenburg Line, they ran into a heavy German counter-bombardment. Bacon, one of the soldiers with Bent in Battalion Headquarters, later described what happened: "the enemy's counter fire became intense and many casualties were caused…. Despite…obstacles and the enemy's stout defence, our men…eventually got into the hostile works and hung on for several hours; and desperate hand to hand fighting took place."

Shortly afterwards, the British attack was called off, but not before suffering casualties. In July, the Leicestershire Brigade went into divisional reserve until early September, when they entrained for the north and Bent's date with destiny. The Leicesters moved to Belgium for the third time since arriving on the continent, occupying an area in the rear of the Ypres Salient. By this point, in late September, the Third Battle of Ypres had been underway for two months and the whole region resembled a vast waterlogged and cratered lunar landscape. To add to the soldiers' suffering, mustard gas, first used by the Germans that summer, had saturated and dissolved in pools of water. Anyone attempting to use shell-hole water for washing or drinking, even if boiled beforehand, was likely to be poisoned. A 7th Battalion soldier summed it up succinctly: "Foulest place we have yet struck."

By October 3, two days after Bent's act of self-sacrifice at Polygon Wood, the British and Australians suffered another thirty thousand casualties. Though they renewed their assault on October 4, attempting to seize the higher—and drier—ground of Passchendaele Ridge, the Germans stopped the concerted attacks of the British and the Australian and New Zealand Army Corps (Anzac) cold in their tracks. By October 12, they could advance no farther, having run themselves literally into the ground. In the face of a revitalized German defence, which had earlier seemed on the verge of faltering, Field Marshal Haig persisted in the operation, as he had at the Somme, long after any hope of achieving the original objectives had disappeared. The assaults continued as the weather worsened, and the fall rains and endless artillery barrages continued to churn the marshy, low-lying ground into a muddy quagmire. But before he could carry on, Haig had to look elsewhere for fresh troops to renew the attack.

Private James Peter Robertson
27th Battalion, Canadian Expeditionary Force
Passchendaele, Belgium, November 6, 1917

In mid-October, with conditions at their worst, Field Marshal Haig summoned the Canadian Corps from the Vimy area to capture Passchendaele Ridge, the low rise of ground a few metres above the devastated landscape which gave its German defenders a significant advantage. Lieutenant-General Sir Arthur Currie, the new corps commander, objected vigorously to what he considered a futile mission, but was over-ruled by Haig. Currie advised the British commander that in his estimation the advance of twenty-five hundred metres would cost some sixteen thousand casualties and was not worth it. In fact, he confided in his diary, "Passchendaele is not worth one drop of blood." Indeed, by the time the twelve-day battle ended on November 6, the Canadians had suffered thousands of casualties to gain the ridge, ground that served no tactical or strategic purpose whatsoever. But the Canadians' bravery in the most appalling conditions imaginable also earned nine VCs within two weeks, two of them posthumously. This is an amazing number, especially when compared with the Second World War, when a larger Canadian Army earned ten VCs over the course of the entire conflict.

The Canadian Corps started to take over the Ypres area on October 18. The assault began at dawn eight days later, as twenty thousand Canadians attacked across the desolate, muddy quagmire of No Man's Land towards the German lines, situated along the slight rise that commanded the battle-field. Marking the enemy's positions was a new type of fortification designed to overcome the problem of digging into the low-lying, water-logged ground—the pillbox—so-called because their low, round shape resembled the common drugstore article. These heavily armed steel and concrete emplacements, surrounded by barbed wire, were formidable obstacles.

PASSCHENDAELE BECAME A BYWORD FOR THE HORRORS OF THE FIRST WORLD WAR, ITS WOODS BLASTED INTO SHATTERED STUMPS, ITS EARTH CHURNED INTO A STINKING, MUDDY MORASS.

Over the next few days, the Canadians slowly pushed forward through the mud, first attacking and then pausing to regroup and bring up fresh battalions for the next phase. During the final attack to capture the village of Passchendaele on November 6, 2nd Canadian Division's 6th Brigade advanced with three battalions up: the 28th (North West), the 31st (Alberta) and the 27th (City of Winnipeg). The Winnipeggers objective was the village itself, while its sister battalions were to drive the Germans off the ridge. The brigade moved forward behind a creeping barrage that advanced at the rate of 140 metres every eight minutes. The first trench line was taken before the enemy could scramble out of their dugouts after the barrage lifted, and the soldiers of the 27th went to work with their bayonets. No prisoners were taken.

Nearer the village, they ran into increasing enemy machine-gun fire and a single German machine gun held up the advance of Private Pete Robertson's platoon in the 27th Battalion, killing many of his comrades. When volunteers were requested to attack the enemy position, Robertson was one of the first to come forward. He was also the first to reach the gun. He ran ahead of the others, dashed around to the flank, jumped the barbed wire and killed four Germans with his bayonet. When the rest tried to run, he turned the captured gun on them, allowing his platoon to advance. Still carrying the machine gun, Robertson led a charge into the village, firing on

SOMEHOW, CANADIAN SOLDIERS MANAGED TO FIGHT WHILE STRUGGLING THROUGH THE MUD OF PASSCHENDAELE.

the retreating Germans and keeping the enemy snipers down as Passchendaele was cleared of the enemy, house by house. Robertson's actions contributed significantly to the platoon's success and inspired his comrades.

During the rest of the day, the 27th consolidated their position, as carrying parties brought forward ammunition and other supplies. The Germans reacted, as usual, with heavy shelling and local counterattacks. Shortly thereafter, Robertson heard of two badly wounded Canadian snipers left in No Man's Land. Without awaiting orders, he immediately went to their aid. Robertson brought the first man in under intense fire and was returning for the second when he was felled by a bullet. Getting up, he carried on through the muddy morass and reached the other soldier. Wounded and exhausted, he somehow summoned the strength to pick him up and carry him towards the Canadian lines. He almost reached safety when a shell exploded nearby, killing him instantly. For these brave acts, the thirty-four-year-old Robertson received the posthumous award of the VC. His VC citation was published in the *London Gazette* on January 11, 1918.

For all their efforts, the Allies had succeeded only in deepening the Ypres Salient by just over seven muddy kilometers, at a staggering cost of an estimated three hundred thousand casualties. Besides Robertson, the 27th Battalion lost another 250 officers and men. Sadly, General Currie had foreseen the results with amazing prescience. The final Canadian count of 15,654 casualties was not far off his prediction to Haig of sixteen thousand losses.

James Peter Robertson was born in Albion Mines (now Stellarton), Nova Scotia, on October 26, 1883, and moved with his family to Springhill four years later, where he received his early education. On February 21, 1891, a violent explosion occurred on the east slope of the Cumberland Railway and Coal Company's colliery at Springhill, where seven-year-old Pete and his fourteen-year-old brother, Daniel, were working. Danny was hauling empty coal boxes with his horse, Jenny. He was sitting on the front box, when a terrific blast of flame knocked him backwards into it. It blew out his light and instantly killed Jenny. After lying in the box dumbfounded for a few minutes, the crashing of timbers and roof-falls all round him brought him to his senses. He jumped from the box and discovered his clothes were on fire.

Danny tore off his blazing coat and vest, painfully burning his hands and arms in the process, and started groping through the darkness to find his way out of the pit. He had only gone a short distance when he heard pathetic cries coming through the blackness. It was twelve-year-old Judson Farris, huddling in a corner, frightened almost to death. Although Danny could not pick up the boy because of the burns on his arms, he managed to coax Judson onto his back and brought him to safety. When Danny learned Pete was still underground, he decided to go back and get him, but a rescue party instead took Danny to the pithead, where he found Pete already waiting for him. Altogether, the explosion took the lives of 125 men and boys.

R. A. H. Morrow, a contemporary author, called Danny the "Hero Boy," and wrote, "As the heroism of this brave boy is, perhaps, unparalleled in history, an effort should be made at once to reward his bravery in some suitable way." Danny was eventually rewarded with a gold cross, purchased with pennies collected from the surrounding area by children, and presented by Sir Charles Tupper, a native of nearby Amherst. The obverse was inscribed "In Admiration of Danny Robertson's Bravery." Danny's courageous act eerily foreshadowed his brother Pete's heroism a quarter-century later.

In 1899, the family moved to Medicine Hat, Alberta, where Danny, Pete and their father joined the Canadian Pacific Railway. Pete eventually became an engineer. It was here he earned the nickname "Singing Pete" because of his habit of singing and whistling cheerfully, day or night, no matter where he was. In June 1915, he enlisted at MacLeod, Alberta, in the 13th Battalion, Canadian Mounted Rifles, and was sent overseas. In England, Robertson was transferred to the 27th (City of Winnipeg) Battalion, part of 6th Brigade, 2nd Division.

PRIVATE PETE ROBERTSON OF STELLARTON, NOVA SCOTIA, EARNED HIS VICTORIA CROSS FOR CAPTURING A GERMAN MACHINE-GUN NEST AND ATTEMPTING TO SAVE THE LIVES OF TWO FELLOW SOLDIERS DURING THE CLOSING STAGES OF THE BATTLE OF PASSCHENDAELE ON NOVEMBER 6, 1917. HE SUCCEEDED IN SAVING ONE, BUT WAS KILLED BY AN ARTILLERY EXPLOSION WHILE CARRYING IN THE SECOND SOLDIER.

The 27th Battalion had been raised in response to the mobilization of a Second Canadian Contingent in late October 1914. The existing militia of Military District No. 10, comprising Manitoba, Saskatchewan and Northwest Ontario, had already contributed to four infantry battalions of the First Canadian Contingent, and was now called upon to form three more, plus an artillery brigade. Manitoba's six infantry regiments were assigned quotas to form the 27th Battalion, which were easily met. The battalion concentrated in Winnipeg for preliminary training, and proceeded to England in May 1915.

Towards the middle of September, after further training, 2nd Division, including 27th Battalion, arrived in France under Major-General Richard Turner, a VC recipient from the Boer War with the Royal Canadian Dragoons. With two divisions in the field, a Canadian Corps was formed under British Lieutenant-General Sir Edwin Alderson; at the same time, Major-General

Arthur Currie replaced Alderson commanding 1st Division. For the first time in history Canadian officers commanded Canadian divisions. At the end of December, the corps's strength was increased, when 3rd Division arrived under Major-General M. S. Mercer.

After a period of familiarization, Private Robertson entered the line with his battalion in the Kemmel Hill Sector of the Ypres Salient on October 1. The Winnipeggers' first casualty occurred three days later, when a German sniper killed a sergeant directing a work party repairing a section of trench. After a week in the front line trenches, Robertson and his comrades marched out to the 27th's rest billets in the rear. They stayed in the Kemmel area with the Canadian Corps until February 1916, when they moved to the nearby Saint-Eloi Sector, a more active area. There, the men of the 27th were about to experience one of the most confused and frustrating battles in Canadian history, and the most serious engagement for Canadian troops since the Second Battle of Ypres.

Just before the Canadians took over, the British units in this sector had been ordered to "straighten out the line" along a five hundred metre section due south of the town of Saint-Eloi, in an attempt to eliminate a slightly elevated German position projecting into the British line. The British blew six large mines, obliterating landmarks, collapsing trenches on both sides and creating four massive craters about fifteen metres deep in the centre, flanked by three smaller ones, one to the west and two to the east.

The four large craters, each surrounded by a muddy lip fifty metres wide and six metres high, were a barrier to both movement and visibility. The sector of front line assigned to the 27th Battalion stretched the entire length of the craters. But no trenches existed to take over; the front was nothing more than a line on a map. Unfortunately, due to the destruction of the landscape, even that was wrong. The actual locations of the Canadian and German lines were shown incorrectly on the maps—and error that would have disastrous results.

In the pre-dawn hours of April 4, Robertson and the soldiers of the 27th slogged forward through waist-deep water and mud, trying in the dark to make sense out of terrain, which had been blasted out of recognition, and occupy the "line." The few existing front-line trenches were little more than water-filled indentations in the mud, which were revealed in daylight to be in full view of German artillery observers, who wasted no time in pressing their advantage. The shelling that followed, that day and the next, was the heaviest ever experienced in the salient to date.

As soldiers struggled to build up parapets and establish machine-gun posts, much of their time was soon occupied with clearing the dead. Congestion became so great that each company had to send about forty men to the rear simply for protection. By noon on April 4, over half the soldiers in the forward companies had been killed or wounded, but somehow they still hung on. Finally, on the night of April 5–6, the greatly depleted 27th was ordered to pull back, to be replaced by the 29th (Vancouver) Battalion. Then, at 3:30 in the morning, before the relief was complete, the Germans attacked.

Under such circumstances, the Canadians were unable to put up much of a defence, and the Germans succeeded in capturing the four large centre craters within three hours. Robertson and his exhausted mates in the 27th struggled to the rear, having endured sixty hours of continuous battering without rest, sleep or any form of respite. While the Winnipeggers were out of the fight, the Canadians were not and the battle continued for another two weeks. Confusion over the location of the craters led the 31st Battalion to claim they occupied Craters 4 and 5, when in fact they were in the much smaller 6 and 7, a mistake that took a week to clarify and undoubtedly led to more confusion. By the time Major-General Turner called off further attempts to take the craters, his division had suffered twenty-four hundred casualties. Almost a tenth of these were in the 27th, which had to endure a second turn in the sector before the confused action ended. Second Division's introduction to battle had been a most unsatisfactory experience.

Casting about for scapegoats, the British initially wanted to relieve the senior Canadian commanders, Turner and Brigadier-General Ketchen, the commander of 6th Brigade. In the end, it was the corps commander, Lieutenant-General Edwin Alderson, a man who had been associated with the Canadians since their arrival in England over a year and a half earlier, who was relieved of his command. On May 28, Lieutenant-General Sir Julian Byng, another Briton, replaced him. For the 27th, the issue of removing commanders hit close to home. Their CO, Lieutenant-Colonel I. R. Snider, had been replaced on April 15, in an act the troops regarded as making a sacrificial lamb of him; they knew their commander had done all he could during the battle.

During the spring and summer of 1916, Canadian battalions received three new pieces of equipment that would significantly improve their fighting efficiency. At the end of March came the first issue of the new metal helmets, which took the place of the totally impractical soft cloth caps previously worn. This was followed two weeks later by the first Lewis machine guns, replacing the older Colts. Lastly, to the great relief of all Canadian soldiers, the much despised Canadian Ross rifle—which was the pet project of Colonel Sam Hughes, Minister of Militia and Defence—was finally replaced by the more reliable British Lee-Enfield. It would be impossible to calculate how many Canadian lives were lost because of Hughes's intransigence over the Ross's replacement and an earlier lack of resolve on the part of the government to force the issue. Furthermore, the Ross rifle was far from the only instance of the egotistical Hughes creating difficulty for the Canadian Army by his continual interference.

For example, a large part of the problem with reinforcements rested squarely on the shoulders of Sam Hughes. His mobilization of the Canadian Expeditionary Force (CEF), eventually reaching 260 battalions in the infantry alone, took no account of battle casualty replacements. As these units were formed, they were sent to England with the expectation

EVEN FOR EXPERIENCED SOLDIERS, RIFLE INSPECTION WAS AN ESSENTIAL PART OF DAILY ROUTINE. SOLDIERS OF ROBERTSON'S 27TH BATTALION HAVE THEIR LEE-ENFIELDS, WHICH EARLIER REPLACED THE MUCH-HATED CANADIAN-BUILT ROSS RIFLE, CHECKED IN JULY 1917 IN A VILLAGE IN THE LENS SECTOR.

that a given battalion would reach the front intact. But the Canadian Corps, even when it reached its greatest strength of four divisions, each with three infantry brigades, only needed forty-eight front-line infantry battalions.

As a result, virtually four-fifths of the CEF infantry battalions formed in Canada—like Robertson's original unit, the 13th Mounted Rifles—were broken up after arrival in England to provide reinforcement drafts to the Canadian Corps in the field. Soldiers were scattered throughout the corps wherever they were needed, with little account taken of their previous affiliations or geographical origin. Not only was this a great disappointment to the units involved, it was an extremely inefficient use of men and money.

For men who had joined and trained together in Canada, then proceeded as a group to England for further training, it was a severe blow to their morale and esprit de corps—essential components of good fighting units. It is a marvelous testimony to the qualities of the Canadian fighting man that he overcame this and went on to establish a clearly unrivalled reputation for the Canadian Corps as the finest formation on the Western Front, approached only by that of the Australian Corps.

For Private Robertson and the 27th Battalion, the summer of 1916 was a time of rest and refitting—new equipment was issued and replacements for their casualties were absorbed—with the occasional stint in the front lines. Then, in early September, Robertson and his mates were transferred to the Somme, in response to Haig's call on the Canadian Corps for help. On September 15, while John Kerr's 3rd Division advanced on the left against Mouquet Farm and the Fabeck Graben, Pete Robertson's 2nd Division moved forward on the right to help capture Courcelette. The Winnipeggers attacked on a 450-metre frontage with three companies leading. Within eighty minutes of zero hour, the 27th reported they had captured all three of their successive objectives, but at heavy cost.

The German reaction was swift, with violent and repeated counterattacks against the decimated 27th. Somehow, the battalion's depleted ranks held out for the next forty-eight hours against these onslaughts, as well as relentless artillery fire. At 8:00 P.M. on September 17, units of 1st Division at long last relieved the 27th. After the debacle at the Saint-Eloi Craters, the men of 2nd Division finally felt vindicated, but at great cost. Unfortunately, they had little time to rest on their laurels. Less than ten days later, on September 26, the Battle of Thiepval Ridge took place, at which Robert Ryder earned his VC.

Although the 27th Battalion was initially intended to be in support, it soon became heavily involved in the battle, and was used to evacuate a number of wounded soldiers from one of the assaulting battalions. Afterwards, Robertson and the 27th remained on the Somme for another month, operating in several minor roles. By the time the Canadians left the area in mid-October, the 27th had lost nearly six hundred men, in effect its complete fighting strength. It was time for another period of rest and refitting—as, indeed, it was for the whole of the Canadian Corps. The 4th Division, which had only arrived on the Somme in early October and was the last formation to become a part of the corps, remained behind for another month and a half. By the time it joined the remainder of the corps on the Arras Front, which was rumoured to be a quiet area, the Canadians had suffered twenty-nine thousand casualties on the Somme, nearly eight thousand of them fatal. It was a terrible price to pay for six kilometres of shell-shocked ground.

The Canadian Corps spent the winter of 1916–17 in relative inactivity, due in large part to the coldest winter in thirty-two years. Behind the scenes, preparations were underway for what would be the greatest military achievement in Canada's history: the taking of Vimy Ridge. On April 9, within 2nd Division, 4th and 5th Brigades led the initial assault, with 6th Brigade in support. Once they took their objectives, the first two of four coded lines, 6th Brigade assumed the lead, with the 27th supporting the brigade's other three battalions. When those units captured the third line (the actual crest of Vimy Ridge), the 27th leapfrogged through to attack and capture the fourth and final line, a defensive trench on the ridge's eastern slope. In the process, they took nine enemy field guns as well as three hundred prisoners. With Vimy Ridge firmly in Canadian hands, the 27th was relieved at dawn on April 11, having lost almost 150 men in Canada's most famous battle.

Early that summer, Robertson and his comrades moved to the Lens Sector, in preparation for an attack that Field Marshal Haig thought would prevent the Germans from using their strategic reserves against the British in the Ypres Salient. General Currie, the Canadian Corps Commander, changed the initial objective from the town of Lens to Hill 70, a much more appropriate target. The 27th fought in this battle, advancing against a position known as Cinnibar Trench on August 21, at 4:36 A.M. The Winnipeggers soon found themselves ahead of the units on their flanks and subjected to enfilade fire from both sides. Casualties mounted, but the men of the 27th persevered and reached Cinnibar Trench, along with one company from a flanking battalion.

The Germans quickly mounted local counterattacks throughout the day to force the Canadians back, but the line held. Unfortunately, Division HQ could not exploit the day's hard-won gains and ordered the 27th to return to their former front line that night. Over three hundred officers and men had become casualties in the battle, a heavy price to pay with nothing to show for it. Then, in mid-October, 1917, the Canadians were summoned to Ypres by Field Marshal Haig, where Pete Robertson's gallantry earned him VC.

Private Robertson is buried not far from where he fell, at Tyne Cot Cemetery, the largest and most visited of the many Commonwealth War Graves Commission cemeteries worldwide, where he rests forever with 11,871 of his warrior comrades, including two other VC recipients. Seventy percent of those buried at Tyne Cot are unidentified, a testament to the appalling consequences of fighting in the Passchendaele mud.

Robertson's tombstone bears an epitaph chosen by his mother: "Behold how good and how pleasant it is for brethren to dwell together in unity." Robert G. Brett, the lieutenant-governor of Alberta, presented Robertson's mother with her son's VC in April 1918, in a public ceremony in Medicine Hat. During the presentation he noted that, "While money can buy many things, the Victoria Cross can only be won by valour and service." Robertson's VC was last known to be in the possession of his family.

At one time, "Singing Pete Robertson" was a hero among railroad engineers the world over. For several years, his picture hung in the former CPR station in Montreal, the only individual so honoured. At a post-war convention of the Brotherhood of Locomotive Engineers held in Cleveland, Ohio, the 77,000 delegates present rose to their feet out of respect for his heroic deeds. They also voted unanimously to publish his story and photograph in *The Locomotive Engineer Journal*. In Medicine Hat in 1969, a branch of the Royal Canadian Legion was named after him. Additionally, a street— Robertson Way—a library, memorial park and swimming pool in the prairie city have all been named after him.

More recently, Robertson's hometown of Stellarton decided to recognize their hero in some way. A group of community leaders from the town and throughout Pictou County began seeking financial assistance to build a park and memorial in his honour, beside the town's present cenotaph. Plans for the project, which is expected to cost about $220,000, were announced in 2004. Fundraising is underway, with the sale of inscribed bricks for a memorial wall.

After Passchendaele, the 27th went on to fight in the great offensive at Amiens in the summer of 1918, after first being sent north as a decoy in a grand deception scheme to make the Germans think the Canadians were in Flanders. The Battle of the Hindenburg Line followed, with the 27th leading in the initial assault on August 26, before participating in the final phase of the attack on Cambrai, which was the battalion's last fight of the war. By this point, the 27th had regenerated itself five times, with over five thousand men passing through its ranks. Only 147 remained from the original one thousand who had initially formed the battalion, and over half of the 147 had been wounded.

When the 27th Battalion returned to Winnipeg in 1919 it had won twenty-three battle honours and two VCs, a very respectable record. Regiments and corps whose soldiers have earned VCs show great pride in these men and continue to honour their memory annually in various ways. Sadly, this is not the case for Pete Robertson and Bob Combe (the unit's other VC recipient). Although attempts were made after the war to perpetuate the 27th by the creation of the Manitoba Regiment in 1920, the unit existed only on paper until it was formally disbanded by the army in 1936. Veterans of the 27th did commemorate their heroes' exploits at numerous reunions over the years, with the final one held in 1981. During the 1990s, the last survivors of the 27th joined their former brothers-in-arms, leaving no one to carry on the unit's name and honours, or formally remember the deeds that earned two of their number the Empire's highest award for gallantry.

CHAPTER 5

"THE BLACK DAY
OF THE
GERMAN ARMY"

Private John Bernard Croak
& Corporal Herman James Good
13th Battalion, Canadian Expeditionary Force
Amiens, France, August 8, 1918

German Chief of the General Staff, Field Marshal Paul von Hindenburg and his deputy, General Erich Ludendorff, planned a series of offensives for the spring of 1918 that they hoped would lead to a decisive German victory. Despite their numerical superiority—192 divisions to the Allies' 173—the Germans were not strong enough to mount a general offensive along the entire front. Instead, Ludendorff conceived of a succession of coordinated, massive attacks that he believed would either smash through the Allied front or break their will to resist. The British were chosen over the French as the object of these attacks, on the theory that the British had less room to manoeuvre in northern France than the French did further south, thereby limiting their options.

In planning these offensives, Ludendorff adopted the new "Hutier tactics" pioneered by German General Oskar von Hutier. These tactics were an attempt to break the stalemate of trench warfare, using a short, intensive artillery bombardment, immediately followed by attacks by shock troops to capture previously identified weak points in the Allied defences, with heavily armed units then moving in with machine guns and mortars to focus on strong points. For the first of his offensives he chose the old Somme battlefield stretching south from Arras. The ground here most favoured an attack and it had the added bonus of being the location where the British and French armies met, always a potential weak spot.

On March 21, three German armies attacked two British ones on a hundred-kilometre front. The Germans advanced steadily, especially against Fifth Army in the south, eventually gaining a great salient seventy kilometres deep before they ran out of steam and Ludendorff called off the offensive, on April 4. This impressive advance was the closest Ludendorff would come to realizing his plans. The losses on both sides were roughly equal, a quarter of a million men each, but for the Germans this number included a high proportion of their elite shock troops. For the Allies, there was also a lasting effect. Alarmed over the German advances, they finally appointed an overall Commander-in-Chief, French General Ferdinand Foch, to command all Allied troops in France.

During the period April to July, Ludendorff launched four more great offensives that succeeded in gaining territory, but failed to achieve any strategic results. The Germans could push the Allies back and create a salient, or bulge, but they could not make a decisive breakthrough. Additionally, of course, once a salient was established, it became vulnerable to counterattack at numerous points—much more than a "straight line" position would be.

By the time Ludendorff called a halt to his stalled spring offensives in July, he had lost a half a million men in five months. Since the US entry into the war in April 1917, some three hundred thousand American soldiers a month were replacing the Allied casualties, while the Germans had used up all of their troops released from the Eastern Front after the peace treaty with Russia.

Because General Ludendorff had couched his battle plans in terms of total victory, when this was not achieved it had a great demoralizing effect on Germany. A turning point had been reached: the Allies had regained the strategic initiative and would keep it to the end of the war. For their part, the Germans were reduced to simply trying to prevent a military defeat. The full Allied counterattack began in August 1918, at Amiens, in what the renowned British historian J. F. C. Fuller has called "the most decisive battle of the First World War."

John Bernard Croak was the fourth and last Nova Scotian to earn the VC in the First World War, and the third soldier to be awarded it posthumously. He also has the distinction of being claimed as a native son by two Atlantic Provinces—Newfoundland and Nova Scotia. Born in Little Bay, Newfoundland, on May 18, 1892, he moved with his family to New Aberdeen, now part of Glace Bay, on Cape Breton Island, when he was four years old. After attending the New Aberdeen School and St. John's School, Croak worked in the coal mines at No. 2 Colliery.

PRIVATE JOHN BERNARD CROAK, THE FOURTH AND LAST NOVA SCOTIAN TO EARN THE VICTORIA CROSS IN THE FIRST WORLD WAR, WAS BORN IN NEWFOUNDLAND, BUT MOVED TO CAPE BRETON WITH HIS FAMILY WHEN HE WAS ONLY FOUR YEARS OLD.

In early 1914, Croak went out west, where he apparently did some fur trapping. During a trip back home, he joined the 55th Battalion in Saint John, New Brunswick, on August 7, 1915. (Although he is now known by the name "Croak," which is how he signed his attestation papers, on his baptismal certificate his surname is listed as "Croke," a not uncommon spelling in Newfoundland.) After basic training at nearby Camp Sussex, he sailed to England with his battalion on the SS *Corsican*, arriving on November 9, 1915, at which point he underwent additional training at Bramshott and Westenhanger Camps.

Croak was not what would be called a "parade ground" soldier. From the time of his arrival in England, his Record of Service attests to monthly brushes with military authority:

-*November 12, 1915* [three days after arriving in England]: *detention for being drunk;*
-*December 30: six days Field Punishment No. 2* [kept in irons and

made to perform labour as if he were undergoing imprisonment with hard labour] *for being in possession of whiskey and forfeited $6.60;*

-January 20, 1916: six days Field Punishment No. 2 for resisting arrest and forfeited $6.60; fined $6.00 for drunkenness;

-February 19: twenty-one days Field Punishment No. 2 for breaking camp while under quarantine and forfeited $23.10;

-March 13: twenty-eight days Field Punishment No. 2 and fined $6.00 for drunkenness; leaving range without permission, breaking escort, breaking camp, absent without leave three days and forfeited $40.10.

Croak's pattern of behaviour only ended with his transfer to an active unit, the 13th Battalion (Royal Highlanders)—the famed Black Watch—in France on April 15, 1916. From then on, his record is clear, the only entry being his admittance to 51 General Hospital in Etaples on August 25, 1917, and his subsequent discharge on September 12.

The 13th Battalion was recruited in Montreal in the early days of the war, based on the Royal Light Infantry of Montreal (later the Royal Highlanders of Canada), which was established in 1862. The 13th became part of 3rd Brigade, 1st Canadian Division, along with the 14th (Royal Montreal Regiment), the 15th (48th Highlanders) and the 16th (Canadian Scottish) battalions. With its heavy Scottish component, 3rd soon became known as "The Highland Brigade." After training at Camp Valcartier, the Highlanders arrived in England as part of the First Canadian Contingent in October 1914. By mid-February 1915, the unit was at the front in France, and it entered the trenches shortly afterwards. The Black Watch distinguished itself in numerous battles. At Second Ypres, in April, it experienced the first use of gas on the Western Front and stood firm during the attack in spite of losing almost half its strength. For his valour during the battle, Lance Corporal Fred Fisher was later awarded the VC, the first Canadian recipient of the medal in the war (see Introduction).

After Ypres, the Highlanders fought in several battles and occupied front line trenches at Festubert, Givenchy, Ploegsteert and Messines during the spring and summer. Meanwhile, recruiting for two more Black Watch battalions was taking place in Montreal: the 42nd Battalion arrived in France in mid-October 1915 to join 3rd Division's 7th Brigade (the same formation to which Private John Kerr's 49th Battalion belonged) and the 73rd arrived in August 1916, and was assigned to 12th Brigade, 4th Division.

This gave the regiment the unrivalled status of having three battalions in the Canadian Corps, each in a different division.

When Croak joined the Highlanders in mid-April 1916, they were in trenches in the Ypres Salient, though they moved out shortly afterwards. On June 13, the battalion successfully took part in a counterattack against Mount Sorrel. The rest of the summer was taken up with a series of trench tours and reserves until August, when the Highlanders began training for a monumental battle that was taking place to the south—on the Somme.

Croak and his comrades reached the town of Albert on the Somme on September 1. The next day, they were immediately thrown into battle to support the Australians in their attack against Mouquet Farm—"Mucky Farm" to the Aussies. With the Highlanders' assistance, the position was taken, and the Canadians remained in the line for another four days. When they came out, they had suffered over three hundred casualties.

Croak's battalion did not take part in the attack on Courcelette, but after its capture the 13th occupied trenches in front of the village, also participating in the assault on Regina Trench on October 8, alongside the Canadian Scottish. After being held up by uncut wire, which resulted in many soldiers being slaughtered, the attack eventually succeeded. By the time the Highlanders left the Somme, Croak and his comrades had completed three tours in the line, sustaining casualties greater than the battalion's strength when it arrived in the area a month earlier.

In October, Croak and 13th Battalion moved to winter quarters on the Vimy Front, where weekly tours of duty in the trenches began immediately. By the spring, the unit had rebuilt and retrained, and it was ready to participate in the Allied plans for the resumption of offensive operations in 1917. The Battles of Arras were designed to break through the German defences north of the newly built Hindenburg Line and outflank them, in support of French attacks farther to the south. The Canadians had a supporting role: they were to seize Vimy Ridge, a task that neither the British nor the French had been able to accomplish in over two years of fighting.

For the first time in its short existence, the four divisions of the Canadian Corps would attack together, rushing forward simultaneously to capture the heights from which the Germans dominated the landscape, supremely confident in their impregnability. The Canadians began an intense period of preparations and rehearsals, unequalled in previous attacks.

The four divisions of the Canadian Corps, some thirty-six thousand strong, were to assault on a frontage of 7,250 metres and penetrate the enemy defences to an average depth of around 3,250 metres. When the assault went in on April 9, the Highlanders were in support, behind the 14th Battalion. They had an easier go of it than most units, but encountered heavy machine-gun fire as they advanced towards the final objectives. When the battle ended, the Canadians had captured four thousand prisoners, 54 guns, 105 mortars and 125 machine guns. The corps instantly became the darling of the British press.

CROAK PARTICIPATED IN THE ATTACK ON VIMY RIDGE ON APRIL 9, 1917, WITH HIS UNIT, THE 13TH BATTALION (ROYAL HIGHLANDERS). CANADIAN SOLDIERS ARE SEEN HERE ADVANCING OVER THE CREST OF THE RIDGE.

Although Vimy Ridge had been captured, the Battles of Arras continued, and Croak and the Highlanders were in action in the area for the next three months. In mid-July, they moved north in preparation for the attack on Hill 70. On August 15, the 13th Battalion was in the assaulting wave, and captured their first and second objectives despite heavy enemy shelling. The next day, they held off several German counterattacks with the help of their own artillery, resorting to the bayonet once their ammunition and grenades ran out. When the Highlanders were relieved two days later, they had suffered forty percent casualties. For the next two months, the battalion served in and out of the line as its strength was rebuilt.

In October, the Canadian Corps moved yet further north and returned to the Ypres Salient, summoned by Field Marshal Haig to help bail him out once again. Fortunately for Croak, the Highlanders were spared the agony of attacking through the muddy morass of Passchendaele, spending only one day in the front line near Gravenstafel Ridge at the end of the battle. For the Canadians, it was the last time they saw action for several months; they were being saved for something big.

Nineteen-year-old Charlie "Bubbles" Hughes served alongside Croak in A Company of the 13th Battalion and had the greatest respect for him:

> *Now this Johnny Croak was a remarkable man. There was not a phoney bone in his body. He was a roly-poly guy, feared nothing, and didn't give a shit for anybody. He always carried a revolver on his hip and I don't think he would have been afraid to use it on anyone who crossed him. It was a saying in our company that if you went out on a patrol or a working party with Johnny Croak you'd come back.*

Croak was obviously the type of soldier who did much better in the field than in garrison. As it turned out, in the Canadian's next big battle he did the utmost that any soldier could—he earned the Victoria Cross.

During the first seven months of 1918, the Canadians were kept out of major battles. Instead, the corps was built up and trained to spearhead what the Allied High Command hoped would be the beginning of the final assault against the German enemy. On August 8, 1918, the powerful and experienced Canadian Corps led the final advance of the war at Amiens, beginning the period that would later be known as Canada's Hundred Days. The Germans' name for the initial assault was different: Ludendorff dubbed it the "Black Day of the German Army." This massive assault was like no other that the Allies had ever launched before.

Amiens marked an end to the uninspired tactics that had dominated much of the war. Operations actually began to resemble those that would occur over twenty years later during the Second World War in such areas as command and control, indirect fire, mechanization, tactical air support, logistics, chemical weaponry and electronic warfare. With the advances in these areas, the Battle of Amiens was the beginning of a series of victories that pushed the Germans inexorably back over one hundred kilometres. It was a blow from which they never recovered; the Germany Army was saved from total annihilation only by an eleventh-hour armistice.

When British infantry brigades were reduced from four battalions to three in 1917 due to manpower shortages, Canadian brigades retained their four battalions. As a result, the Canadian Corps was far stronger, in the final stages of the war, than any comparable British formation. It was called "the most powerful self-contained striking force on any battle front" and was virtually the equal of a small British field army (the next larger formation) in both men and firepower. The Germans certainly agreed with this assessment. They regarded the Canadian Corps as shock troops, and viewed their positioning in an area as a sure indication of an attack to follow.

In fact, due to the Canadians' reputation as harbingers of battles, in the days leading up to the offensive at Amiens the Allies resorted to a massive deception plan to fool the Germans into thinking the Canadians were elsewhere. Two battalions, the 4th CMR and the 27th (Private Pete Robertson's unit), plus a signals company, marched north to the Ypres area and simulated the presence of the Canadian Corps there through a trench raid and radio message traffic, before returning south. The ruse was effective and the Germans were caught entirely by surprise by the Allied attack.

By the end of the day on August 8, the efforts of Croak and his comrades had resulted in the corps advancing an unparalleled thirteen kilometres and capturing eight thousand prisoners, 161 artillery pieces and an uncounted number of machine guns, at the cost of exactly 3,868 casualties. Unfortunately, Croak was one of these casualties. But his gallantry, and that of three of his fellow Canadians, earned the VC that day.

Under a massive artillery barrage and supported by tanks, the Canadians advanced on a 7,775-metre front east of Amiens and were soon engaging the Germans who had survived the opening artillery fire. However, the 13th Battalion was hit by its own artillery and lost thirty men within minutes. The first obstacle facing the Highlanders was Hangard Wood, which was strongly defended by several machine-gun nests. In the wood, Croak, now an experienced soldier with two years in the trenches, became separated from his platoon. Encountering an enemy machine-gun nest in Ring Copse, he threw several Mills bombs into it and then attacked it at bayonet point, putting the German weapon out of action and capturing

CROAK'S BATTALION JUMPED OFF FROM THESE TRENCHES (PICTURED IN THE SPRING OF 1919) NEAR THE VILLAGE OF HANGARD ON AUGUST 8, 1918—THE "BLACK DAY OF THE GERMAN ARMY," IN THE WORDS OF GERMAN GENERAL ERICH LUDENDORFF.

its crew. As he was collecting prisoners he was shot in the right arm, but carried on and rejoined his unit.

Croak's platoon soon ran into another enemy position of several machine guns and was held up. Croak (who should have been having his wound dressed) immediately charged forward, inspiring the rest of the platoon, including Bubbles Hughes, to follow in a rush. With his bayonet Croak once again routed out the enemy, capturing three machine guns, killing several Germans and taking others prisoner. Hughes recalled, "I jumped into the trench—of course we had our bayonets fixed—and when I came down I skewered a German in the neck. He had been lying there wounded already, so I gave him a drink and a cigarette and tried to patch him up."

During the fight, Croak was wounded by machine-gun fire, this time fatally. Knowing he did not have long to live, a popular legend has it that Croak said to a comrade, "Do you wish to show your gratitude? Kneel down and pray for my soul," and then died. He was only twenty-six.

Whatever the truth behind Croak's dying moments, his alleged final words live on. They are carved on his tombstone in nearby Hangard Wood Cemetery, twenty kilometres southwest of Albert.

Indeed, Croak may be the VC recipient who is buried closest to the scene of the deed that earned him the medal. Hangard Wood Cemetery lies in the little opening that separates the two parts of Hangard Wood, and it is virtually unchanged from the time of the war. It contains 161 burials—sixty-one Canadian, fifty-eight British, seventeen Australian, five South

African and twenty French—reflecting the main Allied combatants fighting in that area. Of the Canadians buried there, twenty-nine are from the 13th Battalion, with twenty-three of them, including Croak, in one row along the back wall.

Croak's mother, Cecilia, received a letter from the 13th Battalion chaplain shortly after her son's death. The chaplain wrote: "He was a splendid soldier, had done more than one brave deed in clearing out enemy machine-gun nests, he could not have done more gallantly, and I am stating the truth when I tell you that the Battalion could not honour his action more highly than is done. Death came to him quite instantly, and he is buried with his comrades near the place where he fell."

CROAK'S REMAINS, MARKED BY A CARVING OF THE VICTORIA CROSS ON HIS HEADSTONE, LIE IN HANGARD WOOD, NOT FAR FROM THE SITE WHERE HE WAS MORTALLY WOUNDED.

The citation for Croak's VC was published in the *London Gazette* on September 27, 1918. On June 20, 1920, Cecilia Croak received her son's VC from Lieutenant-Governor McCallum Grant at Government House in Halifax. After remaining in the family for several years, it was purchased for $10,000 from Croak's grandson (who was named John Bernard, after him) in 1976. The grandson was then living in New Hartford, Connecticut, and in poor health. The medal is on display at the Army Museum in the Halifax Citadel.

CORPORAL HERMAN JAMES GOOD CAME FROM BATHURST ON NEW BRUNSWICK'S NORTH SHORE. HE SERVED TOGETHER WITH JOHN CROAK IN THE 13TH BATTALION, AND EARNED HIS VICTORIA CROSS ON THE SAME DAY IN THE SAME BATTLE.

In Glace Bay, several tributes honour Croak's bravery. An Imperial Order of Daughters of the Empire chapter and a branch of the Royal Canadian Legion were named after him. Also, in 1976, a new elementary school replacing the one he attended in the New Aberdeen area was christened the John Bernard Croak Memorial School. On the anniversary of his hundredth birthday, on May 18, 1992, the John Bernard Croak VC Memorial Park was dedicated a short distance from where he grew up. At the same time, a cenotaph, built by the Croak Memorial Foundation, was unveiled in the park in his honour. Some three hundred war veterans, including six from the First World War, attended the ceremony, as well as the preceding church service and parade. John Croak would probably be surprised at all the attention paid to him.

As the 13th Battalion attack against Hangard Wood continued, during the opening phase of the Allied offensive at Amiens, another Highlander's gallantry came into play. When Corporal Herman Good's company was held up by heavy fire from three machine guns near the wood, he unhesitatingly dashed forward alone, killing seven Germans and capturing the remainder. Later, when the Canadians penetrated deeper into former enemy territory, Good came upon a battery of 5.9-inch guns, firing as fast as they could reload, pinning down the Canadian advance and hammering positions in the rear. Gathering three men, he issued orders for an assault.

A direct, frontal attack on three large guns by four badly outnumbered soldiers might not seem like a winning tactic. However, the battle-wise corporal later explained he reckoned the gun crews were probably "not trained in hand-to-hand fighting and that, once at grips, he and his stout-hearted companions would have the advantage." Accordingly, with the element of surprise on their side, Good and his men charged. As the regimental history notes, "What the German gunners thought when this assault was launched, no man will ever know. Perhaps in the drill and text books they had studied

OUTNUMBERED, GOOD LED HIS THREE MEN IN A SURPRISE CHARGE AGAINST A GERMAN BATTERY OF 5.9 INCH GUNS, TAKING ITS THREE ARTILLERY PIECES AND THEIR CREWS. SOLDIERS OF THE 13TH BATTALION ARE SHOWN WITH A CAPTURED GERMAN GUN.

no instructions were given as to procedure when four Canadian highlanders charged a battery with the obvious intent of doing bodily harm." The sudden assault so unnerved the Germans they immediately surrendered; Good captured the three artillery pieces and their crews without any losses.

For his two courageous acts, Good earned the VC, the citation for which was published in the *London Gazette* on September 27, 1918. King George V pinned the medal on Corporal Good's chest at an investiture ceremony at Buckingham Palace on March 29, 1919. Today, it is on display at the Royal Canadian Legion in Clinton, Ontario, on loan from Good's family.

The attack at Amiens was perhaps the most complete surprise attack of the war. Not only were the Canadian divisions transferred to the area with the utmost secrecy, the normal preliminary artillery barrage was foregone in favour of a sudden surge forward of 456 tanks. By the end of the day, Fourth Army, of which the Canadians were a part, took 12,412 prisoners. Indeed, many German units, worn down as they were by attrition, were demoralized and surrendered with little or token resistance. The famous and powerful German fighting machine had sustained an irreversible decline from which it could not recover. As Ludendorff later wrote in his memoirs, "our war machine was no longer efficient." Even though the tremendous advances on August 8 were slowed over the next few days, as the Germans rushed reserve divisions forward, the outstanding tactical victory at Amiens changed the course of the war.

Herman James Good was the first New Brunswicker to earn the Victoria Cross in the First World War—and, in the view of those who do not consider William Nickerson Canadian, Good was the first New Brunswicker ever to achieve the distinction. He is also the only non-officer from New Brunswick to earn the VC, as well as the only army non-commissioned officer in all of Atlantic Canada to achieve this high award.

Good was born in Big River on November 29, 1887. After graduation from the Big River School he went into the lumber business. He and his brother Ernest joined the army in 1915, enlisting in the 55th Battalion together. In the fall of that year they sailed for England on the troop ship *Corsica*. Herman served with the 2nd Pioneer Battalion before ending up in the 13th Battalion (Royal Highlanders) in France with his brother.

Ernest described his first impressions of France in a confident letter home:

Dear Mother:

Received your letter a few days ago and was glad to hear from you. We are only beginning to receive our mail these last few days since we came to France, as we were put in the 13th Battalion and moving about all the time and the mail could not find us.

Herman is wounded but is back with us again. We are having lovely weather here now. I like it better here than when we were in England. It is not so very dangerous in the trenches, and we are not in them all the time, we have to have our rest. We always have lots to eat here too, and it is nice in the trenches when it is fine. We wear the kilts and I like them fine. I suppose you never see any of them around Bathurst, they are fine and cool in the hot weather.

The crops look good over in this country, they have grain over six feet high.

I don't care how soon the war would end for I would like to see you all again. I will close for this time as news is scarce.

From your loving son,
Ernest Good
13th Battalion, France

Sadly, Ernest was not to survive the war. Herman's first letter home after he was wounded expressed an optimism much like his brother's:

Dear Mother:

I now take the pleasure to answer your letter which I received yesterday, and was glad to hear from home. I am well at present and getting on fine. I was wounded but I am nearly better and back with my battalion again. We are out of the trenches now for a few days rest.

Well mother don't worry about us, we will look after ourselves, and when our time comes we will have to go, but we are all living in hopes to come through safe.

Ernest and I are both together so far. All the rest of the Bathurst boys, except a couple, went to reinforce other battalions. I never thought we would be divided up so much over here, after working together for so long, but it may be all for the better. We may all meet again after this war is over. Did any more of the Big River boys enlist? Write to me as often as you can for I can't tell you much that is going on over here, and I have not got time to write many letters. Remember me to all inquiring friends. No more for this time, from your loving son,

Herman Good
In the trenches

Like John Croak, Herman Good also participated in the capture of Vimy Ridge in March 1917. There he saw his brother Ernest fall under a hail of German machine-gun fire when their company was pinned down. Instantly springing into action, he attacked the nest of three machine guns single-handedly. Good had already experienced the viciousness of hand-to-hand combat, killing a number of the enemy with his bayonet at Courcellette on the Somme in 1916, and now he did the same, killing or capturing the machine-gun crews.

After Vimy, in August of that summer, Herman wrote a long, almost philosophical letter home to his father. It so eloquently and simply express-es his thoughts that it bears repeating in full:

Dear Father:

One would never realize but for the casualties that occur that there was a war on at the present moment. 'Tis just the time between the dark and daylight. The birds are singing their joy to the Almighty for an almost per-fect day. Silent are both guns and rifles, the whole atmosphere having a feeling of peace which at any moment may be shattered by either of the warring nations facing each other some hundred yards apart. Little would someone realize who has not been here long that death lies at almost every course, and should one be careless in keeping his head over the parapet too long the Golden Gates would open for him, earth knowing him no more for-ever. 'Tis a shame when one stops to think, still the Great God must surely see some mighty good for the world as a whole to sacrifice some of our finest and best on this lovely summer day. Have been very unfortunate this time in losing my Sgt. this morning, he being hit through the head. We were afraid it was fatal but he soon proved to us that he had a chance so we hus-tled him right out to the hospital. The four men took him first to one dress-ing station, then another until they found one that the ambulance could reach in daylight. That's the kind of thing which appeals so strongly to me. The men will work themselves to the breaking point to give another a chance for his life. Carrying a man on a stretcher is no light task, and these fellows carried that man at least five miles that his chances of recovery might be greater. In many cases they exposed themselves to danger but their one thought was for the wounded. Know full well that should I get hit no trouble will be spared on their part to give me a fighting chance for my life. As time goes on many are the lessons we learn by rubbing shoulders with men of all kinds. At the bottom, be he rich, poor, uneducated or educated he is governed by the same motives that make us all kin. Oh! the marvel of it. Surely this lesson can be taught to mankind without so much bloodshed and sorrow. Am hoping to go on pass very soon when I shall have the delightful luxury of sleeping between clean white sheets. Sleep in the day-time now on sandbags, my boots for a pillow. 'Tis wonderful what one can do without when he has to, yet his sleep is nonetheless pleasant or comfort-able. From those who eventually get through this war the dross will be taken away and they shall review their own lives on the lessons learned with a new idea of their importance in the great scheme of things. 'Twill make a mighty difference in the ideals and lives of future generations which [I] am sure will not be for the worse. How much we will appreciate the joy of living. Here where all luxuries are withdrawn from us we are nonetheless happy. We have our friends and loved ones, nature in all its beauty, music, pictures, what more can a man ask for? We feel 'tis a joy to be alive at all. Just now the birds are singing. In this new haven, war-stricken land where there is hardly a branch to perch on, they are happy. Why should we not be as happy when God has given us greater scope to enjoy His wondrous works. In the midst of our many pleasures we are apt to complain at our own selfish sorrows. We cannot have the green fields we love so much with-out the rain. The real sorrows we have only help us to enjoy to the full the pleasures that pass our way. Thus the world goes on. We are ever learning of the wonders and mysteries of the Almighty.

This is a very wandering, unsatisfactory letter, but it expresses just what I feel this morning.

Your loving son,
Herman
France, August 20, 1917

The successes achieved at Amiens and elsewhere in August 1918 convinced the Allied High Command that further strategic offensives, rather than purely local operations, were warranted. Accordingly, a plan was prepared for three converging attacks coming from the north, centre and south. In the centre, the British objective was the Hindenburg Line, a great fortified zone consisting of a number of defensive belts. As the last major position left to the Germans, they reinforced it with every means at their disposal, creating one of the strongest positions on the entire Western Front. The Canadian Corps had to break through the northern hinge of this formidable position, known as the Drocourt-Quéant Line—a task which General Currie assessed as likely the most difficult his corps had ever undertaken.

The offensive opened with the Battle of the Scarpe on August 26, involving one British division, plus 2nd and 3rd Canadian divisions. By the end of the month, the Canadians had successfully advanced to within eighteen hundred metres of their objective, the Drocourt-Quéant Line. At 5:00 A.M. on September 2, the Canadians, supported by tanks, surged forward in an all-out assault on the enemy's well-prepared defences of the Drocourt-Quéant Line, all of which was in Canadian hands by mid-afternoon. Among their great achievements that day was a feat unrivalled by any other nation of the Empire during the First World War—seven Canadians earned the VC for their conspicuous bravery in the battle. Good and the Highlander companies advanced behind a rolling barrage, leading 3rd Brigade's advance, with the 16th Battalion on their right. The 13th Battalion took its objective with minimal casualties and, at eight o'clock, 14th Battalion passed through and assumed the lead. However, the advance slowed as German resistance stiffened, and both units began to suffer heavy casualties until they could go no further. Fresh troops from 1st Brigade replaced them to resume the attack. The Highlanders had captured a thousand prisoners, but lost 230 killed, wounded or missing.

Good went on to fight in the final battles of the war with the 13th Battalion, during Canada's Hundred Days. By this point, he was an experienced three-year veteran, having fought in the famous battles of Ypres, the Somme, Vimy Ridge and Amiens, among others. He had been gassed, shell-shocked, wounded three times, promoted corporal and had earned the VC.

In his final letter to his father, Good's tone was less optimistic and his desire to return home was clear:

Dear Father:
   I must now answer your welcome letter which I received last night.
   I was glad to hear you were all well at home.
   We are having beautiful weather over here now, and the fighting is pret-

ty heavy. Well father I came through another pretty rough battle, but near went it, just a bomb I had in my pocket stopped the bullet, and lucky for me the bomb did not explode.

There were quite a few of them went under, but we got great satisfaction. Fritz counterattacked pretty heavy. Their general came up on horseback and was driving his troops with a revolver into the jaws of death. As fast as they came they fell with their brave general by their side. They are still counterattacking, but can never gain a foot of ground.

We just came out for a few days rest and are going back at it again. All the boys are cheerful and don't care for anything.

One thing is that Fritz can't stand before the Canadians, and they know it too, for their officers got to drive them into battle with revolvers. There are thousands of Germans laying dead in no man's land, but they still come on. They have to give it up for a bad job before long.

Well I would like to be on my old farm once more, I am getting tired of the war. You say my colt is growing fine, I may need him someday.

I have no more news to tell in my letter, but I could give quite a spill if I was allowed to write it.

Give my best regards to all inquiring friends. No more news at present.

From your loving son,
Herman

After the Armistice of November 11, Good and the Highlanders formed part of the Army of Occupation in Germany and crossed the Rhine on December 13. They remained in Germany only a short time, leaving for Belgium on January 6, 1919. In mid-March, the battalion arrived in England and on March 29 Good received his VC from the hands of the king. In April, Good returned to Canada, to his native north shore of New Brunswick, as a sergeant. He received a hero's welcome in Bathurst, when the largest crowd ever seen there turned out to greet him at the railway station. The VC recipient was taken through the town's streets in a carriage, followed by a brass band, war veterans and a procession of cars, carriages and citizens on foot.

Back in the woods of Big River, Good farmed and cut lumber, and for twenty years served as a fish, game and fire warden. Hired by the New Brunswick Travel Bureau in 1927, he assisted in arranging exhibits at sportsmen's shows in Boston and Philadelphia. In 1931, at the White

House, in uniform, Good presented President Herbert Hoover with a hamper filled with products from his province's fields and streams—moose steaks, venison and Atlantic salmon.

In 1939, during the royal tour of Canada by King George VI and Queen Elizabeth, Good was presented to Their Majesties when they visited Fredericton. A short time later, Hitler's forces invaded Poland and the century's Second World War began. In 1941, Good's wife, Martha (Moore), passed away at only forty-one years of age. She had born the brave man three sons.

Good was a lifelong member of the Gloucester Branch of the Royal Canadian Legion and laid the cornerstone of the new building for the branch in 1962; four years later it was renamed the Herman J. Good Branch in his honour. After a brief five-day illness, he died on April 18, 1969, aged eighty-one. The north shore hero is buried in St. Alban's Cemetery in Bathurst, where his headstone incorrectly shows his date of birth as 1888.

CHAPTER 6

KILTED CANADIANS

Lance Corporal William Henry Metcalf
16th Battalion, Canadian Expeditionary Force
Arras, France, September 2, 1918

Lieutenant-Colonel Cyrus Wesley Peck
16th Battalion, Canadian Expeditionary Force
Villers-lez-Cagnicourt, France, September 2, 1918

During the assault on the Hindenburg Line, after the Battles of Amiens and the Scarpe (see Chapter 5), two soldiers of the same unit—the 16th (Canadian Scottish) Battalion—earned the VC on the same day for their gallant actions: an American, Lance Corporal William Metcalf, and his CO, Lieutenant-Colonel "Cy" Peck. After midnight on September 2, 1918, as troops moved to their assembly area for the attack, their greatest problem became direction keeping in the darkness. The Canadian Scottish were meant to be the right forward battalion, with the 13th Battalion on their left within the brigade. However, a few minutes before the 5:00 A.M. zero hour, it seemed as if the 16th was in the wrong place, as the unit on its right flank knew nothing about an attack. Just then Colonel Peck appeared on the scene, accompanied by his piper. "Well, it doesn't make any difference, we've got to go forward whether they do or not," he said, sorting the matter out in his typical no-nonsense fashion.

As dawn broke and the artillery barrage fell, the 16th advanced into No Man's Land. Peck, his piper and Battalion HQ personnel were in the centre of the leading troops. Through the smoke, crowds of Germans could be seen with their hands in the air, surrendering in large numbers. However, as the advance continued, strong uncut wire and intense machine-gun fire held up the two right hand companies. They suffered heavy casualties, including all eight of their officers. Then a valiant soldier intervened and got the advance going again.

Lance Corporal Bill Metcalf and his comrades, hopelessly pinned down by enemy machine-gun fire, were waiting for a supporting tank before proceeding any further. However, when one finally appeared, though several soldiers waved their helmets, the tank's crew did not see them. When the tank was ninety metres from the German wire, it came under heavy fire. Metcalf jumped up from his shell hole, rushed forward alone under concentrated machine-gun fire and led the tank towards the enemy's trench, directing it to the German positions with signal flags he carried. The Germans continued to fire on the tank and, when it got closer, began to throw clusters of bombs at it.

The tank eventually overcame the German position, and Metcalf's comrades moved forward to join him. When they reached the enemy trench, they found seventeen machine guns. Though Metcalf was wounded, none present could understand how he had survived the murderous hail of bullets. For his exceptional display of courage he received the VC. His citation was published in the *London Gazette* on November 15, 1918, and King George V pinned the medal on him at Sandringham, the royal country estate, on January 26, 1919.

William Henry Metcalf was born in Waite, Washington County, Maine, on January 29, 1894, a barber by trade. When Canada mobilized for war in August 1914, Metcalf crossed into New Brunswick and, without telling his mother, enlisted in a militia unit at Fredericton, the 71st York Regiment. He added nine years to his age, giving his year of birth as 1885, presumably to ensure his acceptance. At Valcartier, Quebec, he transferred to the 12th Battalion on September 22. By the time his unit sailed for England in October, Metcalf's mother learned he had joined the Canadian Army and was inundating Canadian and American government officials with letters, in an attempt to have him sent home.

When he arrived in England, Metcalf was confronted by the American ambassador, who asked if he was the Metcalf about whom he had received all the letters. Metcalf claimed, "I'm not the man, I'm from St. David

Ridge, a little farming town outside St. Stephen, New Brunswick," just across the international border from Maine. When his CO backed him up, the ambassador could do nothing, so Metcalf remained with the Canadian Expeditionary Force. After several months training in England, Metcalf transferred to the Canadian Scottish Battalion on May 13, 1915, joining the unit in France. He received two wounds, the first just two months later. He became a signaller and made lance corporal in October 1916, the same month that saw him awarded the Military Medal (MM) for his bravery on the Somme, to which he later added a Bar.

Even as Metcalf was displaying his exceptional courage under fire, Peck, advancing with the two left flank companies, met little resistance. The leading sections found a wide lane through the wire and signaled the rest to follow. Led by Peck, the two companies reached the main Drocourt-Quéant Line trenches as the artillery barrage lifted to the rear. Peck rushed forward and reached a trench containing about twenty-five to thirty Germans. A German NCO pointed his rifle at him, about to fire, when the man behind him knocked the weapon out of his hands. The Germans surrendered, although they outnumbered the Canadians present about three to one. After disarming the prisoners, the 16th advanced to the Drocourt Intermediate Support Line, about 225 metres beyond the main

LANCE CORPORAL WILLIAM HENRY METCALF WAS AN AMERICAN CITIZEN SERVING WITH THE 16TH (CANADIAN SCOTTISH) BATTALION. HE EARNED THE VICTORIA CROSS ON SEPTEMBER 2, 1918, MAKING HIM ONE OF FOUR AMERICAN RECIPIENTS OF THE VC IN THE FIRST WORLD WAR.

defences, reaching it without difficulty. Germans continued to surrender without a fight, raising their hands en masse whenever the Canadians pointed a weapon at them. Peck was unimpressed. "I never saw the enemy so cowardly," he said. "Prisoners surrendered in shoals. They outnumbered us vastly, but they were in a demoralized condition."

Down a slope and across a hollow, the Intermediate Support Line overlooked the battalion's next objective: the Drocourt Support Line in front of the village of Villers-lez-Cagnicourt. As the 16th scrambled forward, it immediately came under ineffective machine-gun fire from high ground to the south. The battalion continued on, but additional fire forced it to take cover about 180 metres from the Support Line. It was now sometime between 8:00 and 9:00 A.M. and the enemy had excellent visibility. Just as Peck ordered smoke bombs thrown to provide concealment, he heard additional machine-gun fire on the right. Raising his head, he saw a nearby

THE CANADIAN SCOTTISH WERE HELD UP BY GERMAN POSITIONS NEAR THE VILLAGE OF VILLERS-LEZ-CAGNICOURT ON SEPTEMBER 2, 1918. THE RUINS OF THE TOWN ARE PICTURED IN THE SPRING OF 1919, A FEW MONTHS AFTER THE CANADIAN ATTACK.

British tank in difficulty and drawing enemy fire. He decided he could best sort out the situation from the Intermediate Support Line and prepared to return to it. Just then, a second British tank appeared on the scene; this tank should have been moving forward in support of the 16th's attack, but its commander seemed to have other ideas. An eyewitness described his colonel's actions and Peck's seemingly charmed life:

We were firing smoke bombs in an endeavour to conceal our positions as much as possible, when a tank, which had been following us up stopped, possibly thirty yards in our rear, and proceeded to turn around to go back.

An attempt was made to stop the tank but with no success. Colonel Peck, observing what had happened, left the shell hole where he was taking cover and under heavy machine-gun fire ran back to the tank. He stood directly in front of it. He forced it to turn around. But directly he returned to shelter, the tank instead of continuing towards the Drocourt Support, turned about and proceeded to move back towards the Drocourt-Quéant Intermediate Support.

I do not know how the Colonel escaped being riddled by bullets.

Abandoned by the tank, the 16th's situation became critical. Peck realized something must be done, and quickly. With his scout officer he dashed back to the Intermediate Line under withering machine-gun fire. Safely there, Peck directed troops from another battalion to put machine-gun and artillery fire onto the enemy positions holding up the advance. He then gathered up the rest of the battalion and led them to the forward troops that were sheltering in shell holes. Under Peck's leadership, the two forces linked up, advanced to and occupied their objective on the Drocourt Support Line. His coolness, tenacity and valour in the face of devastating enemy fire earned Peck the VC. Along with Metcalf's award, this gave the Canadian Scottish the rare distinction of two VCs received for the same engagement. Peck's VC citation was published in the *London Gazette* on November 15, 1918.

After taking the Drocourt Support Line, the Canadian Scottish became brigade reserve and Peck moved them into a nearby sunken road to reorganize. The situation remained volatile, but finally an attack on the left succeeded and Peck ordered an advance. The battalion moved forward, and by 1:00 P.M. occupied its final objective for the day. That night, fresh troops relieved it and the 16th moved back into divisional reserve. General Currie called a halt to the attack for the evening, well satisfied with another successful operation by his corps. The Canadians had taken most of their objectives, and Currie issued orders for the advance to resume the next day. As always, success came at a price: for the Canadian Scottish, that one day's fighting resulted in 154 casualties, a quarter of them fatal.

Cyrus Wesley Peck was forty-seven when he earned his Victoria Cross, the oldest Canadian to earn the VC in the First World War. He was born at Hopewell Hill, New Brunswick, on April 26, 1871, of Massachusetts Loyalist stock, the second son of Wesley Peck, a shipbuilder, and May (Rogers) Peck. He completed his schooling at Hopewell Hill and Toronto, moving with his parents to New Westminster, British Columbia, in June 1887, where his father carried on his trade. Peck went to the Klondike during the gold rush, returning to BC where he became involved with salmon canneries, sawmills and lumber towing operations.

Peck possessed an instinctive love for soldiering. He joined the militia and took every course available at the various militia schools of instruction in Toronto in the 1890s. He even travelled to England to enlist in the British Army. When viewed at close quarters however, British Army life was very different from the picture that Peck had imagined, so he returned home. He remained in the militia and volunteered for the Boer War in 1900, but was not accepted.

When the First World War broke out, Peck and his family were living in Prince Rupert, British Columbia. He enlisted in the 30th Battalion, CEF, on November 9, 1914, with his cousin, Donald Moore. A newspaper account of Peck's award of the VC described him as "a comfortably built, middle-aged man." Both Peck and his cousin received their commissions as captains and sailed for England in February 1915, where Peck was promoted major. Moore was later killed in action, on May 22, 1915. His body was never found.

The Canadian Scottish arose as a Highland battalion composed of a company from each of four existing militia Highland regiments. At Valcartier, the battalion became part of 1st Division's 3rd Brigade—the same "Highland" brigade to which Private John Croak and Corporal Herman Good's 13th Battalion belonged.

The battalion was in divisional reserve on April 28, 1915, when Peck and his company arrived as reinforcements in Belgium's Ypres Salient, immediately after the first German gas attack. A wild counterattack by the 10th and 16th Battalions had helped restore the situation by driving the enemy from their newly won positions in Kitchener's Wood. For the first time, overseas troops of the Empire assaulted and defeated the troops of a European army on European soil. It was not to be the last. Although they were decimated in the attack, the intervention of the 10th and 16th battalions at a critical time had prevented a disaster. The new reinforcements would shortly become as battle-experienced as their comrades, for the Canadian Scottish were about to re-enter the line.

On May 18, at Festubert, Peck's company initially supported an attack and then set to work digging hasty trenches in a nightmarish landscape littered with the bent and broken bodies of dead soldiers. On the night of May 20, Peck's objectives were an orchard, to be captured in a flank attack with another company, and a house code-named M10, surrounded by barbed wire about 140 metres south of the orchard. At 7:45 P.M. the troops of the two companies went over the parapet "in magnificent style." On the left flank, a British Guardsman noted: "The Canadians went into the attack...just as if they were drilling in Hyde Park. I never saw anything like it. Each man at about two paces interval going at the walking pace with the enemy's machine guns and rifle fire on a wide front turned on them. In fact no better example could be shown by any regiment under the British flag." Troops quickly took the orchard, while

LIEUTENANT-COLONEL CYRUS WESLEY PECK WAS THE COMMANDING OFFICER OF THE CANADIAN SCOTTISH DURING THE ASSAULT ON THE HINDENBURG LINE. HIS WAS THE SECOND VICTORIA CROSS FOR THE UNIT THAT DAY.

Peck's company made a dash for M10, but was forced to withdraw after coming under heavy machine-gun fire.

Fresh troops relieved the two attacking companies early the next morning, which withdrew to their pre-attack positions. Two days of battle cost 277 casualties, one-quarter fatal. Peck was among the injured: he had been wounded in both legs. Three days later he was on his way to England for treatment and recovery. He had received a "Blighty," a wound ensuring evacuation to England, which was much sought after by many soldiers, especially if it meant not returning to the front. For the pugnacious Peck, such a possibility would have caused him great distress. He need not have feared; he would be back with his beloved battalion in a few weeks.

In late June, the battalion moved to Ploegsteert—known to the British as "Plug Street"—a village north of Armentières. The battalion spent the next eight months in a forward area routine of front line trench duty, support and reserve; it was necessary work, but of mind- and body-numbing monotony. Towards the end of July almost four hundred replacements arrived, bringing the unit up to strength. Officer changes also occurred and Peck, back from convalescence, became second-in-command.

At the end of March, 1916, the battalion again entered the Ypres Salient, overlooked from dominant positions on Mount Sorrel and elsewhere by the Germans. The salient had no intrinsic strategic importance and, surrounded on three sides by the enemy, the position made no sense tactically. The logical action would have been to "straighten out the line," a sound and accepted tactical procedure. But in this war, the holding of ground assumed an almost mythical significance and the British bulldog would not even consider withdrawal. Altogether it was a far more dangerous sector than Festubert. In the Ypres Salient British Empire troops suffered fully one-fifth of *all* their casualties on *all* fronts during the entire war—a staggering 570,000, with 160,000 fatal. This grim statistic flowed down to the Canadian Scottish; just over one-quarter of its total casualties in the First World War occurred there.

With the CO on leave in early June, Peck became acting commanding officer with the battalion in corps reserve. After an enemy attack on June 2, the order came to move forward. Peck reported to Brigade HQ, where the situation was confused. During the afternoon, the Germans seized Mount Sorrel and Observatory Ridge, pushing patrols forward. In the early evening, Division HQ ordered 3rd Brigade to counterattack before dawn and assist in re-establishing the front line. The Canadian Scottish would be in support. Brigade HQ fired the attack signal well after dawn and the two attacking battalions, the 14th and 15th, struggled forward, up the slopes of Observatory Ridge, only to be engulfed in a wall of artillery fire.

The HQ of these battalions quickly lost contact with their companies, though the few reports of their progress that filtered through indicated that they had reached their objectives. When Brigade HQ ordered the 16th to reinforce them, Peck pointed out that from what they could observe, in fact, none of the Canadian units had reached their objectives. Confirmation of this fact postponed any further action until nightfall. At 7:00 P.M. the enemy began another heavy barrage, throwing the Canadian plans for a counterattack into confusion. By the time commanders realized no enemy attack was forthcoming, it was too late for a brigade attack. Peck, as acting CO, had performed well.

The CO returned from leave on June 4 to find his battalion preparing for a counterattack in hastily dug shallow trenches in the pouring rain, under full observation and intermittent shelling by the enemy. By the time the 16th completed these preparations, none of the assaulting troops were in any fit state to carry out the mission. Recognizing this, 1st Division HQ sent the assault units to the rear for a period of rest, before resuming the attack on June 12. Moving up under cover of darkness that evening, the battalion occupied its assembly area less than one hundred metres from the closest German trenches.

Promptly at 1:30 the next morning, in a violent wind and rainstorm, the Canadian Scottish assaulted on a two-company frontage in four waves. The battalion attacked over conditions of muddy and broken ground such as had not been seen before, comparable only to the desolation experienced later on the Somme and at Passchendaele. Despite this, the 16th advanced inexorably against the Germans. One after another the objectives fell, until the soldiers—with Peck among the attacking waves—occupied their final one at 2:15 A.M. The Canadian Scottish captured 143 Germans and nine machine guns, but at a heavy cost: 269 casualties, including sixty-six killed. On August 9, the Canadian Scottish marched out of the Ypres Salient, hoping never to return.

If the Canadian Scottish were marching out of one cauldron, they were marching straight into another—the Somme, where, mercifully, Canadians had been spared the initial massacres. As the 16th moved towards the Somme on those hot August days, it marked the first time the unit had moved fully out of the front lines since April 1915. On September 1, the battalion arrived outside Albert—marked by the now-famous statue of the Hanging Virgin leaning precariously from the top of the town's church—and moved into the Anzac reserve. The 16th was assigned to 13th Australian Brigade, which was attacking Mouquet Farm. Based on the new "Left Out of Battle" orders, designed to allow a battalion to be rebuilt from key personnel in case of heavy casualties, Peck assumed command when the CO headed for the rear.

At Brigade HQ, Peck dispatched three companies forward under command of the 49th Australian Battalion. The front in this area was particularly confused, with most normal landmarks no longer recognizable, having been blasted and churned into a chaotic mess. When Peck received orders to relieve the 49th the next day, he sent an officer ahead to clarify the situation as he proceeded in the dark and rain with his staff to the 49th Battalion HQ. There the situation should have been sorted out, but became more muddled as the night wore on. Companies stumbled about, saved from destruction only because the Germans had temporarily ceased shelling. The 16th finally succeeded in occupying its positions during the night of September 4–5, eventually holding about three hundred metres more than assigned—a fact unknown to both Battalion and Brigade HQ.

With dawn, the enemy commenced shelling the battalion's salient jutting towards the German lines. By evening casualties began to mount, especially in the most acute part of the salient. The company there was down to fifty-three men, many remaining at their posts although wounded, and the position had large unmanned gaps. Additionally, they had received no water or rations for two days. During the evening, companies asked Peck to reinforce them, but the brigadier would not allow it. Shortly after midnight, when the size of the battalion's coverage became clear, Brigade HQ immediately authorized moving additional men forward, but not enough to fill out the front. The brigadier subsequently called off the Canadian Scottish attack scheduled that night and arranged for the battalion's relief. By the time the 16th finally struggled out of the trenches three days later, they had 349 casualties, almost a hundred fatal.

Apart from the Ypres Salient, the Canadian Scottish suffered its greatest number of casualties at Mouquet Farm. One of the battalion's soldiers wrote: "Mouquet Farm was the most nerve-wracking, hellish time I ever put in; a lifetime in three days.... I shudder at the thought of my experiences there." Division HQ ordered the exhausted 3rd Brigade units out of the line; however, much to their regret, Brigade HQ ordered the 16th forward again on September 15, when Haig, worried over his massive losses with no appreciable gains, decided to renew his faltering offensive. As the 16th moved forward it received almost 350 reinforcements.

For the next two weeks, the 16th was involved in sporadic fighting north of Courcelette, including the Fabeck Graben trench system, where John Kerr had earned his VC ten days earlier (see Chapter 3), and Regina Trench, the scene of particularly heavy fighting. The Canadian Scottish marched out of the Somme on October 11, never to return; the 16th had sustained 827 casualties, its four companies commanded by lieutenants or senior NCOs. The battalion moved north, arriving at its new location behind the Vimy Front on October 25.

In the Vimy area the Canadians began an intensive period of training and re-equipping, and on November 3 the Canadian Scottish received a new commanding officer—Cy Peck. All who knew him well regarded Peck as a picturesque personality, though his most engaging qualities were well hidden from the casual observer by his sturdy, solid exterior. Underneath the surface lay a thoughtful soul, as fond of poetry and music, history and philosophy, as of soldiering. That said, he was a natural, instinctive soldier and leader. Peck was a gallant fighter with a thorough understanding of human nature. He possessed a good sense of humour and a vivid imagination. Perhaps most importantly, he was intensely devoted to his men, who reciprocated his feelings in kind.

Peck believed in leading from the front. Accompanied by his piper, he went forward with the battalion in the attack, and frequently ahead of it. He was often in No Man's Land or the front trenches. Employing bagpipes, Peck strove to inspire an offensive spirit in his men, though this decision caused doubts among the less imaginative. He later wrote that when he proposed to take pipers into action he "met with a great deal of criticism." He persisted however, believing "the purpose of war is to win victories, and if one can do this better by encouraging certain sentiments and traditions" then there was no reason not to do so. He felt "the heroic and dramatic effect of a piper stoically playing his way across the modern battlefield, altogether oblivious of danger, has an extraordinary effect on the spirit of his comrades." From this point on, when the Canadian Scottish went into battle, they were accompanied by five pipers, one for the CO and each company. Peck successfully countered all objections, such as the pipers' conspicuousness. He wrote, "Officers, machine gunners and runners are conspicuous. People get killed in war because they are conspicuous; many get killed when they are not."

For the next few months, the battalion moved through its well-practiced routine of trench duty interspersed with various support and reserve tasks, usually facing Vimy Ridge. Rumours began to circulate of another "big push," which was confirmed in February 1917 by the arrival of maps marked with German positions on Vimy Ridge and four successive colour-coded lines running up and over the ridge from west to east.

REGINA TRENCH WAS FINALLY TAKEN AFTER BITTER HAND-TO-HAND FIGHTING THAT CAUSED HUNDREDS OF CASUALTIES IN THE CANADIAN SCOTTISH. GERMAN PRISONERS CAPTURED BY THE CANADIANS ARE MARCHED TO THE REAR AFTER THE BATTLE.

On April 1, the 16th began practicing on ground resembling Vimy Ridge. The weather contrived to do its worst, as winter blizzards and cold continued into spring, hampering training. Word came down that the attack would go in on April 7. In preparation, Peck gathered his men about him and delivered a stirring battle oration. Shortly thereafter the assault troops began moving forward, only to be told that Corps HQ had postponed the attack until April 9, Easter Monday. At 6:00 P.M. on Easter Sunday the soldiers began moving forward again. Canada was about to come of age on the battlefields of France.

First Division was to form the right flank of the corps attack, with 2nd Division on its left. First Division had the farthest distance to advance, thirty-six hundred metres, and planned to assault with two brigades forward, 3rd on the left. Within 3rd Brigade, from right to left, the 15th, 14th and 16th battalions would attack with the 13th in support. Peck's unit would assault on a two-company frontage, each company extending about 135 metres. His mission was to seize and occupy the first two colour-coded lines within his boundaries, Black and Red. With this accomplished, 3rd Brigade would move into reserve and 1st Brigade would assume the lead against the final two lines, Blue and Brown, exploiting beyond if possible. At each objective line, a planned pause permitted reorganization for the next phase.

Throughout the night, the Canadian Scottish assembled in a vast complex of tunnels dug into the French chalk. Despite being seriously ill with gastritis, a stomach ailment, Peck was determined to command, as always, from the front. Just before midnight he and a party of five began to make their way forward to their battle HQ. Finding the subterranean approach too crowded, Peck opted to proceed overland. They had not gone very far when a German shell landed in the middle of the group, killing three instantly and wounding two others. Peck, miraculously untouched, proceeded ahead alone.

With all companies in location, troops settled down in the frosty predawn to await the start of the preliminary artillery barrage at 5:30 A.M. Cold squalls of hail and sleet replaced the previous evening's mildness, chilling everyone to the bone. As the men emerged from their cover, they immediately came under machine-gun fire that momentarily checked their advance. However, they soon surged forward and to the flanks, overcoming machine-gun nests by bayonet and bomb. Additional enemy machine guns opened up from the front and flanks and a running fight ensued, as soldiers, singly and in small groups, dashed from shell hole to shell hole to overwhelm these posts. For the 16th, the company on the right proceeded with little difficulty, but a machine gun held up the company on the left. Finally, after numerous attempts to outflank it ended in failure, a soldier managed to crawl close and kill the entire crew with Mills bombs.

The troops captured the main German trench, the Black Line objective, on schedule, and a pre-arranged forty-minute artillery barrage gave the Canadians an opportunity to reform before proceeding towards the second objective, the Red Line. Soldiers quickly dispatched two machine guns holding up the advance and, as the 16th approached the Red Line, the Germans' morale collapsed and they scrambled out of their trenches, retreating eastwards. Up and down the line, the soldiers of the 16th could see other units experiencing similar successes. As the Canadian Scottish savoured their victory and dug in, Peck approached from the rear, accompanied by two pipers "playing lustily," the RSM and two other soldiers. The last soldier carried a jar of rum under each arm. Scattered cheering broke into a loud roar, probably more for the rum than for the colonel. The battalion's part in the Battle of Vimy Ridge was over.

The 16th suffered 341 casualties, over one-third fatal. For the next few days, relentless German artillery and gas attacks hit the unit, causing additional casualties and leading the Canadians to expect an assault at any moment. Peck's stomach inflammation became so bad that he was evacuated and eventually invalided to England, not to return until June 4. His superiors recognized his personal bravery and devotion with the award of the DSO, published in the *London Gazette* the same day he returned to duty. As was often the case, there is no citation, simply the annotation "awarded on the occasion of His Majesty's Birthday." Coming as soon as it did after the Canadian triumph at Vimy Ridge, it is clear that at least part of the reason for the honour was Peck's service in leading his battalion during that momentous battle.

Four days after Peck returned, the Canadian Corps welcomed its third and final commander of the war, a homegrown leader who progressed through successful brigade and divisional command in battle—Lieutenant-General Sir Arthur Currie. Currie's appointment and promotion particulaly pleased the Canadian Scottish. They always regarded him as one of their own, as Currie had been CO of one of the founding units of the 16th in 1914. Major-General Archie Macdonell, known affectionately to the troops as "Batty Mac" because of his many eccentricities, replaced Currie in command of 1st Division.

In mid-July, the battalion was called to participate in a two-division attack slated for the next month against Hill 70, between Lens and Loos in northeastern France. Prior to moving off, Peck addressed his soldiers. While he was speaking the new division commander arrived, unknown to him. Macdonell overheard the last part of Peck's stirring talk to his men: "The Brigade Commander, the Divisional Commander, the Corps Commander knows, and God knows you are the best of men—none ever better." Macdonell, who had come to the unit to speak to Peck about certain problems he noticed, felt he had been euchred. He said nothing, as "criticism seemed out of place, and it was difficult to see what more could be said in the way of praise."

When the attack went in against Hill 70, 3rd Brigade was left forward, attacking with three battalions up, with the 16th on the brigade's right flank. At 4:25 A.M. on August 15, the battalion, led by its pipers, rose up out of its trenches and moved into No Man's Land in virtually the same attack formation it used at Vimy Ridge. Within twenty-five minutes the leading companies captured the first objective, the Blue Line, having encountered little German resistance. After a forty-minute pause, the battalion moved off again towards its second objective, the Green Line. This fell as quickly as the first. For some reason, the expected German counterattack never materialized. Although the 16th had relatively light casualties, enemy shelling took its toll until fresh troops relieved the battalion.

In September, the Canadians learned they were needed elsewhere in support of a major offensive. Accordingly, the battalion began moving north during the third week of October. For the third and final time they moved to an area to which they fervently hoped they would never return—the Ypres Salient. A Canadian Scottish soldier described the scene in a letter to a friend: "I look back on the Passchendaele show as a nightmare. The ground was strewn with our dead. I have never seen anything to compare with the holocaust." Fortunately, the battalion's stay in this hellhole was short, and the 16th did not participate in a major attack during that time. On November 10, the 16th moved north of Arras, near Hill 70.

In Canada, on December 4, polls opened for the so-called "Khaki" general election of 1917. Prime Minister Robert Borden, concerned over the growing problem of finding sufficient recruits to replenish the Canadian Corps, had introduced conscription in August and faced defeat by opposition leader Wilfred Laurier on this issue. To enhance national unity, Borden proposed a coalition government with his Liberal opponent, which Laurier promptly rejected. Undeterred, the Conservative prime minister approached back-bench Liberals with the same proposal. With the votes counted, Borden's new Unionists won 153 seats to Laurier's eighty-two (all but twenty of which came from Quebec). Not only were the seeds planted for yet another divisive English–French conscription crisis twenty-five years later, conscription itself became a dismal failure. Of the more than four hundred thousand men registered, fewer than twenty-five thousand actually made it to the CEF in France. Cy Peck was one of the successful candidates, elected Unionist MP for Skeena *in absentia*—the first time any member of parliament was elected while overseas.

The men of the Canadian Scottish welcomed 1918, unaware that it would be their final year in the trenches. To them it was simply another cold, wet, blustery winter in dreary surroundings. The soldiers of the 16th spent the next few weeks alternating between trench duty and reserve, while Peck was acting brigade commander. In this appointment he became ill and spent some time recovering. He rejoined the battalion on March 27, by which time HQ ordered it forward in anticipation of a German break-through. Although still quite ill, Peck assumed command over the protests of his medical officer.

The first German spring offensive of 1918, employing the new "Hutier tactics," began on the Somme, on March 21. It quickly drove a seventy-kilometre deep salient into the British lines, before the attack ran out of steam. While the success of this first onslaught created panic for the Allied High Command, the Canadian Scottish and their CO were stalwart. The battalion's spirits were up, as one soldier recorded: "The Colonel says we are in for a wonderful battle...we are sure to be attacked, and we are to hold

GENERALS HAIG AND CURRIE DISCUSS THE COURSE OF THE WAR WITH PRESIDENT RAYMOND POINCAIRE OF FRANCE.

on as long as the last man is able to resist. Feel quite thrilled at the role we are to play." On the day German General Ludendorff called off the attack, Peck advised brigade HQ: "I think a raid now would keep up the keenness of our men and impress the enemy with the fact that we are not downhearted."

The CO got his wish three weeks later, when the battalion carried out the most successful raid in its history, northeast of Arras. By the time the hundred and fifty raiders returned, they had destroyed several dugouts, causing many casualties. They had also captured twenty-eight prisoners, three machine guns, communications equipment and numerous documents and maps, at a cost of five killed and seventeen wounded.

The 16th Battalion now entered a long period of rest and training—a prelude to the last hundred days of the war when the Canadians would spearhead the Allies' astonishing advances. As well as training with the tanks, the 16th also received additional Lewis guns, weapons in which they placed much more faith than they did in the armoured monsters. Each infantry battalion now carried thirty-eight such guns: two with each platoon and six at Battalion HQ. At this time, the Allies also introduced new "infiltration" tactics, modeled after the German Hutier ones.

By mid-summer rumours were circulating that something big was about to happen. On August 4 the soldiers entrained under conditions of great secrecy, and, three days later, after liaison with the 49th Australians holding the front southeast of Amiens, the 16th marched to their assembly area. Early the next morning they were in position, along with the rest of the Canadian Corps. The long-awaited "big push" was about to begin, spearheaded by the Canadians and Australians. The Black Day of the German Army had begun.

Although Field Marshal Haig's original intention for the Battle of Amiens was that it be a local offensive with limited objectives, in the end it became one of the turning points of the war. While Private Croak and Corporal Good earned their VCs with the Royal Highlanders (see Chapter 5), attacking in the centre of a three-battalion frontage, the Canadian Scottish advanced on their right. At 4:20 A.M. the Canadian Scottish began moving forward on a two-company front, supported by seven tanks. Advancing in darkness and through a sudden ground mist that sprang up twenty minutes before zero hour, over rough ground and with the sounds of tanks rumbling disconcertingly nearby, the fighting quickly became confused. After a few hundred metres Peck, in the centre of the battalion, came up against a high, dark mass looming out of the fog. Taking it as a strong enemy fortification, the CO immediately gave the order to charge. The men rushed forward instantly, only to find themselves up against an almost perpendicular bank of earth, part of the valley walls sloping down to the River Luce to the south.

Successfully negotiating this obstacle, the battalion continued its advance. A piper mounted a nearby tank, appropriately named "Dominion," and began to play the regiment's march past, "The Blue Bonnets over the Border." Thus led, the soldiers moved towards the enemy. Once the fog began to lift it became possible to see German anti-tank guns and trench mortars scattered about in the open, unmanned and still under their canvas covers. Then, as the battalion moved up a grassy slope the mist lifted altogether. Peck, in the first wave, ran forward to the crest when a machine gun opened fire, killing the piper standing beside him, who had been on the tank. Before a quick attack could be mounted, shots rang out and the battalion intelligence officer appeared in the enemy machine-gun post. He had outflanked it and killed its crew.

German resistance began to stiffen and the Canadian Scottish launched quick attacks to take positions stretching across their line of advance. The 16th captured numerous prisoners, including a battalion commander and his headquarters. The advance continued towards the village of Aubercourt, about nine hundred metres short of the Canadian Scottish's final objective, the Green Line. The 16th quickly took Aubercourt in a small action personally directed by Peck, but on the high ground north of the village things were not going as well. Here, the CO ordered a small party to outflank the enemy to the rear, and when heavy fire soon held this group up, Peck directed a passing tank forward to assist them. When the Germans saw the tank, they surrendered, with a regimental commander, his staff and a large number of men all taken prisoner. By this time, troops overcame the enemy on the high ground and the battalion continued to the Green Line, reaching it before 9:00 A.M.

In less than seven hours, the Battle of Amiens was over for Peck and the Canadian Scottish. It was one of their finest showings of the war. For his actions in leading the attack, Peck received a second award of the DSO, published in the *London Gazette* on January 11, 1919. A new feeling was in the air, a heady sense that the Allied armies were finally on the road to ultimate victory. On August 25, the 16th Battalion entrained and moved north to Arras, where Metcalf and Peck would earn their VCs.

After the success at Arras on September 2, patrols discovered that during the night the Germans had withdrawn over six kilometres to the east, to strongly entrenched positions behind the Canal du Nord. All along the British front, troops discovered that similar withdrawals had taken place, with the canal's bridges blown up as the Germans retreated. Beyond the canal stretched the daunting defences of the main Hindenburg Line. On September 24, with the 16th Battalion in brigade reserve, the brigadier sent Peck to the rear for a much needed and deserved rest. On September 30, the 16th received orders to participate in an attack the following day to seize the high ground north of Cambrai. Under the second-in-command the battalion successfully achieved its initial objective, seizing the village of Cuvillers; however, the Canadian Scottish were soon outflanked and forced to withdraw. Sometime before being forced back, the acting CO went forward to link up with patrols and was never seen again.

Meanwhile Peck, anxious over the fate of his battalion, was riding forward. Near Sancourt, from where the attack had been launched, he came under machine-gun fire in an area supposedly well behind front lines. He proceeded ahead on foot under heavy fire, eventually establishing a clear picture of 3rd Brigade's dispositions. Advising his brigadier of the situation by telephone, he was ordered to take control of the brigade's front line. As day turned into night, the Canadians made no further progress. After advancing nearly five kilometres that morning, the battalion ended the day only sixteen hundred metres past its jumping-off line, a disappointing result.

At 4:00 A.M. the next morning, fresh troops relieved the remnants of the battalion, which was down to three officers and seventy-five soldiers, who moved into brigade support. The unit had suffered 345 casualties, nearly one-quarter fatal. The Canadian Scottish had just fought their last major engagement of the war. With his troops now bordering on exhaustion and with casualties mounting, General Currie broke off the attack on October 1. On October 4, a gas shell wounded Peck, and sporadic fighting continued on the Cambrai front. Then, on October 9, the Canadian attack resumed. A general corps advance began all along the front on October 11, with the German forces retreating towards Valenciennes. Wanting to save the lives of his men, Currie gave orders to avoid decisive engagements. The corps advanced cautiously towards Valenciennes, with the 16th Battalion playing its part.

On October 19, Peck left his second-in-command in charge so he might roam the countryside:

I rode into the towns we occupied—sometimes alone, sometimes with my groom. The people seemed stunned. For four years they had been under the heel of the enemy who had left that morning, and the spell still seemed to be upon them.... The Germans had left them with terrible threats, and they seemed cowed and uncertain until we were actually among them....

In one of the towns I entered I saw the inhabitants coming out of a house bringing with them six or seven German military police who had overslept themselves. The police were being savagely menaced by the population, and I had to take them under my protection and hand them over to the leading troops of my Battalion when they arrived. These were the only prisoners we captured that day.

I don't know whether the presentations of flowers started here or farther on, but by the time we got to Erre my groom and myself had to discharge our floral load of huge bouquets, only to be loaded up again at a later stage. Wines and liqueurs were hastily dug up from gardens at short notice and insistently pressed upon us.

The first large town we came to was Somain.... I rode in and halted before a huge crowd. One man seized the hem of my dirty trench coat and kissed it passionately. I shouted "Vive la France!" The people shouted back, and went wild with enthusiasm.

The gentleman who had kissed my trench coat escorted me first to the mayor's place, where we partook of wine and exchanged salutations in pigeon French, and afterwards to the doctor, who was a great dignitary and lived in a fine house. I felt quite imposing as the deliverer of Somain.

...Further exhibitions of the intense feeling with which the French inhabitants regarded their release were witnessed.... Leaving Erre,...I saw five Uhlans [German mounted troops] *armed with lances, retiring over the ridge in front.... I rode rapidly towards them for a space, a bouquet of flowers in one hand and holding the reins and my revolver in the other.*

...I shortly afterwards rode off with my groom towards Hornaing, a town about a mile short of the line which the 16th was ordered to occupy for the night 19th/20th.

The German rearguard scouts had only passed through a short time before. A large crowd had assembled in the square and seemed quite uncertain as to just who I was. I again shouted "Vive la France!" but this time met with no response. Noting a street sign (Kaiser Wilhelm Strasse) nailed against the wall, I rode up to it, tore it off, spat on it and hurled it to the ground, exclaiming, in what I thought to be French, "To hell with the Germans!" This produced the desired result and the crowd went wild with enthusiasm.

The Battalion arrived shortly afterwards.... Thus passed my most enjoyable day in the War; bloodless withal, but most moving, witnessing the unbounding joy of a delivered people.

Battalions passed through each other, cautiously attempting to avoid any casualties. The Canadian Corps drove the Germans steadily back, pressing on to the Belgian city of Mons, which the Canadians reached on daybreak of November 11, Armistice Day. A few hours later hostilities ceased, a surprise to most soldiers, accustomed to the fighting of the last few years. When word reached the Canadian Scottish, they immediately made arrangements to mark the end of the war in style. That night the unit and its sister battalions celebrated around a giant bonfire, as pipe bands played and rockets and flares arced into the heavens.

On Sunday, November 17, in Peck's absence, word arrived that he would be awarded the VC, possibly the only occasion it has ever been earned by any elected member of parliament in the British Empire or Commonwealth. On Peck's return that evening the entire battalion, led by the pipe band, marched to Battalion HQ and demanded their CO and a speech. Peck appeared, delivered his speech, and his men then carried him on their shoulders to Brigade HQ, where the jubilant troops finished off the brigadier's whisky in short order.

The next day, the Canadian Scottish began their long march to the Rhine. For the first time during the war, support units did not deliver rations because the troops outran their supply lines. When this happened repeatedly, three platoons of one company refused to parade, falling in only after being addressed by their company commander. When word of this incident reached Peck, he delivered a stern rebuke to the soldiers in question, leaving no doubt how repetitions of such conduct would be handled.

At mid-afternoon on December 6, the unit crossed the German border to the sound of "The Blue Bonnets" being played by the battalion's piper. One week later, the Canadians crossed the Rhine at Cologne as the division commander, Batty Mac, took the salute from 3rd Brigade's battalions. While the brigade remained in the Cologne area it bade farewell to its CO: after over two years in command, Peck left on January 3 to take up his parliamentary responsibilities as a new MP. On the way home, Peck stopped off in England to receive his Victoria Cross. On January 26, 1919, King George V invested him with his VC at the royal estate at Sandringham, along with Bill Metcalf.

When the 16th Battalion arrived at Quebec City on May 4, Peck met his soldiers there, to entrain with them for Winnipeg and disbandment. Three days later, after marching up Portage Avenue and giving a salute to the district officer commanding, Peck dismissed the 16th. The Canadian Scottish's part in the Great War was over, as was Cy Peck's. His distinguished leadership was recognized by a number of awards. During the First World War, only one other Canadian received the VC as well as the DSO and Bar, while a total of five officers earned the VC and DSO. During the course of the war Peck also received an amazing five Mentions-in-Dispatches.

On his return to Canada, Peck took his seat in Parliament and became active in veterans' affairs. Defeated in the 1921 election, he commanded the Canadian Bisley rifle team that same year. He entered provincial politics and became Conservative Member of the Legislative Assembly for the British Columbia riding of The Islands from 1924 to 1928. He was re-elected in the next election, but resigned partway through his term on appointment to the Canada Pensions Commission. He later served as aide-de-camp to two governors general.

In June 1956, Peck and his wife attended the centennial celebrations for the Victoria Cross in London, England. A few weeks later, after his return to Canada, Peck died on September 27, 1956, at "Hopewell," his home in Sidney, on Vancouver Island, which was named after the village of his birth. His family cremated his body, scattered his ashes in Rupert Sound, off the coast at Prince Rupert, and erected a marker in the family plot in the Fraser Cemetery in New Westminster, outside Vancouver. Sir Arthur Currie, the greatest general Canada ever produced, said of Peck: "No braver or kinder heart ever beat in the breast of a man."

From 1930 to 1966, the 155-tonne passenger and car ferry *Cy Peck* plied the waters between Saltspring Island and Vancouver Island's Saanich Peninsula, perhaps the longest serving vessel in the fleet. The Sidney Heritage Post Office bears a plaque dedicated to him, and the federal government erected a plaque in the House of Commons in Ottawa in memory of his time as an MP. His VC remained with his wife for a number of years, eventually becoming the property of his three sons. The family loaned it to the Canadian Scottish for a number of years, until 1993, when the last surviving son, Edward, formally presented it to the Canadian War Museum in

Ottawa, where it forms part of the national VC collection and is viewed by thousands each year.

After the war, Bill Metcalf lived in Eastport, Maine, where he worked as a motor mechanic. During the 1920s and '30s, he served as a second lieutenant in C Company of the York Regiment, a New Brunswick militia battalion, in St. Stephen, across the border from Calais. When he died in South Portland on August 8, 1968, fifty years after he earned the VC, the Union Jack draped his cas-

On January 2, 1919, King George V presented Peck and Metcalf with their Victoria Crosses at Sandringham, a rare occasion when two members of the same unit received their Victoria Crosses for their heroic actions on the same day.

ket, with over forty members of the Royal Canadian Legion in attendance at his funeral service. At his request, Metcalf was buried in the Bayside Cemetery, Eastport, in a spot overlooking the mouth of the St. Croix River, which forms the border between Maine and New Brunswick. Crossed American and Canadian flags mark his grave and annually, on the anniversary of his death, New Brunswick members of the Royal Canadian Legion journey to his grave for a small ceremony. In 1998, his son, Stanley, donated Metcalf's VC and other medals to the Canadian Scottish Regiment; they are on display in the regimental museum in Victoria, British Columbia.

CHAPTER 7

"THE MOST UNLIKELY HERO ONE COULD IMAGINE"

Lieutenant Milton Fowler Gregg
The Royal Canadian Regiment, Canadian Expeditionary Force
Cambrai, France, September 27–October 1, 1918

Milton Fowler Gregg was the third and last New Brunswicker to earn the Victoria Cross in the First World War, gaining his medal in the final weeks before the Armistice. He went on to become one of the best known native sons of his home province and was arguably the most famous of all Atlantic Canadians to be awarded the VC. As well, he was one of only two junior officers from Atlantic Canada to earn this rare distinction. Gregg was born in the small rural community of Mountain Dale (now Snider Mountain), Kings County, on April 10, 1892, the son of farmer George Gregg and Elizabeth Myles. He received his education locally, afterwards attending the Provincial Normal School in Fredericton, where he received his teaching certificate. He graduated from Acadia University with a Bachelor of Arts degree and attended Dalhousie University before teaching school in Carleton County, in his home province, for three years.

Gregg joined the militia in 1910, enlisting in the 8th Princess Louise's New Brunswick Hussars. The Hussars were one of the province's oldest regiments, tracing their roots back to eleven independent cavalry troops that were attached to county and city infantry battalions. In April 1848, these troops were amalgamated into the New Brunswick Regiment of Yeomanry Cavalry. By the time of Confederation, the regimental establishment was reduced to four troops, all located in Gregg's home county of King's. Shortly afterwards, the unit was renamed the 8th Regiment of Cavalry. In 1879, when Her Royal Highness Princess Louise visited the Maritimes, the regiment acted as her escort. As a result, a few years later her name was added to the unit's title.

When war broke out, Gregg enlisted as a private in the 13th Battalion (Royal Highlanders) and went overseas with 1st Canadian Division, which formed the First Canadian Contingent to be dispatched abroad. The battalion trained in England, then went to the front in February 1915. Beginning April 22, Gregg participated in the Second Battle of Ypres, which saw the first German gas attack on the Western Front. Then, on May 22, he was wounded twice while serving as a stretcher-bearer in the Battle of Festubert. While in England convalescing in hospital, Gregg was recommended for a commission. He subsequently attended the Imperial Officers' Training School at Cambridge, graduating third in a class of over two hundred. After receiving his commission as a second lieutenant in 1916, he was posted to the British Army's King's Own Royal Lancaster Regiment, but only served there for four months before being sent to the Royal Canadian Regiment.

The RCR was Canada's senior Permanent Force infantry regiment, formed to replace the British Imperial troops withdrawn after Confederation. It was established in 1883 as the Infantry School Corps, with three independent companies at Fredericton, New Brunswick, St-Jean, Quebec, and Toronto, Ontario, to instruct the militia in all aspects of infantry drill and warfare. Shortly after the corps' formation, its mettle was tested for the first of many times when Toronto's C Company, with a strength of five officers and eighty-five rank and file, participated in the Northwest Rebellion of 1885. It fought at Fish Creek, Batoche and Cut Knife Hill, suffering the regiment's first fatalities (two killed and seven wounded) and earning its first battle honours (Saskatchewan and Northwest Canada, 1885).

Through the 1890s, the corps went through a number of name changes, became a regiment under one commanding officer, and in 1901, acquired its present title. The regiment contributed over half of the 216 personnel of the Yukon Field Force, created to assist the Northwest Mounted Police in maintaining law and order during the Klondike Gold Rush of 1898–1900.

During the Boer War (October 1899–May 1902), the government mobilized the 2nd (Special Service) Battalion, Royal Canadian Regiment. Formed before the parent regiment's duties in the Yukon ended, the 1,019-man battalion was built around a core of about one hundred and fifty officers and men from the Permanent Force unit and additional volunteers from eighty-two different militia units across the country. On February 27, 1900, the 2nd Regiment participated in its most celebrated battle in South Africa and helped defeat the Boers at Paardeberg, the first great British victory and the turning point of the war. A few months later, the regiment was part of the victorious British column that entered the Boer capital of Pretoria on June 5. Although the war dragged on for two more years before the Boers finally surrendered, the RCR's role was almost over—the volunteer soldiers' contracts of "six months, or one year if required" were coming to an end.

The last of the regiment left South Africa on November 7, 1900, arriving back in Canada two days before Christmas. At a cost of sixty-eight dead and 115 wounded, two more battle honours (Paardeberg and South Africa, 1899–1900) had been added to the regiment's list. On the way home, the regiment was feted and entertained in London and journeyed to Windsor Castle, where an ailing Queen Victoria inspected and thanked the Canadians. It was one of the eighty-one-year-old queen's final public appearances; she died less than two months later.

In March 1900, while the 2nd Battalion was on the South Africa veldt, a 3rd Battalion of 1,004 men was raised to replace the Imperial infantry garrison in Halifax, freeing the latter to go to South Africa. The 3rd served in Halifax until September 1902, when a British battalion was able to relieve it, after the end of the Boer War. However, the losses the regiment suffered in the Canadian northwest and South Africa were about to pale in comparison to the next war in which the RCR participated.

On the outbreak of the First World War, the RCR was still the Dominion of Canada's only regular infantry regiment. Since the withdrawal of the last of the Imperial garrison in 1906, the RCR consisted of ten companies, with Regimental Headquarters and six of its companies stationed in Halifax. Prior to Britain's declaration of war on August 4, 1914, the regiment was ordered to occupy various port defences in Halifax and elsewhere, as a part of the existing defence scheme. Fully expecting to be sent overseas with the

First Contingent, the regiment was surprised at being sent to garrison duties in Bermuda—the first Canadian troops to be sent abroad during the war—to relieve a British unit there. The RCR served in the tiny island colony from September 1914 until the following August, when another Canadian unit replaced it.

The regiment sailed from Halifax for England at the end of August 1915, arriving in Plymouth on September 5. After a brief period of training, the unit, 1,042 strong, went to France in November. By this time the Canadian Corps, consisting of 1st and 2nd Canadian Divisions, had been formed under the command of British Lieutenant-General Edwin Alderson. Meanwhile, the war was settling into a great struggle of attrition, with masses of infantry fighting and dying for a few shell-torn metres of ground. After a brief period, during which time individual platoons served in the trenches learning this new form of warfare from battalions of 1st Canadian Division, the RCR was incorporated into the newly formed 3rd Canadian Infantry Division. The regiment ended up as a unit of 7th Brigade, the senior of the division's three brigades and the same one to which Chip Kerr's 49th Edmonton Battalion belonged.

MILTON FOWLER GREGG WAS THE LAST NEW BRUNSWICKER TO EARN THE VICTORIA CROSS DURING THE FIRST WORLD WAR. DURING ATTACKS NEAR CAMBRAI OVER A FIVE-DAY PERIOD IN THE FALL OF 1918, HE DISPLAYED CONTINUOUS BRAVERY AND INITIATIVE WHILE SERVING AS A LIEUTENANT IN THE ROYAL CANADIAN REGIMENT.

In January 1916, the RCR took over a portion of the front lines for the first time, in the Kemmel Sector. Nearly three years of wretched and lethal trench warfare were to follow. But the troops' spirits were high. When the soldiers of the RCR proudly maintained their regular force customs in the filth and dirt of the trenches, the other units in 7th Brigade referred to them derisively—and perhaps a bit enviously—as "the shino boys." They said the RCR were so fond of spit and polish they even used to shine the barbed wire in front of their trenches.

In March, 3rd Division moved to the Ypres Salient in Belgium, where the regiment earned its first battle honour of the war (Mount Sorrel) and suffered its first heavy casualties. This was followed by a move to the Somme in September, to participate in General Haig's ill-fated campaign that commenced on July 1. After its unsuccessful attack on Regina Trench with Kerr's 49th Edmonton Battalion during the Battle of Ancre Heights in October, the regiment was reduced to a staggering 140 officers and men. Later that month, the Canadian Corps, now four divisions strong, was transferred to the Vimy Ridge area to build up its numbers and prepare for the great assault there.

Six months later, the attack on Vimy Ridge on Easter Monday 1917 saw all four Canadian divisions operating together for the first time. The RCR took its first and second objectives in a timely fashion, only to suffer casualties from the high ground to its left flank, where 4th Division had failed to capture its objectives according to schedule. This setback, however, did not detract from the brilliant victory that the capture of the ridge represented, one of the few bright moments for the Allies on the Western Front that year.

When Lieutenant Milton Gregg joined the RCR in France as a platoon commander in C Company, one of his first operations was a night trench raid at Lens involving three battalions of 7th Brigade. It was termed a raid as opposed to an attack because it was not intended that any captured enemy territory would be held, although at the soldier level the distinction was somewhat lost. The RCR were to attack on a narrow front astride the Vimy-Avion railway embankment with two companies, Gregg's C Company on the right and D Company on the left. For this operation, C Company was divided into three parties with a total strength of four officers and ninety-two soldiers. The intention was to advance just over seven hundred metres, hold the captured ground for an hour and a half to bomb dugouts, trenches and strong points, then commence a withdrawal.

At about 10:00 P.M. on the evening of June 8, 1917, the companies deployed to their jumping-off positions, with an artillery barrage on the

German front line trenches commencing at 11:45. The attacking companies advanced behind this barrage and soon entered the enemy's forward positions. Both companies made good progress until a German machine gun, occupying a strong position unaffected by the preliminary bombardment, held up the advance of C Company. Gregg realized the threat this position posed to his company, and moved forward to take action, leading a party of bombers in a successful flank attack against the machine gun. The raid continued, gaining all of its objectives while inflicting heavy casualties and destroying many enemy dugouts.

At 1:15 A.M. on June 9, some ninety minutes after the attack was launched, the RCR began to withdraw from the German trenches they had seized. This withdrawal was carried out under heavy fire, especially from German trench mortars. When Gregg saw a fellow lieutenant fall, mortally wounded, he ignored his own wounds, hoisted the officer onto his back and carried him through the pitch black of No Man's Land to the regiment's front line, all the while under heavy fire. The raid was deemed a success, with considerable damage inflicted upon the enemy's troops and trenches.

On July 25, 1917, the *London Gazette* announced that Gregg was awarded the Military Cross for his actions during the raid. The MC was normally awarded "for distinguished and meritorious services in time of war." As a decoration (as opposed to an order, such as the DSO), it was first in precedence after the VC, and awarded only to army captains, lieutenants and warrant officers—the leaders of men. The white and purple ribbon of the MC symbolizes initiative and outstanding courage. During the First World War, 2,885 members of the CEF, or those detached from the CEF, received the MC. Only fifteen of them received both the VC and the MC.

Gregg spent the next fourteen months in the trenches as a platoon and company commander. The regiment moved back to the Ypres Salient to participate in yet another of recently promoted Field Marshal Haig's futile offensives. (It was this same battle in which Philip Bent and Pete Robertson were killed earning their VCs.) King George V, acting on his own initiative, had made Haig field marshal at the beginning of 1917 without consulting the British cabinet; the king considered the promotion as a New Year's gift from himself and the country. At Passchendaele in the Ypres Salient, the RCR was not among the Canadian battalions from 3rd and 4th divisions that assaulted the ridge on October 26, acting instead as support troops and reinforcements. Despite their support roles, by the time the ridge was captured on November 10, the regiment had suffered 258 killed, wounded or missing.

After the meat grinder of Passchendaele, the Canadian Corps returned to the scene of its earlier victory at Vimy Ridge. It remained there for the next eight months, defending the ridge and turning it into one of the most heavily fortified positions on the entire Western Front, Allied or German. With the Russian Revolution taking Russia out of the war, the Germans were able to move troops from the Eastern to the Western Front; accordingly, the Allies expected a massive German offensive in the spring of 1918, before the full power of the United States could be brought to bear on the war.

During this period the RCR took on a much-needed draft of one hundred men and two officers from the 185th Battalion (Cape Breton Highlanders). This unit had been raised from across Cape Breton Island in April 1916, trained in the Annapolis Valley's Camp Aldershot that summer, sailed to England in October and was used there as reinforcements for the Canadian Corps until February 1918, when it was finally disbanded. Its CO throughout the war was Lieutenant-Colonel Frank Parker Day, who would later write *Rockbound*, a classic novel of Nova Scotia's South Shore first published in 1928. In 2005 the book was the winner of CBC Radio's "Canada Reads" contest. Although the 185th never fought as a unit, the majority of its soldiers fittingly went to two battalions of the Black Watch, the 42nd and 73rd, both of which had several Maritimers in their ranks, or to Nova Scotia units, such as the 25th (Nova Scotia Rifles), the 85th (Nova Scotia Highlanders) and the RCR. Day himself ended up in the 85th Battalion, having reverted to major to become the unit's second-in-command.

On August 26, 1918, Gregg's actions resulted in his receiving a Bar to his Military Cross for leading another bombing attack, this time against two German machine guns at Monchy-le-Preux during the Battle of the Scarpe. Wounded again, he carried on, killing the entire crews of both guns. Advancing with his platoon, he soon found himself and his men isolated, so he dug in, and conducted a personal reconnaissance to connect with the left flank. He carefully positioned his men to enable a counter-attack to be repulsed. In the words of his *London Gazette* citation, which was published on February 1, 1919, Gregg's "courage and good leadership saved a critical situation." Two hundred and ninety-four members of the CEF received a second award of the MC, with only three awarded the VC as well as the MC and Bar.

In front of the city of Cambrai and nine kilometres beyond, the Hindenburg Line consisted of two separate German trench systems, the

Marquoin and the Marcoing, immediately behind the Canal du Nord. Nothing less than a full-scale assault would be required to breach these formidable defences. As the corps commander, General Currie, made a detailed reconnaissance of the area in preparation for the attack, the Canadians established a defensive line along the western bank of the canal.

Before attacking the Marquoin and Marcoing lines, the Canadian Corps first had to cross the Canal du Nord. Currie ascertained that the canal was a formidable obstacle: nearly one hundred metres wide with an additional four hundred metres on either side of flooded swampland. The open ground on both sides of the canal was also completely dominated by strong enemy positions on the heights on the eastern side. However, to the south of the area from which the corps was meant to attack was a four-thousand-metre stretch where the canal was still under construction, with a dry bed and firm ground on each side. Currie asked for and received an adjustment to his boundaries to include part of this dry area, to permit his crossing to take place here. His plan was to cross in this narrow sector—an operation of considerable risk, with the corps bunched together in a small zone of only twenty-four hundred metres frontage— and then fan out laterally towards the northeast to a front of fourteen thousand metres, before advancing towards Cambrai.

The attack was launched at 5:20 A.M. on September 27 and within an hour the troops

ARTHUR CURRIE WAS THE GREATEST GENERAL CANADA EVER PRODUCED. A MILITIA COMMANDING OFFICER WHEN THE WAR BEGAN, HE ROSE THROUGH BRIGADE AND DIVISION COMMAND TO BECOME THE FIRST AND ONLY CANADIAN TO COMMAND THE CANADIAN CORPS.

had seized a two thousand metre deep bridgehead, meeting only light opposition. By night, the advance penetrated as far as the Marcoing Line, the last remaining trench line in the area. Canadian lieutenants earned three VCs that day for capturing enemy strong points. For their part, the Germans rushed seven more divisions into the area, determined to halt the Canadian tide before it reached Cambrai.

THE CANAL DU NORD WAS A FORMIDABLE OBSTACLE TO THE ALLIED ADVANCE, BUT IT HAD TO BE OVERCOME BEFORE THE ATTACK ON CAMBRAI COULD OCCUR. CURRIE'S INNOVATIVE—AND RISKY—PLAN TO CROSS THE CANAL WAS A COMPLETE SUCCESS. CANADIAN ENGINEERS ARE SHOWN IMPROVING CROSSING SITES FOR SUPPLIES.

The Marcoing Line was attacked on September 28 and both in this assault and in the days that followed, Lieutenant Gregg continuously displayed a high level of "bravery and initiative," in the words of the *London Gazette*. When the advance was held up by fire from both flanks and by heavy, uncut wire, Gregg crawled forward alone and probed the wire until he found a small gap, large enough for one man at a time. He guided his men through it and, gaining entry into a German trench that was part of the Marcoing Line, Gregg led his soldiers in an attack with bombs on the

first German strong point. Although outnumbered, the Canadians overcame the enemy machine-gun crews and forced the occupants of a deep
dugout, some three officers and forty-five men, to surrender. With reinforcements, Gregg and his men moved on, taking position after position
until about one-half of the Marcoing Line in their sector had been captured.

When the enemy counterattacked, the situation soon became desperate
due to lack of bombs, as the Canadians used up their own and all the
German ones they could find. Although badly wounded, Gregg returned
alone to his own lines under heavy fire and collected more bombs, before
rejoining his men. Despite being wounded again, he re-organized his small
force and led it against the enemy trenches. Gregg personally killed or
wounded eleven Germans and took twenty-five of them prisoner, capturing
twelve machine guns. By day's end, the Marcoing Line had fallen. Although

CAMBRAI, AN IMPORTANT COMMUNICATIONS HUB, WAS THE LAST MAJOR OBJECTIVE OF
THE CANADIAN CORPS DURING THE WAR. THIS VIEW WAS TAKEN FROM THE CANADIAN
FRONT LINES ON OCTOBER 1, 1918.

wounded, Gregg remained with his company and led them in another attack on September 30. He was so seriously wounded on this occasion that he was evacuated and hospitalized. Gregg returned to his unit in time to take part in one of the final battles of the war, the advance to Mons. For his courage and determination during this period Gregg was awarded the VC. His citation was published in the *London Gazette* on January 6, 1919, and Gregg received the medal from the king at Buckingham Palace on February 26, 1919.

"Milt" Gregg returned to Canada in the spring of 1919, married Dorothy Alward in August and began a distinguished post-war career. He held positions in the Soldiers' Civil Re-establishment (the predecessor of the Department of Veterans' Affairs) and the Soldiers' Settlement Board, followed by various civilian jobs at the Halifax *Herald*, a mining company and

THE ROYAL CANADIAN REGIMENT DEPARTED FROM LIVERPOOL, ENGLAND ON MARCH 1, 1919, ON THE SS ADRIATIC. GREGG (RIGHT), NOW THE BATTALION ADJUTANT, STANDS NEXT TO HIS COMMANDING OFFICER AND THE COLOUR PARTY BEARING THE UNIT'S ENCASED COLOURS.

THE SOARING MAJESTY OF THE VIMY RIDGE NATIONAL MEMORIAL COMMEMORATES THE MOST FAMOUS CANADIAN BATTLE OF THE FIRST WORLD WAR. IT TOOK 11 YEARS TO BUILD AT THE THEN UNHEARD OF COST OF $1.5 MILLION. GREGG WAS IN CHARGE OF THE ROYAL CANADIAN REGIMENT CONTINGENT AND COMMANDED THE GUARD OF HONOUR AT ITS UNVEILING IN AUGUST 1936.

an automobile dealership. Gregg maintained his military connections after the war and remained in the militia while pursuing a business career. In 1934, he was acting brigade major of 16 Infantry Brigade (Militia) when he was appointed sergeant-at-arms in the House of Commons, a job he held until 1939. The previous year, Gregg had taken the salute on Warriors' Day at the Canadian National Exhibition as the Old Comrades of the Royal Canadian Regiment from Toronto formed the Guard of Honour.

On August 26, 1936, the magnificent Canadian war memorial at Vimy Ridge was unveiled by King Edward VIII in one of the few public acts of his short reign. Over six thousand former soldiers and their relatives made the pilgrimage to Vimy for the occasion. Major Gregg led the RCR contingent and commanded the Guard of Honour. There were several ex-members of the regiment in the Guard, and Gregg detailed Corporal G. W. Horne, who had won the Military Medal and Bar, to lay the wreath, as Horne was "a particularly valuable and popular member of the overseas regiment."

On the outbreak of the Second World War, the RCR mobilized for active service and began recruiting to bring its strength up to war establishment. First Canadian Division was reformed, its three brigades each with three infantry battalions (as opposed to the four of the First World War). The RCR, as Canada's senior infantry unit, occupied pride of place in 1st Canadian Infantry Brigade. The other units in the brigade, an all-Ontario formation, were two Militia battalions, the Hastings and Prince Edward Regiment, and the 48th Highlanders of Canada. The 2nd Brigade was based on Western Canada, while 3rd came from Quebec and the Maritimes. On November 10, 1939, the RCR received orders to concentrate at Camp Valcartier, outside Quebec City.

Gregg re-enlisted in the Permanent Force and in early December was posted to the RCR at Valcartier as second-in-command of the battalion. Shortly afterwards, the regiment entrained for Halifax and boarded His Majesty's Transport *Almanzora*, bound for England. Gregg was going overseas as he had in the First World War—part of 1st Canadian Division. While still anchored at Halifax, Gregg had intervened on the soldiers' behalf to solve an accommodation problem on board that saw sixty men herded into sleeping space for half that number. A reallocation soon provided ample accommodation space for all 1,281 other ranks on board.

The troop ship disembarked the regiment at Gourock, on Scotland's Clyde River, on December 30; Gregg was the first man ashore. The troops entrained that afternoon, arriving at their new home of Aldershot after an overnight journey south. In early February, as the regiment settled into the worst winter in forty years, Gregg's appointment as CO of the West Nova Scotia Regiment, one of the battalions of 3rd Brigade, was announced.

The West Novas had mobilized in Bridgewater with soldiers from the Annapolis Valley and South Shore of Nova Scotia in September 1939, proceeding overseas in the same convoy that brought the RCR and Gregg to Britain. On February 5, the brigade commander, Brigadier Charles Price, assembled the officers of the West Novas in their mess and introduced their new CO to them. Over the next two days, Major Gregg gathered the officers and senior NCOs in the band room of the soldiers' canteen for a series of personal talks. They were impressed. The First World War record of courage and decisiveness by the "slim, dark, dynamic" Gregg was known to all. For the next few months of "hard monotonous training" in England, he "made himself the heart and soul of the Regiment."

Soon promoted to lieutenant-colonel, Gregg took the regiment through its work-ups for war, with exercises, range shoots and the introduction of new equipment. There was also a steady stream of visitors to the unit. In late April, Norman Rogers, a native of Amherst and the Minister of National Defence, inspected the unit. Speaking of the visit by radio to Canada, Gregg said: "The Honourable Norman Rogers has inspected the West Nova Scotia Regiment and was greatly pleased with their appearance. On my own part I wish to say to the fathers and mothers in Nova Scotia that your boys put on a great show today. They will give an excellent account of themselves, whatever they may be called upon to do. All ranks in my Regiment send to all of you in Nova Scotia our best wishes."

Indeed Gregg was correct and the West Novas went on to establish an admirable record for themselves as they fought in Sicily, mainland Italy and the Netherlands. Unfortunately, the First World War hero was not to command them, nor was Rogers to see his native province's regiment go on to glory. At an officers' mess dinner that night, at which Rogers was the guest of honour, Gregg proposed a toast to him. In response, Rogers congratulated the regiment on its "worthy representation" of the founding races of Nova Scotia, adding, "This is the proudest day of my life." On June 10, shortly after his return to Canada, he was killed in an airplane crash. Coincidentally, another Amherst native, James Ralston, replaced him as Minister of National Defence, serving until November 1944 when Prime Minister Mackenzie King forced his resignation over Ralston's outspoken support for overseas conscription.

Another visitor later that summer in August was the premier of Nova Scotia, Angus L. Macdonald. He presented the unit with the flag of Nova Scotia, bearing the same St. Andrew's cross of Scotland emblazoned on the regiment's cap badge. Gregg himself hoisted the flag with proper ceremony at a parade at the unit's camp in Kent. From then on, the Nova Scotia flag marked the location of Regimental HQ, no matter where the West Novas served, for the rest of the war.

Towards the end of October, Gregg was taken ill and was away from his regiment for almost two weeks. In early December, Major-General George Pearkes, general-officer-commanding 1st Division and a VC recipient from the First World War, inspected the regiment. Gregg, whose health had been failing for some time and was still recovering from his most recent stay in the hospital, stayed on his feet during the inspection only by sheer will power. Immediately afterwards, the unit medical officer sent him back to the Bramshott Hospital, where he remained for several months.

At the end of April 1941, Gregg returned from a period of convalescent leave and resumed command of the regiment. However, it was not to be for long. On May 9, he was promoted colonel and appointed to command the Canadian Officer Cadet Training Unit in London. His second-in-command, who had stood in for him during his long convalescence, replaced him. The regiment was sad to see him go, and he visited each of the companies in turn to say farewell. Gregg was regarded as an extremely capable commander and it was unfortunate that his illness deprived him of the chance to lead the West Novas into battle.

On July 10, 1943 at 4:00 P.M. the West Nova Scotia Regiment landed on the beaches of Sicily. From then to VE Day it successfully fought in twenty-one actions across the island of Sicily, up the boot of the Italian mainland and in the Netherlands, where it was transferred for the final few weeks of the war, in the process earning twenty-six battle and campaign honours. Though Gregg was not there to lead the regiment, the stamp of his personality was definitely on it. He helped to shape the untrained soldiers and officers into an effective fighting machine.

In 1942, Gregg returned to Canada as commandant of the Officers Training Centre (Eastern Canada) at Brockville. In 1943, he was promoted to brigadier and appointed chairman of the Officers' Selection Board, charged with selecting appropriate candidates for officer training at various Officer Training Centres across Canada. Later that year, Gregg was selected to organize and command the Canadian Infantry School in Vernon, BC. He ended his full-time military career at Sussex, NB, not far from where he was born and where his military service had commenced in the 8th Hussars. At Sussex, he commanded the Canadian Infantry Training Centre (Reinforcement).

Among his responsibilities was the training of CANLOAN officers. Canadian Loan, or CANLOAN, was a plan that saw 622 surplus Canadian infantry lieutenants and captains (plus fifty-one Ordnance Corps officers) loaned to the British Army on a voluntary basis. These officers were in excess of Canada's requirements due to the disbandment of two Home Defence Divisions, and the fact that the Canadian Army was only fighting on one front at the time, the Italian. Meanwhile, the British Army, fighting on several fronts and experiencing several shortfalls due to casualties, was preparing for the new front in Normandy, and Britain desperately needed an influx of trained lieutenants and captains. On the whole, the CAN-LOAN officers acquitted themselves extremely well. Many went directly into action on the Normandy beaches on D-Day, and almost all of them were involved in the heavy fighting that followed the invasion of France as the war was carried on the ground into the German homeland.

In the summer of 1944, Gregg's career took a different turn, when he was invited to become president of the University of New Brunswick (UNB). On being offered the presidency, Gregg confessed to being "astonished," and confided that he thought the Presidential Search Committee was "scraping the bottom of the barrel." The committee disagreed: the university was expecting a large influx of returning veterans to enrol as students as the war drew to a close, and realized the administration would have to adapt to this older, tougher and more sophisticated student body. However, not all faculty and staff at UNB agreed with the choice of an army officer as president, and a few wondered, at least initially, if he was the right man for the job. For a time, a rumour even circulated that the post had mistakenly been offered to Gregg, and that the recommendation for "young Greg" had actually been meant for Gregory Bridges, an eminent New Brunswick lawyer and graduate of the university.

In any case, Gregg's organizational and administrative abilities were soon put to the test as returning veterans, many married and some with children, flooded UNB's classrooms. As he set about learning his role in administering the university, he soon discovered that disorganization was the norm and decision making slow, inconsistent and occasionally chaotic.

For the next three years, the "Brigadier," as he was known, met these challenges and guided the university through one of its most trying times, though not in the way that those who held a stereotypical view of military men expected. Rather than barking orders and issuing demands, he delegated responsibilities and duties, presided over faculty meetings where he listened attentively to opinions and established a clear chain of command from department chairs to faculty deans to himself. To deal with the large increase in student population, he converted army huts into classrooms and living quarters, established proper facilities for women undergraduates and brought in more faculty, library facilities and laboratory equipment.

In recognition of his wartime services, Gregg was appointed as a Commander of the Order of the British Empire in its Military Division. His appointment was announced in the *London Gazette* of December 28, 1945, along with several other senior Canadian officers.

In 1947, aware of his many talents, Prime Minister Mackenzie King personally asked Gregg to join his Cabinet. Elected as MP for York-Sunbury, Gregg served in three cabinet posts successively. While Minister of Fisheries, 1947–48, he renewed close connections with the unit in which he served during the First World War and was guest of honour for the military ball held by the regiment on New Year's Eve 1947.

When Gregg became Minister of Veterans' Affairs in January 1948, veterans and their organizations were delighted. The magazine of the Royal Canadian Legion, *The Legionary*, wrote of the appointment: "Gregg will champion the cause of his fellow veterans and their dependants to the utmost of his very great ability...with the never ceasing sympathy of one who himself has fought, bled and suffered hardship on the battle fields with his comrades." Gregg became Minister of Labour in August 1950, during a bitter national railway strike, as 125,000 railway workers threatened to walk off the job. His abilities came to the fore once more and he settled the strike in nine days.

On January 31, 1952, shortly after the RCR was warned for service in Korea, Gregg was appointed Honorary Colonel of the regiment, much to the delight of all ranks. When the 1st Battalion returned from Korea, Gregg was there to welcome them home on behalf of all Canadians as they marched through the streets of Ottawa to Parliament Hill.

In 1956, Gregg attended the VC centenary celebrations in London along with some of the surviving Canadian VC recipients. The VC Association (now the Victoria Cross and George Cross Association) was formed at the time, and he was an enthusiastic supporter of it, becoming its first overseas chairman. When the Liberals were defeated in 1957, after ten years as a cabinet minister, Gregg moved from politics to diplomacy at the age of sixty-five. On the regimental side of things, he resigned as Honorary Colonel on January 31, 1958, after serving in the appointment for six years. (When the army had reorganized such appointments the previous year, his position disappeared, to be replaced by Colonel of the Regiment.)

Between 1958 and 1964, Gregg was involved with the United Nations, first with the its Technical Assistance Board in Iraq (1958–1959), then with the UN International Children's Emergency Fund in Indonesia (1960–63) and finally as Canada's representative at the UN (1963–64). When he returned to Canada from Iraq in 1959, he was named warden of Medway

Hall at the University of Western Ontario. In December of that year, Dorothy, his wife of forty years, died after a lengthy illness. In 1964, at seventy-one, he remarried, to Erica Deichman, and became Canadian high commissioner to British Guiana as it transitioned to independence, an appointment he held until 1967.

Duncan Fraser, Acadia University professor, Second World War veteran, journalist and long-time friend of Gregg's, recalled visiting him in Guyana during the troubles that marked the new country's independence:

> *His coolness under difficult circumstances was confirmed to me in a very personal and direct way by the singular events of June 1964 in British Guiana.... I was staying with him in Georgetown when the Guianese disturbances erupted into a civil war in Georgetown. I was due to leave Georgetown that night, but was forbidden by the Commissioner of Police to attempt to drive the 24 miles to Atkinson Air Field because I was a guest of the Canadian [High] Commissioner and therefore a sensitive visitor to the colony. Milton got me to the airfield in his own official car. The situation was extremely tense, and as we made our tortuous way through the slums and back alleys of Georgetown, we were frequently exposed to cross fire and rocks and bottles. These were not intended for us, but for the contesting elements in Georgetown, but we were in the unhappy position of peacemakers everywhere. I was naturally enough a bit apprehensive, but Milton said to relax, as [he] had been through much worse than this before, and that he in fact had (out of curiosity) gone through the Kassim riots in Baghdad during the revolution there in the early 60s. He was as cool as a cucumber and I can understand fully why he was the gallant and valorous man he was.*

Gregg officially retired to his native province of New Brunswick during Centennial Year in 1967. On December 22 that year, his appointment as one of the first recipients of the newly created Order of Canada was announced "for his services to Canada as a soldier, and public servant." Gregg received the Order's Medal of Service during an investiture ceremony on April 26, 1968. In 1972, the Medal of Service was abolished, and all holders were appointed to the new level of Officer of the Order of Canada.

As a board member for the New Brunswick League for Urban Renewal, Gregg helped launch the New Horizons programme for the preservation of his province's many covered bridges. In 1968, he became president of the Canadian Council for International Co-operation and the following year he served as the first honorary president of the newly-formed Conservation Council of New Brunswick. In 1981, after his death, the Conservation Council established an annual award in his name to recognize significant contributions to the health of the province's environment. He became the first grand patron of the New Brunswick Command of the Royal Canadian Legion in 1975 and also served on the board of Katimavik, Canada's national youth outreach programme.

Gregg died at his home on March 13, 1978, at eighty-five years of age. A few months earlier he had attended a reunion of the West Nova Scotia Regiment in Kentville, a matter of great joy to his regimental comrades. On a "desperately cold and damp" St. Patrick's Day, after "a hell of a wake" the night before, his funeral procession slow marched from the funeral home to Fredericton's Christ Church Cathedral. Duncan Fraser recalled, "The instruments were frozen, we all had ice picks between our eyes and the

MINISTER OF VETERANS' AFFAIRS THE HONOURABLE MILTON F. GREGG (CENTRE) EXAMINES A MODEL HOUSE TYPICAL OF THOSE BEING BUILT BY VETERAN CONTRACTORS, WHILE DEPUTY MINISTER W.S. WOODS LOOKS ON.

combination of the lack of music and the bad streets made it into a penitent's progress." Several senior military and civilian dignitaries, two hundred members of the RCR, a number of former CANLOAN officers and many Legionnaires attended. Burial followed in a family plot in the United Baptist Church Cemetery at Snider Mountain, near Gregg's birthplace and close to his parents' graves, with only Minister of Defence Barney Danson and the immediate members of the family in attendance. His headstone bears the biblical inscription from the Gospel of Matthew: "Blessed are the pure in heart, for they shall see God. Blessed are the peacemakers, for they shall be called the children of God."

Although no eulogies were said at his funeral, Danson, who was one of the honorary pallbearers, later penned the following: "The most unlikely hero one could imagine. An outstanding soldier who looked like someone's older uncle, yet won the nation's highest award for bravery. A far from accomplished speaker who could inspire the best in each of us. An indifferent administrator who built some of the most efficient organizations which served this nation."

Three days after the funeral, Duncan Fraser noted, "He was quite the bravest man I have ever known—and I have known quite a few. It is, I suppose, in comparison to Gregg's achievement, easy to win a Victoria Cross in half an hour when the red fire comes down in front of your eyes—but it took Gregg four days to win his VC.... Few others have received the award for such a sustained effort."

One aspect of Gregg's funeral upset Fraser:

I was shaken however, when I realized there were so few spectators on the streets of Fredericton. I simply cannot understand why this should be so, for Milton Gregg was one of the ten or twelve greatest men ever produced in this country at any time. Perhaps indeed, despite the all-encompassing nature of his life, he was too modest and only his military, political and university friends realized the full extent of this great man. Sic transit Gloria!

Gregg's family donated his VC to the RCR in London, Ontario, in 1978. On Christmas Eve that year, it was stolen from the Regimental Museum during a function and, unfortunately, has never been recovered. That same year, the RCR donated the Gregg Trophy to the Canadian Forces Small

Arms Competition in his honour, to be awarded to the Regular Force member who obtains the highest aggregate score in pistol matches during the annual competition. A bursary is also given annually in his name to a University of New Brunswick student who shows promise in environmental management or international affairs.

Outside of Fredericton, at nearby Canadian Forces Base Gagetown, the infantry barracks, which have housed the 2nd Battalion of Gregg's old regiment for many years, were named in his honour. On the same base, at the entrance to the Combat Training Centre's Infantry School, stands a memorial commemorating Gregg's relationship with the CANLOAN officers and dedicated to the members of the group who fell. It was erected by the CANLOAN Association and unveiled by Erica Gregg, his widow.

Perhaps the mild-mannered hero should have the last word on his VC: "When you are looked upon with favour," he said, "you wonder whether it was anything of intrinsic value in yourself or whether it was because you happened to have a special decoration." In Milton Gregg's case, it was definitely the former.

CHAPTER 8

THE FIGHTING NEWFOUNDLANDERS

Acting Lieutenant-Colonel James Forbes-Robertson
1st Battalion, The Border Regiment, British Army
Near Vieux Berquin, France, April 11–12, 1918

Private Thomas Ricketts
1st Battalion, The Royal Newfoundland Regiment, British Army
Ledeghem, Belgium, October 14, 1918

James Forbes-Robertson holds a unique place among the VC recipients associated with Atlantic Canada—he never set foot in the region. His Atlantic connection comes about because he was a British officer attached to the Newfoundland Regiment (which became the Royal Newfoundland Regiment in December 1917) during the First World War, serving first as its second-in-command, then later as commanding officer. The Newfoundland Regiment had been formed in response to the colony's desire to contribute to the war effort, along with two thousand Newfoundlanders who joined the Newfoundland Royal Naval Reserve and several hundred who formed a Forestry Corps that operated in Scotland from the summer of 1917 onwards. The government originally intended to provide five hundred men for the regiment. However, by the end of the war over six thousand had served in its ranks.

The First Five Hundred was the name given to the initial group of Newfoundland volunteers that sailed to Britain (although their true tally was 537). The regiment's other nickname was the "Blue Puttees." When the war started, there were no stocks of uniforms in the colony, nor any khaki serge from which to make them. The only woolen material available for making leggings was navy blue, so the first soldiers were outfitted with puttees of that colour. The makeshift item of clothing quickly became a badge of distinction; to be a Blue Puttee was to be a member of the famous First Five Hundred.

The convoy carrying the First Canadian Contingent sailed to England on October 3, 1914, and the SS *Florizel* with the Newfoundland Regiment aboard joined it as it passed Newfoundland three days later. The regiment spent its first winter in training camps in Scotland before moving south in the spring to Aldershot, the home of the British Army. In September, the British sent the Newfoundlanders off to the Mediterranean for their first taste of battle, in the disastrous Gallipoli campaign against Turkey.

The Turks entered the war in October 1914 as an ally of the Central Powers. The Allied High Command decided to attack Turkey in the hopes of opening the Dardanelles as a supply route to Russia via the Black Sea, perhaps convincing some of the Balkan states to join the Allies in the process. It did not achieve either aim. A large force of British, Australian and New Zealand troops landed in Gallipoli in late April 1915, but never succeeded in making it off the Turkish beachheads. The area soon resembled the Western Front, with both sides dug in and engaging in vicious trench warfare.

After spending some time in Egypt for training and acclimatization, the Newfoundland Regiment landed at Suvla Bay, on the western side of the Gallipoli Peninsula, on the night of September 19. There, they joined 29th Division, the British formation they were to be part of until the last six months of the war. The Newfoundlanders walked right into the middle of a maelstrom. From the commanding heights overlooking the shallow beachheads, the Turks poured down continuous artillery, machine-gun and rifle fire onto the unit lines, inflicting several casualties. Resupply was difficult in this position and water and rations often ran short. In early November, the regiment participated in an attack that advanced the division's front and in tough fighting on the aptly named Caribou Hill (the regiment's symbol was a caribou, proudly displayed on its cap badge), two soldiers won the Distinguished Conduct Medal (DCM) and an officer the Military Cross.

By the end of the month, the weather surpassed the Turks as the main enemy. Three days of torrential rain and sleet caused flash floods that swept away complete trenches and much of the soldiers' equipment with them. Temperatures fell to below zero and a severe blizzard struck. Water bottles froze, food ran out and shelter was non-existent. By early December, the regiment was reduced to a quarter of its strength, some of its men having died from exposure. Even the indomitable British had had enough and decided to withdraw. The Newfoundlanders left Suvla Bay on December 20, pressed by the Turks as they departed. They moved to Cape Helles at the southern tip of the peninsula and assisted in the British withdrawal until January 12. Those Newfoundlanders still fit to fight sailed to Egypt, to rebuild and retrain the unit there before it went to France.

As part of the rebuilding process, the Newfoundland Regiment received a new second-in-command, a Scottish officer by the name of James Forbes-Robertson. Forbes-Robertson was born on July 7, 1884, in Strathpeffer, Ross and Cromarty, Scotland, the son of Farquhar Forbes-Robertson and Laura Ann Macauly. He was educated at Cheltenham College, Gloucester, from 1897 to 1902 (he was one of fourteen "Old Cheltonians" who earned the VC). He was commissioned into the Border Regiment (now The King's Own Royal Borderers) in 1904 and was promoted lieutenant in 1906. His older brother, Kenneth, a fellow Cheltonian, also enlisted in the army. He was serving as a captain in the 2nd Battalion, Seaforth Highlanders, when he was killed in action on November 7, 1914—four days after James received his promotion to captain. Forbes-Robertson was a staff captain when he joined the Newfoundland Regiment as a temporary major on June 15, 1916, shortly before the regiment's second disastrous battle—the first day on the Somme.

The Allies had planned a great Anglo-French offensive on the Somme for the summer of 1916—an all-out attack that they hoped would knock Germany out of the war. However, by the time the operation began on July 1, French participation had been drastically reduced from thirty-nine to five divisions, as the slaughterhouse of Verdun drew off the majority of the French Army.

At nine o'clock on the evening of June 30, the Newfoundland Regiment, some eight hundred strong, marched up to the line from their billets in the village of Louvencourt, leaving ten percent of its strength behind under Forbes-Robertson. This reserve policy had been adopted in 1915, so that attacking battalions that suffered severe losses could be more easily rebuilt. The policy also decreed that commanding officers should not be part of any initial assault, and should not move forward until enemy trenches had been captured, to prevent a breakdown in command and control.

The regiment arrived at the front line support trenches just after 2:00 A.M., six and a half hours before they made their attack. The Newfoundlanders did not form part of 29th Division's initial assault, but were in the second wave. They were to pass through the first wave in their sector—made up of the 2nd Battalion, South Wales Borderers, followed by the 1st Battalion, the Border Regiment (Forbes-Robertson's old unit)—and then advance to the division's final objective for the day, Puisieux Trench, some three kilometres further on.

In preparation for the attack, the Newfoundlanders had trained intensively for months on ground selected for its similarity to that where the offensive would take place, near the village of Beaumont Hamel, with tapes laid out to show the exact locations of German trenches. As it happened, no training could prepare them for the first day on the Somme. On July 1, after a hot breakfast brought forward by the soldiers left under Forbes-Robertson, the regiment watched the explosion of a large mine, about a kilometre away, at 7:20 A.M. Ten minutes later, the first wave went in.

A large German salient, called Y Ravine, jutted forward towards the British lines. Those German soldiers in the ravine who survived the artillery barrage were in an excellent position to enfilade the attacking troops. So it was that the attack of the South Wales Borderers at 7:35 collapsed within five minutes, its ranks decimated by machine-gun fire from Y Ravine. When the Border Regiment followed at 8:05, they suffered the same fate and their attack ground to a halt within ten minutes as bodies piled up at the gaps in the wire. Now it was the turn of the Newfoundland Regiment.

One of the ongoing problems throughout the war was the lack of instant communications to enable commanders to modify orders quickly. Without this capability, once troops were launched in the attack, it often became very difficult, if not impossible, to change the orders issued to them and their supporting arms. By far, the most important supporting arm was the artillery. For an attack, artillery usually followed pre-planned barrages with a strict minute-by-minute timetable, lifting fires forward at a pre-determined rate to keep just ahead of the advancing infantry. This procedure usually worked very well, providing the infantry were able to move at the right pace. However, at Beaumont Hamel, the artillery was soon far beyond the leading elements of the British assault.

To make matters worse, the communications problem was compounded by a deadly misinterpretation. The British saw white flares on the division's right— the signal for the capture of the first objective; unfortunately, the Germans used the exact same signal to indicate their artillery was dropping short. The division commander, Major-General Beauvoir de Lisle, seeking to reinforce what he perceived to be success, ordered Brigadier-General Cayley, commanding 88th Brigade, to commit two battalions to capture the German front line to support the "success" on the right. At 8:45, Cayley

MAJOR JAMES FORBES-ROBERTSON (RIGHT) POSES WITH THE COMMANDING OFFICER OF THE NEWFOUNDLAND REGIMENT, LIEUTENANT-COLONEL HADOW.

ordered the Newfoundland Regiment and the 1st Battalion, the Essex Regiment, to attack as soon as possible. The Newfoundlanders faced an unenviable task. They had to advance down an open slope, vulnerable from the front and sides to German fire, without any artillery support. Lack of communications and the urgency of the situation meant they could not coordinate their attack with the Essex Regiment, not even knowing what time the Essex planned to attack.

The Newfoundland Regiment set off at 9:15, following the procedures they had rehearsed in training. The CO led, followed by A and B companies line abreast, with C and D companies in the same formation forty paces behind. The soldiers had to cross their own front line trench system and wire before they entered No Man's Land, some 230 metres under deadly enemy shell and machine-gun fire. Many were killed before they even reached their own front trenches. On the Newfoundlanders' right, the Essex attack stalled immediately among the dead and wounded of the South Wales Borderers who clogged the forward trenches, making it impossible for the Essex to form up for the advance. Soon the only unit moving forward in that sector of the battlefield on that July morning was the Newfoundland Regiment.

Dead and wounded also filled the forward trenches in the Newfoundlanders' area, but the regiment scrambled past the bodies and out of the trenches—and into a hail of bullets. The enemy fire was particularly devastating when the Newfoundlanders bunched to get through the gaps in the wire. The CO, Lieutenant-Colonel Arthur Hadow, stopped near the front line to let his men pass by so he could follow, in accordance with procedures. The Newfoundlanders moved on, down the slope, which was bare except for a few scraggy trees about halfway across the 550 metres

ALL THAT REMAINS TODAY OF A FEW SCRAGGY TREES IN NO MAN'S LAND AT THE PRESERVED BATTLEFIELD OF BEAUMONT HAMEL IS THE PETRIFIED "DANGER TREE," WHICH THE GERMANS USED TO MARK THEIR ARTILLERY FIRE.

of No Man's Land. (All that remains of them today is the petrified "Danger Tree," which the Germans used to mark their artillery fire.) In the face of overwhelming fire and without proper support, some Newfoundlanders amazingly made it to the German wire, but to no avail. By 9:45 that morning, the battle was essentially over for them.

Lieutenant-Colonel Hadow, who had observed the decimation of his regiment, went to tell Brigadier-General Cayley the attack had failed. Unbelievably, the brigadier directed him to gather up any fit men he could find to make another attempt. Fortunately, a corps staff officer who observed the battle from a nearby ridge overruled him and called off any further operations in the area. Hadow collected those who made it back to the front lines and, with Forbes-Robertson and the ten percent of the Newfoundlanders left behind, occupied a support trench to the rear.

The regiment held this position until July 6, while they buried as many of their dead mates as they could find. Those Newfoundlanders trapped in No Man's Land suffered terribly in the blazing sun—the wounded bleeding and in pain, the injured and uninjured alike thirsty and unable to move because of German fire. They lay there all day. At nightfall, those who could crawled back to the British lines in between German Very flares lighting up the battlefield, and stretcher bearers recovered the wounded.

Inside half an hour, the proud Newfoundland Regiment had almost been completely wiped out. Every officer who walked into the maelstrom that day became a casualty: fourteen were killed and twelve wounded. Of the other ranks, 219 were killed and 374 wounded, with another ninety-one missing. Only sixty-eight of those who went into action remained uninjured when the roll was called. Remarkably, on July 5, a soldier crawled in from No Man's Land, where he had survived for four days. He must have wondered what he had gotten himself into: he had only arrived with a new draft hours before the attack and missed all the preparatory training for it.

Colonel Hadow, a strict, unbending disciplinarian, had definite ideas on how to train and run a battalion. His ways were initially unpopular with the easygoing Newfoundlanders, and they even made a little song up about him. It stated in part: "I'll make them or break them, I'll make the blighters sweat." Yet one of the most frequently asked questions from the wounded filling the dressing station was whether the CO was satisfied with their efforts.

After Beaumont Hamel, Hadow's only concern was the rebuilding of his regiment, a task that fell to Forbes-Robertson. The Newfoundlanders

NO SINGLE UNIT HAS AS MANY MEMORIALS TO ITS MEMORY ON THE BATTLEFIELDS OF THE FIRST WORLD WAR AS THE ROYAL NEWFOUNDLAND REGIMENT—FIVE MAGNIFICENT AND DISTINCTIVE CARIBOU MONUMENTS. THE LARGEST AND MOST IMPRESSIVE OF THESE IS AT BEAUMONT HAMEL, WHERE THE REGIMENT WAS VIRTUALLY WIPED OUT ON JULY 1, 1916, THE FIRST DAY OF THE INFAMOUS BATTLE OF THE SOMME.

moved to a tented camp to the rear on July 8, to begin training under the direction of the new second-in-command. The regime Forbes-Robertson immediately established, with training from 5:30 A.M. to 7:30 P.M. daily, made even the most hardened soldier complain. However, Hadow knew he had only a short time to build the regiment up again, and that was his only priority. In the end, he succeeded.

In 1916, the population of the colony of Newfoundland was only a quarter of a million, and the losses at Beaumont Hamel reverberated across the island. Hardly any extended family was unaffected. To this day, July 1 in Newfoundland is still referred to as Memorial Day in memory of Beaumont Hamel, as well as Canada Day. After the attack, General de Lisle, the divisional commander, wrote to the prime minister of Newfoundland about Beaumont Hamel. "It was a magnificent display of trained and disciplined valour," he said, "and its assault only failed because dead men can advance no further."

Today, no other unit has a more striking commemoration of an attack than the caribou monument at Newfoundland Memorial Park near Beaumont Hamel, inaugurated in 1925. The impressive memorial stands atop an artificial hill, the caribou gazing over the ground on which so many Newfoundlanders gave their lives. It is one of five such memorials placed at various locations on the Western Front where the regiment fought, but the one at the park is the most impressive. At the base of the hill are tablets listing all Newfoundlanders who fought in the war, but have no known grave, including those lost at sea. Probably no part of the Western Front receives more visitors than this small corner of the Somme battlefield.

Unfortunately, the regiment returned to the front lines in mid-July, long before it was ready to fight again; it mustered only eleven officers and 260 soldiers. As additional reinforcement drafts arrived, the Newfoundlanders moved north at the end of July and spent the summer in the Ypres Salient. Some of their time was spent manning front line trenches, but they also worked on a new support position known as the X Line, about eight hundred metres east of Ypres's famed Menin Gate. In early October, the regiment left the salient—they would see it again—and entrained for the south, back to the Somme. They were going into battle once more.

In the Newfoundlanders' absence, the planned breakthrough had not occurred and the battle was reduced to an agonizing war of attrition. However, by October, a few Allied successes had convinced the Commander-in-Chief of the British Expeditionary Force, General Douglas Haig, to renew the offensive. The Newfoundland Regiment's role was to capture German positions north of the village of Gueudecourt, not far from where Captain Philip Bent and the 9th Leicesters had attacked two and a half weeks earlier. With the 1st Essex on their left, the Newfoundland Regiment advanced at 2:05 P.M. on October 12. They attacked with two companies in the lead and two more following—their first use of the recently introduced rolling artillery barrage. They had about 365 metres to cover to reach their first objective, designated the Green Line, beyond Hilt Trench. The regiment quickly reached the German trench; it was in their possession by 2:30, after some hand-to-hand fighting.

The Newfoundlanders reorganized and began the advance towards their second objective, the Brown Line, another 365 metres beyond the Green. However, they soon came under concentrated enemy fire and were forced to fall back to Hilt Trench. Unfortunately, the Essex Regiment had also been forced to withdraw and vacated their portion of Hilt Trench. Ignoring orders to retire to Gueudecourt, the Newfoundlanders held on through repeated German counterattacks and were relieved in the pre-dawn hours of the next day.

The two days at Gueudecourt resulted in 239 casualties for the Newfoundland Regiment, 120 of them fatal. Two MCs (one a Bar), three DCMs and eight Military Medals (MM) were won. Two of these medal winners also received the French *Croix de Guerre*. Today, a caribou memorial stands alone in a small grove in the middle of the fields outside Gueudecourt, marking the farthest point reached by the regiment on October 12.

On November 27, 1916, Lieutenant-Colonel Hadow, badly rundown, was invalided home, not to return until early May 1917. Forbes-Robertson replaced him, and was soon made acting lieutenant-colonel. Shortly afterwards, the battalion began a month in reserve with a series of long marches to the rear areas. Regimental lore relates that on one of these marches, Forbes-Robertson came upon a private resting in a shell hole with two packs—the soldier's and his own. When the CO asked what was wrong, the soldier replied that he was too tired to go on. With what is described as his "good nature" and "characteristic kindness," Forbes-Robertson immediately picked up what he thought was his own pack and carried on down the road for several kilometres.

The battalion intelligence officer then came upon the private and asked him the same question, to which the soldier again replied he was done for— and had to carry the CO's pack as well. Without delay, the officer shouldered the pack, which was the CO's, and headed off. Following at a discrete distance behind him came a smiling soldier, unburdened by any pack at all. The comments of Forbes-Robertson when he discovered he had been carrying the private's pack remain unrecorded.

Under Forbes-Robertson, the regiment spent its third Christmas overseas, thankfully out of the line. On December 29, the *London Gazette* announced Forbes-Robertson's receipt of a so-called "periodic" (i.e. awarded not for any specific incident) MC. The Newfoundlanders re-entered the trenches in mid-January and their CO led them into battle at Sailly-Saillisel, followed by a rest and training period at Méaule. The instruction there included something new—the start of training for open warfare, as opposed to the trench warfare of the past. They would need it. The

Newfoundlanders were about to participate in Haig's great spring offensive, launched on a twenty-two kilometre front east of Arras. Their part in the battle would result in heavy losses, exceeded only by those at Beaumont Hamel. And Lieutenant-Colonel James Forbes-Robertson and a handful of men would save the day.

At 5:30 A.M. on April 14, 1917, the Newfoundland Regiment, with the faithful 1st Essex again on their left—and an open, unprotected right flank—advanced behind a rolling barrage from the salient around the town of Monchy-le-Preux, which is perched on a conical hill, towards the enemy's front line at Shrapnel Trench. After this initial objective, the regiment was to carry on to Infantry Hill, about seven hundred metres further to the rear. Forbes-Robertson, who had established his headquarters in the centre of the town, received revised orders at 3:00 A.M. and only briefed his company commanders at 4:45, just behind the front line.

In ninety minutes, the Essex captured their part of Infantry Hill, but the Newfoundlanders ran into difficulty almost immediately. They were raked by extreme machine-gun fire as they advanced, but made it to the German trenches. As they pushed onwards, up Infantry Hill, a fresh German battalion met them, quickly followed by two more. Under pressure and counterattacks from three sides, the Newfoundland Regiment quickly disintegrated into little knots of men, who fought until they were killed or captured.

All telephone communication with the attacking companies was soon cut off and no company runners got through, so Forbes-Robertson sent an officer to find out what was happening. Within twenty minutes, at ten o'clock, the officer reported that there was not a single unwounded Newfoundlander east of Monchy and that some two to three hundred Germans were advancing on the village from less than five hundred metres away. Forbes-Robertson quickly collected sixteen available men from his headquarters and led them to a trench on the edge of Monchy-le-Preux, collecting weapons and ammunition from dead and wounded soldiers along the way. As they ran, they came under enemy fire. By the time they got to the trench, there were only ten men left.

Forbes-Robertson and his men opened up with rapid-fire rifle bursts on the advancing Germans. The enemy immediately went to ground, assuming they were facing a strong defending force. For the next four hours, in the words of the Official British History, the ten determined Newfoundlanders were "all that stood between the Germans and Monchy, one of the most vital positions on the whole battlefield." The defenders ensured every bullet they fired found its target, taking care to shoot any German scouts sent forward to keep the enemy misinformed about their true strength.

The CO and his men held off until mid-afternoon, when British reinforcements arrived. Their gallantry and determination had saved the day, but the regiment's losses were heavy. Casualties totalled 460, with one-third of them, some 153, taken prisoner, of whom twenty-eight died in captivity from wounds or other causes. The heroism of "the men who saved Monchy" was recognized: the other officer besides the CO received the MC, while all soldiers received the MM; Forbes-Robertson received the DSO. It was announced in the *London Gazette* of June 18, 1917.

Today, a Newfoundland caribou stands on the eastern edge of Monchy, on top of the ruins of a German pillbox, gazing from the now quiet little farming village towards Infantry Hill. It marks the place where the

"THE MEN WHO SAVED MONCHY," LED BY FORBES-ROBERTSON (THIRD FROM LEFT, REAR ROW), WERE ALL THAT STOOD BETWEEN THE GERMANS AND THE TOWN OF MONCHY.

Newfoundland Regiment was nearly wiped out for the second time during its service in France.

After Monchy, some four hundred survivors of the Newfoundlanders and the Essex, which suffered even greater losses in the battle, briefly formed a temporary composite battalion under Forbes-Robertson, until each unit was slowly built back up to normal strength. Even while severely understrength, the Newfoundlanders fought again under Forbes-Robertson's command that spring during the Second Battle of the Scarpe.

On May 5, Lieutenant-Colonel Hadow returned to duty, and Forbes-Robertson reverted to major and second-in-command. By the end of the month, the regiment was down to 221 all ranks. It was time to rest, recuperate and rebuild. Reinforcement drafts arrived in June and July to bring the regiment up to fighting strength once more. One of these contained a young soldier named Tommy Ricketts, who would later go on to earn the VC.

In June, the regiment, still in the process of rebuilding, returned to the Ypres Salient. While there, Forbes-Robertson spent two weeks training a group of thirty men, known as "The Raiders," in the art of trench raids. Their first raid on the night of July 12–13 proved unsuccessful, but one five nights later resulted in a prisoner and five dead Germans, at no cost in casualties to themselves.

Forbes-Robertson's last battle with the Newfoundland Regiment was Tommy Ricketts's first. The Newfoundlanders were assigned two objectives between two streams east of the village of Langemarck, the Steenbeek and the Broembeek. At 4:45 A.M. on August 16, the Newfoundlanders advanced behind a rolling barrage through a muddy swamp. They secured the first objective within an hour in relatively easy going, but the attack towards the second objective was slower and the soldiers did not capture it until 7:45 that morning. Casualties in the attack totaled 103, of which twenty-seven were fatal. For their bravery, the Newfoundlanders received two MCs (one a Bar), two DCMs and thirteen MMs.

The next day, Forbes-Robertson left the Newfoundland Regiment and returned to the British Army. His inflexible attitude towards training during the rebuilding period after Beaumont Hamel had not initially endeared him to the men, but his actions since then, especially his heroic stand at Monchy, had earned him the respect and esteem of the entire unit. He was appointed to command the 16th Battalion, The Middlesex Regiment, in the neighbouring 86th Brigade, again as an acting lieutenant-colonel, although his permanent rank was still captain. While commanding, he won a Bar to his DSO, announced in March 1918. The *London Gazette* of August 24 carried details of this second DSO:

> *For conspicuous gallantry and devotion to duty. He led his battalion with great dash and determination in a successful attack. Later, during continual enemy attacks, though he was wounded in the eye and unable to see, he was led about by an orderly among his men in the front line, encouraging and inspiring them by his magnificent example of courage and determination.*

Forbes-Robertson subsequently earned the VC for his actions over two days on April 11 and 12, 1918, near Vieux Berquin, France. In that battle, he repeatedly saved the situation, helping to hold the German advance near Estaires. His *London Gazette* entry of May 22, 1918, reads:

> *For most conspicuous bravery whilst commanding his battalion during the heavy fighting.*
>
> *Through his quick judgment, resource, untiring energy and magnificent example, Lt-Col Forbes-Robertson on four separate occasions saved the line from breaking and averted a situation which might have had the most serious and far-reaching results.*
>
> *On the first occasion, when troops in front were falling back, he made a rapid reconnaissance on horse-back, in full view of the enemy, under heavy machine-gun and close range shell fire. He then organized and, still mounted, led a counter-attack which was completely successful in re-establishing our line. When his horse was shot under him he continued on foot.*
>
> *Later on the same day, when troops to the left of his line were giving way, he went to that flank and checked and steadied the line, inspiring confidence by his splendid coolness and disregard of personal danger. His horse was wounded three times, and he was thrown five times.*
>
> *The following day, when the troops on both his flanks were forced to retire, he formed a post at battalion headquarters and with his battalion still held his ground, thereby covering the retreat of troops on his flanks. Under the heaviest fire this gallant officer fearlessly exposed himself when collecting parties, organizing and encouraging.*
>
> *On a subsequent occasion, when troops were retiring on his left, and the condition of things on his right were obscure, he again saved the situation*

by his magnificent example and cool judgment. Losing a second horse, he continued alone on foot until he had established a line to which his own troops could withdraw and so conform to the general situation.

When the award of the VC was announced, Newfoundland newspapers proudly listed Forbes-Robertson as one of theirs—a Newfoundlander. He went on to command a brigade for about six weeks in August and September 1918 as a temporary brigadier-general, followed by a term in battalion command again until August 1919. Besides the VC, DSO and Bar and MC, he received three Mentions-in-Dispatches, one of them for service with the Newfoundland Regiment.

Forbes-Robertson remained in the army after the war, becoming a major in 1921 and a lieutenant-colonel in 1926 (for the fourth time) in command of the Gordon Highlanders. In August 1927, he married Hilda Forster; they had three children, a son and two daughters. He was promoted colonel in 1930 and commanded 152 Infantry Brigade from 1932 to 1934 in 51st Highland Division, a part of the Territorial Army. In 1946, he was appointed deputy lieutenant of the County of Sutherland. He retired to his home, "Chardwaw," in Bourton-on-the-Water, Gloucestershire, where he died aged seventy-one, on August 5, 1955. He is buried in the Cheltenham Borough Cemetery and his name appears on the Roll of Honour at Cheltenham College. His VC is privately held.

Thomas Ricketts was the youngest Canadian ever to receive the VC, although strictly speaking, he did not become a Canadian until thirty years later, when Newfoundland joined Confederation. Additionally, he was the only person born in Atlantic Canada who actually earned his medal while serving in a unit from the region, the Royal Newfoundland Regiment.

Ricketts lied about his age to get into the army. He was born in Middle Arm, White Bay, on April 15, 1901, the son of John Ricketts, a fisherman, and Amelia Castle. His mother died when he was young, and Ricketts's sister helped raise him for a few years. He attended school in Middle Arm and enlisted in the 1st Battalion, Newfoundland Regiment, on September 2, 1916, giving his age as eighteen years and three months, though he was only fifteen. He followed his older brother, George, who had joined over a year before.

On January 30, 1917, Ricketts sailed overseas on the SS *Florizel* (the same ship that brought the First Five Hundred to Britain) arriving in Ayr,

Scotland, to begin training. In mid-June, he crossed the Channel to join his regiment at Rouen on July 2, and immediately went into the trenches on the Western Front. In August, the same month that Forbes-Robertson left the Newfoundlanders, Ricketts saw his first action at the Battle of Langemarck (or Steenbeek) in Belgium, when the regiment returned to the Ypres Salient.

Later, in the fighting to break through the heavily defended Marcoing Line near Cambrai on November 20, Ricketts was wounded in the right thigh by a rifle bullet. He was treated by 89 Field Ambulance, and then transferred to 48 Casualty Clearing Station, followed by 1st Canadian General Hospital at Etaples. On November 28, he was admitted to 1st London General Hospital, at Camberwell in southeast London. While there recovering from his injury, Ricketts's brother was killed in the same battle in which he had been wounded. (George Ricketts has no known grave; his name is engraved on the Caribou Memorial at Beaumont Hamel.) Once his wound had healed, Ricketts was moved through various depots until he was declared fit and joined the 2nd Battalion in early February 1918, at Winchester in Hampshire. From there, he was sent back to France and rejoined the Newfoundland Regiment on April 30.

In Ricketts's absence, the regiment took heavy casualties in an attack on the Masnières-Beaurevoir Line near Cambrai, and held out against repeated German counterattacks between November 23 and December 4, when it was withdrawn. As the only non-regular unit in a division made up of Regular Army battalions, the Newfoundlanders received a rare distinction. For their heroic stand at Masnières, King George V granted the regiment the title "Royal" on December 17—the only time during the entire war any British unit received this honour.

When Ricketts rejoined his unit, the Newfoundlanders had just been withdrawn from the line, along with 29th Division, with which the regiment had served since Gallipoli; after the heavy losses suffered at the Bailleul they were sent for rest and replacements near the base depot at Etaples. The division commander, Major-General D. E. Cayley, noted in his farewell tribute, "I wish to place on record my very great regret at their withdrawal from a Division in which they have served so long and brilliantly.... [T]he battalion has shown itself to be, under all circumstances of good and bad fortune, a splendid fighting unit.... [T]hey have consistently maintained the highest standard of fighting efficiency and determination."

Shortly afterwards, the Newfoundlanders relieved the 1st Battalion,

Honourable Artillery Company, in providing guards for Field Marshal Haig's headquarters at nearby Montreuil. The Newfoundlanders were billeted a short distance away in the village of Ecuires and those selected for guard duty paraded in the village square for inspection every morning.

Ricketts's officers remember him as "a good soldier—smartly turned out, obedient, efficient."

Over the summer, the regiment slowly rebuilt its strength as various drafts arrived to be trained and incorporated into the unit. At the same time, most surviving members of the First Five Hundred were permitted to return home on leave, some to remain there at the Regimental Depot in St. John's. By early September, the unit was ready for action once again and was assigned to 28th Brigade, 9th (Scottish) Division for operations in Flanders, in support of the great offensive spearheaded by the Canadian Corps at Amiens, which had begun on August 8.

On September 20, Ricketts and his regiment relieved a British battalion in the front line trenches just east of Ypres, some eighteen hundred metres behind positions they had occupied two years earlier. They had even dug some of the trenches they now occupied at that

SERGEANT RICKETTS WEARS HIS VICTORIA CROSS AND FRENCH CROIX DE GUERRE AVEC ETOILE D'OR (WAR CROSS WITH GOLD STAR). A SHY MAN, HE SHUNNED PUBLICITY ALL HIS LIFE, AND GENERALLY REFUSED INTERVIEWS OR TO HAVE HIS PHOTOGRAPH TAKEN.

time as part of a support position. To their front stretched the long, curving semi-circle of Passchendaele Ridge, which Philip Bent and Pete Robertson had given their lives almost a year earlier to help seize. Unfortunately, the ridge had subsequently been lost in the German offensive of April 1918 and the Allies were pushed back to the outskirts of Ypres, forfeiting almost all the gains of the earlier battle.

On September 28, Ricketts and his comrades, fifty percent of whom had never been in battle before, advanced in a drenching downpour, in support behind the two attacking battalions of 28th Brigade at Passchendaele. Ricketts's B Company, under Captain Sydney Frost of Yarmouth, Nova Scotia, led on the right. The forward battalions readily dealt with most of the minor resistance encountered and by noon the Newfoundlanders were safely ensconced in Polygon Wood, the scene of Colonel Bent's heroism the previous October (see Chapter 4). At a cost of fifteen casualties, the regiment had advanced nearly five kilometres. Then the sun came out, drying rain-soaked uniforms. Coupled with the rapid advance, this boosted everyone's morale.

The next day, the Allied advance continued, with 28th Brigade in the van of 9th Division's attack. On the left, the Royal Newfoundland Regiment advanced with the 9th Scottish Rifles on their right and the Belgians on their left. The unit formed up on the western slope of Passchendaele Ridge and moved over the top shortly after 9:00 A.M., with B Company on the battalion's left. As soon as they cleared the crest, the Newfoundlanders came under effective artillery fire, which caused many casualties.

Nevertheless, the regiment pressed on, with soldiers moving in short rushes by twos and threes, covering each other as they advanced. As they ascended the next feature, Keiberg Ridge, the soldiers came under direct fire from a 6-inch gun, which was protected on either side by a machine gun, making a frontal attack impossible. Realizing that this enemy position could derail both the British and the Belgian advance, Captain Frost quickly issued orders to one of his platoons, commanded by 2nd Lieutenant Albert Taylor, to work around to the south. Under covering fire from the company's two Lewis guns, Taylor's men stormed the German position, clearing the way for the capture of the village of Keiberg by 10 o'clock. Taylor, who already had won the MC and DCM, added a Bar to his MC for his skilful action, while Frost received an MC. Two weeks later, Taylor was killed in the same action in which Ricketts earned his VC.

The advance eastwards off Keiberg Ridge recommenced shortly, with the Allied troops moving for the first time through country that did not exhibit the effects of wartime devastation. Ahead of the Newfoundlanders lay two successive German lines, the Flanders I and II Stellung, about four kilometres apart and based on a series of strongpoints centred on farmhouses behind thick belts of wire. The first position was taken in concert with flanking units by mid-afternoon, and then the advance continued towards the second line, with Ricketts's 9th Division pushing ahead of its flanking formations.

The Flanders II Stellung was centred on the town of Ledeghem, which was too strongly held for 9th Division to attack until the other units had drawn level. Here, Ricketts and his wet comrades, tired after forty-eight hours without sleep, dug in for the night to await the arrival of the flanking units. The next day, to their great surprise and delight, they were sent to the rear for a period of rest in reserve. The fighting on September 29 brought the Newfoundlanders twelve major decorations for bravery: two MCs and one Bar, two DCMs and six MMs and one Bar. The deeds of the men who won them may have inspired young Private Ricketts, whose actions would soon add his name to Newfoundland's growing list of heroes.

On October 2, Ricketts moved forward with his regiment to the front line. By this time, portions of the Flanders II Stellung had fallen to other brigades in the division, and the Newfoundlanders took over the Ledeghem train station and about 450 metres of track along the western edge of the town, where they dug in. Over the next four days, they resisted repeated German efforts to drive them out, in the process winning four DCMs, five MMs and one Bar before being withdrawn on the night of October 6–7. Bivouacking near Keiberg, the men were able to wash and shave for the first time in over a week. All along the front, the Belgian and British forces making up the Flanders Group of Armies under the King of the Belgians rested and regrouped to lick their wounds. It would be another week before they could renew their attack.

During the next phase of the offensive, the role of Second British Army was to act as a flank guard along the Lys River for operations to their north. Because the Lys flows in a generally northeasterly direction, 9th Division, on the British northern or left flank, had the farthest distance to go to achieve its objective—some eight and a half kilometres to the east. In preparation, Ricketts and his regiment moved forward under cover of darkness along the railway track stretching north from Ledeghem. As they advanced, they came under German artillery fire, as the enemy had previously registered the railway line as a target. Fortunately, casualties were few and shortly after midnight the Newfoundlanders were in position. There they waited in such shelter as the railway embankment provided until zero hour, which was set for 5:35 A.M. on October 14.

At 5:15, British field guns set up only 180 metres behind the infantry opened up with a barrage of shrapnel and smoke, soon joined by heavy machine guns firing over the heads of the troops. At zero hour, the men rose up out of their positions, with Ricketts's B Company leading on the right and D Company on the left. Success came quickly, as three German pillboxes, each manned by fifteen to twenty soldiers, were outflanked and silenced. Suddenly, the battlefield was plunged into darkness. Artillery smoke combined with the typical Flanders heavy ground mist had produced an almost impenetrable fog. Visibility was reduced to less than a metre. Soldiers could not even see their own feet. Split into small groups of two or three, the men kept in touch with each other by shouting.

While the Newfoundlanders could at least continue to stumble forward, the effect on the Germans was far greater. Deprived of their visibility, they were also denied the use of their prime weapon in the defence: the deadly machine gun. As Ricketts's regiment continued to advance—making their way past numerous small streams and several new wire entanglements—a large number of German prisoners were taken and sent to the rear under escort.

By mid-morning a breeze sprang up, strong enough to disperse the smoke and mist. It revealed the Wulfdambeek, a stream winding diagonally across the Newfoundlanders' axis of advance, nearly two-metres deep in some places and too wide to jump. There was no choice but to cross it, in bright sunshine and in full view of the enemy. And so the regiment did, some soldiers swimming and others wading, in the process sustaining heavy losses from artillery fire. Once across, Ricketts and his companions advanced another nine hundred metres to a farm on a ridge, where direct enemy shelling from a battery on a feature known as Drie-Masten, about 550 metres away to the southeast, pinned them down. A call for their own artillery to deal with the Germans went unanswered; the regiment had outrun its own artillery support. Casualties began to mount.

Ricketts volunteered to go forward with his platoon commander, Lieutenant Stanley Newman, and a small group of men with a Lewis gun to try to outflank the German gun position to the right. The soldiers advanced in quick rushes, under heavy enemy fire, until they were about 275 metres from the German battery. Then, within point-blank range of the field guns and under fire from the battery's protective machine guns, they ran out of ammunition for the Lewis gun. At the same time, the Germans brought up gun teams in an attempt to get their guns away before the Newfoundlanders could assault their position.

Quickly taking stock of the situation, Ricketts dashed back ninety metres to the closest section of B Company, picked up some ammunition and ran with it back to his Lewis gun, under concentrated machine-gun fire all the while. With the additional ammunition, Ricketts—supported by some well-placed rifle fire from his section commander, Lance Corporal Matthew Brazil (the only other unwounded Newfoundlander remaining)—forced the Germans back to some nearby farm buildings. Ricketts's platoon was then able to advance on the enemy without sustaining any more casualties. In the process, they captured four field guns, four machine guns and eight prisoners, soon afterwards adding a fifth field gun to the tally.

With the battery out of the way, the regiment reorganized and continued its advance. However, a more heavily defended position about a kilometre and a half to the east soon halted their progress. At dusk, the Newfoundlanders dug in for the night. It had been another successful day; they had captured five hundred prisoners, ninety-four machine guns, eight field guns and a large quantity of ammunition. As always, it came at a cost: the next day the regiment mustered only three hundred men. For his bravery that day, Private Thomas Ricketts earned the VC, while four of his comrades received the DCM and four others the MM.

The next day, 9th Division's advance resumed with another brigade, the 26th, leading and the Newfoundlanders bringing up the rear, able to march along non-tactically in column formation. The British move went well, encountering only a few rearguards here and there as the Germans withdrew across the canalized Lys, blowing its bridges as they went. In the process, a sergeant from the 12th Royal Scots earned the VC in almost the same circumstances as Ricketts had the previous day—single-handedly manning a Lewis gun to overcome an enemy position on a hill, which was then captured by his mates. That night, the Allies paused to regroup before an assault crossing of the Lys, and Ricketts and the Royal Newfoundland Regiment moved into reserve for four days training in various water-crossing operations.

The crossing began on the night of October 19, with the Newfoundlanders following up the assault battalions northeast of Courtrai. The regiment crossed after 4:00 A.M. and continued the advance at dawn, initially against light opposition. That afternoon, the Germans began to put up a stiffer fight and the Newfoundlanders took over the lead. They were stopped at the village of Vichte, just over six and a half kilometres east of the Lys, by a determined German defence and a lack of supporting artillery. The regiment was then ordered back to the Lys for rest and was replaced by other units. But the smell of blood was in the air, and a general

German collapse was expected at any moment. Accordingly, on October 24, Ricketts and his comrades moved forward once again, in an attempt to reach the Scheldt River, eight kilometres beyond Vichte.

At 9 o'clock the next morning, 9th Division's final attack of the war went in, with the Newfoundlanders in support of the lead battalions. German resistance was surprisingly heavy, and the regiment soon found itself in the thick of battle. Two machine-gun battalions, strongly supported by artillery, defended the last ridge before the Scheldt valley. Against this opposition, the division could make little progress as it tried to advance up an open hillside under direct fire. Mercifully, the divisional commander decided that taking the ridge was not worth the loss of life and called a halt to the operation, ordering units to consolidate where they were. On October 26, the Newfoundlanders handed over their front-line positions for the final time and marched to the rear. In B Company, only Ricketts and forty-five others remained.

After the Armistice of November 11, the Newfoundlanders began the long march eastwards as part of the British Army of Occupation. They marched into Germany on December 4 and crossed the Rhine into their assigned bridgehead at Cologne on December 13. Two days before Christmas, the Newfoundlanders received the welcome news on a regimental parade that Ricketts earned the VC for his heroism at Drie-Masten. For their part in the battle, Lieutenant Newman received the MC while Corporal Brazil, who had already won the MM, was awarded the DCM. (Ricketts is often listed as having won the DCM, but this is due to an error on the part of the Newfoundland Record Office, and he in fact never received it.)

On November 27, Ricketts had received a rare honour when the commander of Second Army, Lieutenant-General Sir Claud Jacob, presented him the *Croix de Guerre avec Etoile d'Or* (War Cross with Gold Star) on behalf of the French government at Holickshen, awarded for the same heroism that resulted in his receiving the VC. The *Croix de Guerre* was only established in 1915, and was normally awarded to soldiers Mentioned-in-Dispatches, with the gold star added for corps citations. The award of Ricketts's medal was published without citation in the *London Gazette* on June 19, 1919.

Ricketts's VC investiture was held on January 21, 1919, at Sandringham, the country estate of King George V. Sergeant James Dunphy accompanied him. The ceremony was a private one, as the king and queen were in mourning for their youngest son, Prince John, who had died the day before. John was referred to afterwards as the "Lost Prince," because he had been kept in seclusion for most of his life due to a limited mental capacity and the Royal Family's embarrassment over it. Rather than delay Ricketts's early return to Newfoundland and demobilization, the king agreed to a special investiture at York Cottage on the estate.

The king, dressed in civilian clothes, read aloud the citation for the award that had been published in the *London Gazette* just two weeks earlier, on January 6. He then pinned the VC on Ricketts's chest and turning to the small group assembled, remarked, "This is the youngest VC in my army." By sheer coincidence, one of the oldest living VC recipients was also in attendance. General Sir Dighton Probyn, comptroller to Queen Alexandra, who was then eighty-five, had earned his VC during the Indian Mutiny over sixty years earlier. The next day the king wrote in his diary, "Yesterday I gave the VC to Private Ricketts, Newfoundland Regiment, who is only 17½ now, a splendid boy."

After the simple ceremony, Queen Mary suggested a walk in Sandringham's gardens, and she, the king and Princess Mary (who forty-four years later became the Royal Newfoundland Regiment's Colonel-in-Chief) took their guests outside. In the garden, the queen picked a white rose and gave it to the young hero. Then it was off by car to the train station. As they drove slowly down the gravelled drive, one by one the soldiers of the Royal Guard who lined the driveway came smartly to attention as the car passed—a mark of respect for Ricketts's achievement. What Ricketts thought of the proceedings and the honour bestowed upon him remains unknown. Years later James Dunphy recalled, "He wasn't a man of few words, he was a man of no words at all."

Following the award of the VC, the army promoted Ricketts to sergeant on January 29. In early February, he returned to St. John's on the SS *Corsican*, a few months ahead of the regiment. One of the first people to greet him was a young reporter from *The Evening Telegram*, who rowed out to the troopship as it lay in harbour overnight before disembarking its soldiers the next morning. Ricketts was his normal shy and retiring self, but the reporter manager to get the story of his exploit out of him, including a rough map of the area where it occurred, and spent the rest of the night writing it up. The next day, the story appeared under the largest banner headline possible: "Deeds that Won The Empire! How Ricketts Won the VC.

The Hero interviewed by *The Telegram*." The reporter was a man who was to become a celebrity himself in later years: Newfoundland's most famous son, Joey Smallwood.

The next day, the people of St. John's gave Ricketts a tumultuous reception. He was carried from the Furness-Withy pier up to Water Street, where a sleigh and pair of horses met him to take him to various receptions throughout the city. A number of spectators did not feel this was an appropriate welcome, so they unhitched the horses and pulled the sleigh themselves through the city streets behind several marching bands as the citizenry cheered. Similar receptions followed elsewhere, including presentations of an illuminated address and a purse containing gold.

Ricketts returned to school, entering Bishop Feild College in 1920, followed by Memorial University College. On graduation he was employed at McMurdo's Drugstore in St. John's, where he passed his pharmacy exams.

A RARE PHOTOGRAPH OF TOMMY RICKETTS TAKEN IN THE DISPENSARY OF HIS ST. JOHN'S DRUGSTORE IN 1957. HE COLLAPSED AND DIED OF A SUDDEN HEART ATTACK THERE 10 YEARS LATER.

He eventually opened his own drugstore on Water Street at the corner of Job, where his daughter, Dolda, a trained pharmacist, worked with him for about two years. A modest, quiet and introverted man—perhaps because of his war experience—Ricketts continued to shun publicity, and even seemed to draw further into a protective shell. He refused to give interviews, have his photograph taken or appear in public.

Ricketts did, however, travel to London in 1929 to attend a dinner for VC recipients given by the British Legion in the presence of the Prince of Wales at the House of Lords. The following day, he laid a wreath of poppies at the Cenotaph in Whitehall on behalf of the Great War Veterans' Association of Newfoundland. His refusal to make public appearances even extended to royal visits. He politely declined invitations to functions during the visit of then Princess Elizabeth in 1951, followed by that of Princess Mary in 1964 on her first official visit as the Newfoundland Regiment's new Colonel-in-Chief.

Ricketts was not a well man and had a serious heart attack in his mid-forties. He was in pain much of the time, and his wife Edna Edwards used to drive him to the drugstore daily. On February 10, 1967, shortly after Edna had checked on him, he collapsed and died of a sudden heart attack on the floor of his store. The hero who had survived two years of fighting on the Western Front was two months short of his sixty-sixth birthday. The young reporter who interviewed the returning war hero forty-eight years earlier was now premier of Newfoundland, and Joey Smallwood and his government decreed a full state funeral to honour Ricketts, with the lieutenant-governor, premier, Supreme Court judges and other dignitaries in attendance. On February 13, after lying in state and a funeral at St. Thomas's Church, his coffin was placed on a gun carriage and escorted to the Anglican Cemetery on Forest Road in St. John's, where he was buried. His headstone notes he was "awarded the Victoria Cross in action with the Royal Newfoundland Regiment."

For many years, Ricketts's VC and other medals remained the property of his family and were on display in the Newfoundland Naval and Military Museum in the Confederation Building. Throughout his lifetime, Ricketts insisted that his medals were never to be sold for profit. On October 22, 2003, his ninety-year old widow, son Thomas and daughter Dolda Clarke, donated his VC and other medals to the Canadian War Museum, almost eighty-five years to the day after the act that earned Ricketts the VC. His Victoria Cross forms part of that institution's growing collection of Canadian VCs, which numbered twenty-six in mid-2005.

There are a number of tributes to Ricketts in Newfoundland. Schools and other public buildings in the Middle Arm area were named after him, as was the branch of the Royal Canadian Legion in Lewisporte. In 1972, the mayor of St. John's unveiled a plaque on the site of his Water Street drugstore, which was torn down in the late 1960s. It commemorates Ricketts as "Soldier—Pharmacist—Citizen" and incorrectly notes the award of the DCM.

But perhaps the best testimony to Thomas Ricketts is the biblical quotation engraved at the foot of his black granite headstone, which also bears an etching of the Victoria Cross. It is the motto of the Church Lad's Brigade—"Fight the Good Fight." That he did.

CHAPTER 9

AND THE SEA SHALL
HAVE THEM

Acting Captain Edward Stephen Fogarty Fegen
HMS *Jervis Bay*, Royal Navy
The North Atlantic Ocean, November 5, 1940

The phrase "Battle of the Atlantic" was first used by British Prime Minister Winston Churchill on March 6, 1941, to describe the conflict at sea between Allied merchant ships and their escorts on one side, and German naval and air forces on the other. The Battle of the Atlantic was arguably the most decisive, and certainly the longest, campaign of the Second World War. It ranged across the Atlantic Ocean, although it was mainly fought in the unforgiving North Atlantic, and lasted for the duration of the war in Europe, from September 1939 to May 1945, although it had essentially peaked by March 1943. After that date, Allied losses steadily decreased while Germany's rose. Canadian and British warships, plus RCAF and RAF aircraft, played the major part in the campaign, with some American assistance in the fall of 1941 until their attention was diverted by the war in the Pacific.

By mid-1942 Canada provided about half of the convoy escorts in the North Atlantic and the lion's share thereafter, plus virtually all land-based aircraft from Newfoundland and the Maritimes, as well as seven RCAF squadrons stationed overseas in the RAF's Coastal Command (see Chapter 10). Initially, Germany used a combination of U-boats, mines, surface raiders and airplanes to attack Allied ships, but Allied counter-efforts against these German methods soon left U-boats as the major weapons used by the Germans. The Allies responded with increasing reliance on the convoy system, with protection provided by escorting and patrolling warships and aircraft.

Eventually, Allied tactical and technical improvements—such as better detection and destruction of U-boats, breaking the German "Enigma" code and the introduction of very long range patrol aircraft—coupled with the rising production of replacement and new merchant ships, won the battle. During the campaign, the Germans sank about thirty-five hundred Allied merchant ships, totalling over thirteen million tonnes, the vast majority sunk by U-boats, but over 160 million tonnes of cargo got through to Britain under RCN escort.

On the fine, clear afternoon of November 5, 1940, convoy HX84 steamed towards Britain in the mid-Atlantic, about sixteen hundred kilometres east of Newfoundland and eight days out of Halifax, with vital war supplies of gasoline and food. The convoy's thirty-seven ships, spread out in nine columns, made a steady nine knots under the sole escort of HMS *Jervis Bay*, an eighteen-year-old, thirteen-thousand-tonne, Australian passenger liner converted to an armed merchant cruiser (AMC) fitted out with seven 6-inch guns.

Late that afternoon as he scanned the seas, Midshipman Ronnie Butler reported to his captain, "Ship to port, sir, on the horizon." Captain Edward Stephen Fogarty Fegen, the forty-nine-year-old RN officer commanding *Jervis Bay* got the unknown vessel in his glasses and immediately gave the order: "Sound 'Action Stations.' Enemy raider. Tell convoy to scatter and make smoke."

Various other vessels in the convoy had also reported sightings of a strange ship on the horizon. It was *Admiral Scheer*, a long, lean and fast twelve-thousand-tonne German commerce-raiding pocket battleship, capable of making twenty-eight knots and armed with six 11-inch guns and eight 5.9-inch guns. At the end of October, Captain Theodor Krancke had slipped *Scheer* into the Atlantic through the Denmark Strait north of Iceland, in search of Allied convoys to England. He knew the dates HX84 left Halifax—the main departure point for convoys—and lay in wait for it. Krancke may even have received this information from a German spy, Gottfried Sohar, a steward on one of the Swedish ships in the convoy, who went by the name of Joe Refi. At about 5:10 P.M., at a range of over fifteen kilometres, *Scheer* opened fire, its first rounds landing in the middle of the convoy.

Fegen's old, manually loaded guns with their obsolete fire-control system had a maximum range of nine kilometres. "You wouldn't believe it," Robert Squires, a member of the crew from Saint John recalled, "but our 6-inch guns were made in 1899 and 1900 for the Boer War." Before leaving Halifax, Fegen had told his crew, "If the gods are good to us, and we met the enemy, I shall take you in as close as I possibly can." He was as good as his word and immediately broke out of the convoy, "action stations" clanging. He headed straight for *Scheer* at full speed, firing as he went. Fegen knew there could be but one end to this uneven battle, yet his duty was to protect the convoy. He had to engage the German battleship long enough for the convoy to scatter and escape, as it now did under cover of smoke.

Scheer's third salvo hit *Jervis Bay*'s bridge, setting it on fire and partly severing Fegen's right arm. The one-sided battle quickly turned into a massacre. In quick succession, *Scheer*'s accurate fire knocked out *Jervis Bay*'s fire control, range finder, steering gear and radio. Fegen staggered to the after bridge, blood dripping from his arm, in an attempt to control his ship,

ADMIRAL SCHEER, AN ARMOURED, TWELVE-THOUSAND-TONNE GERMAN POCKET BATTLESHIP, WAS CAPABLE OF MAKING 28 KNOTS. ITS ARMAMENT CONSISTED OF SIX 11-INCH GUNS AND EIGHT 5.9-INCH GUNS.

HMS *JERVIS BAY* WAS AN EIGHTEEN-YEAR-OLD, THIRTEEN-THOUSAND-TONNE AUSTRALIAN PASSENGER LINER CONVERTED TO AN ARMED MERCHANT CRUISER. DURING ITS CONVERSION, IT WAS FITTED OUT WITH SEVEN OLD 6-INCH GUNS.

but when shellfire blew it away he was forced to return to the wrecked fore bridge. *Scheer*'s rounds hit *Jervis Bay*'s superstructure repeatedly and holed her hull in several places, as fires raged from bow to stern.

Despite this, Fegen's few undamaged guns continued to blaze away. To the gun crews' great frustration, even at full elevation they fell short of the German raider, which stayed outside their range. In the after-well deck, Squires served in the crew manning No. 3 gun. When a German shell knocked it out almost immediately, he helped carry wounded to the sick bay. Then a shell hit the small hospital, killing most of the injured.

Soon *Jervis Bay* began to list heavily and her decks were awash. When enemy fire shot her ensign away, a sailor climbed the flagstaff and attached another one. As one survivor recalled, "It was an inferno—flying shell and flame all over the place." On the main bridge, Fegen, severely wounded, gasped out, "Abandon ship!" As the surviving crew scrambled into the four remaining undamaged life rafts, *Jervis Bay* settled by the stern. Even when she lay dead in the water, a burning hulk, *Scheer* continued to send broadside after broadside into her. As *Jervis Bay* slowly went down, Fegen stood on the bridge, arms hanging limply at his side. Her colours still flying, she slipped beneath the waves almost three hours after *Scheer*'s first salvo.

But the terrible ordeal had not ended, as *Scheer* began firing at the men on the life rafts, wounding nearly all of them. Those who were able helped pile the most badly injured in the centre of the largest raft, while they stayed in the water, clinging desperately to the raft's lifelines. Soon the wind approached a hundred kilometres per hour and the sea whipped up into huge waves. The overburdened life raft alternately climbed to the crests of the waves, and then plummeted to the bottom of the troughs. Squires recalled, "When the raft went down, it took your breath away. The men jumped to their feet as the seas swept over, and the raft often flipped upside down, trapping many wounded underneath. Another few hours and no one would have survived."

The gallant self-sacrifice of Fegen and the majority of his crew was not in vain. The delay saved most of the convoy, whose ships escaped in different directions. *Scheer* pursued and sank five of them, but thirty-one got away—three to Canada and the rest to the Britain. One of those sunk was SS *Beaverford*, a nine-thousand-tonne armed freighter, originally a Canadian Pacific cargo ship. After *Jervis Bay* went down, *Beaverford* took up the struggle and gallantly attacked *Scheer* with its small, forward 4-inch gun, holding the enemy warship at bay for almost five hours. With darkness falling, Captain Krancke could not see what was attacking him and erred on the side of caution. He finally dispatched *Beaverford* with a torpedo, sending her with all seventy-seven hands to the bottom at 10:45 P.M.

Of *Jervis Bay*'s complement of 254 offices and men—a mixed bag of RN and RCN regulars and Merchant Navy—another ship picked up sixty-eight, three of them already dead. The Swedish freighter *Stureholm*, one of the vessels in the convoy, had remained in the area looking for survivors rather than scrambling to safety and witnessed the uneven battle. When *Stureholm* arrived in Halifax on November 12, her skipper, Captain Sven Olander, said, "Never will I forget the gallantry of that British captain sailing forward to meet the enemy." Once the survivors told what happened, the story of *Jervis Bay* electrified the free world and became one of the most celebrated naval sagas of all time. Perhaps no other incident symbolizes the courage shown in the Battle of the Atlantic more than Fegen's pluck in challenging a powerful German battleship.

When King George VI learned of Fegen's action, he noted in his diary, "27 ships have now reported out of the shelled convoy. The AMC *Jervis Bay* put up a gallant fight to give the convoy time to disperse." The story of Fegen's sacrifice so impressed the king that he asked the Admiralty to recommend Fegen for the VC. It is the only known instance of a VC nominated by the sovereign, as well as the only VC ever awarded for convoy defence. The award of Fegen's posthumous VC was published in the *London Gazette* on November 22.

Fegen's body was never found. King George VI presented his sister with his VC at Buckingham Palace on June 12, 1941. RN officers reported the bravery of the Canadian sailors aboard as "a wonderful example of the courage and spirit of the Canadian Navy." The thirteen who went down with the ship are commemorated on the Sailors' Memorial in Halifax's Point Pleasant Park, honouring all Canadians lost at sea in both world wars. The London *Times* said, "If ever a ship deserved a VC, that ship is surely the *Jervis Bay*."

SEVEN CANADIANS WHO SURVIVED THE SINKING OF *JERVIS BAY* GIVE A THUMBS UP AFTER THEIR RESCUE. NEARLY TWO HUNDRED OF THEIR SHIPMATES, INCLUDING THIRTEEN FELLOW CANADIANS, PERISHED IN THE SINKING.

Prime Minister Winston Churchill paid tribute to Fegen in the House of Commons on November 13: "The spirit of the Royal Navy [is] exemplified in the forlorn and heroic action...fought by the captain, officers and ship's company of the *Jervis Bay* in giving battle against overwhelming odds in order to protect the merchant convoy which they were escorting, and thus securing the escape of by far the greater part of that convoy." Fegen's brother, a fellow naval officer, summed up his last action: "It was the way he would have wished." Robert Squires later remembered him as "a good, fair skipper—the sort that knew a sailor when he saw one."

Edward Stephen Fogarty Fegen followed in the footsteps of his naval father and grandfather. Born on August 10, 1891, in Portsmouth, England, he joined the RN in 1904 and served at sea throughout the First World War in destroyers and other small ships. As a new sub-lieutenant, he survived his first sinking in August 1914, when his ship, HMS *Amphion*, struck a mine and sank, only twenty-four hours after the declaration of war. Later in the war, he commanded the destroyers *Moy* and *Paladin*. He was promoted lieutenant-commander in 1922 and served in succession on the destroyers *Whitley*, *Somme* and *Volunteer*. In 1925, Fegen was appointed to command the boys' training ship *Colossus*, followed by command of *Forres*. During his time at sea, he received British and Dutch medals for lifesaving and in 1927 attended the Senior Officers' Technical Course at Portsmouth.

At the end of 1927, Fegen was attached to the Royal Australian Navy to command their Naval College for two years. Coincidentally, the college's home was a place whose name would figure prominently in his future—Jervis Bay. While he was in Australia, he was promoted commander in 1928. After returning to England, he served on *Osprey*, *Dauntless*, *Curlew* and *Dragon*, attended the Senior Officers' War Course at the Royal Naval College at Greenwich and completed a three-year tour at HM Dockyard in Chatham from 1935 to 1938. Just before the war broke out, in July 1939, he was appointed executive officer in the 6,850-tonne cruiser HMS *Emerald* under Captain Augustine Agar, who had received the VC for the CMB raid on Kronstadt in June 1919, along with Claude Dobson (see Chapter 2).

In February 1940, Fegen became acting captain and took command of *Jervis Bay*, which spent several months that summer being refitted in dry dock in Saint John, New Brunswick. Shipyard workers tore out *Jervis Bay*'s comfortable cabins and replaced them with austere accommodations, also removing most of the ship's wooden fittings to decrease the risk of fire should it be hit. Twenty-four thousand watertight drums filled its hold, to provide buoyancy in case it was holed below the waterline (they were the reason the ship stayed afloat long enough for convoy HX84 to escape). While in Saint John, Fegen and his crew made many friends and were highly regarded by all they met. *Jervis Bay* came out of dry dock that fall, called back to duty before the refit was complete. Some of the dock-workers sailed to Halifax aboard *Jervis Bay* so they could continue their tasks. HX84 was the ship's third convoy after leaving Saint John.

The courage of Fegen and his crew is widely commemorated. In England, their names are engraved on the Chatham Naval Memorial in Kent. As well, there is a sundial to their memory in Hamilton, Bermuda, and a wreath of copper and gold laurel leaves at the Seaman's Institute, Wellington, New Zealand. In Owen Sound, Ontario, the Jervis

EDWARD STEPHEN FOGARTY FEGEN WAS AN EXPERIENCED ROYAL NAVY OFFICER WHEN HE WAS GIVEN COMMAND OF *JERVIS BAY* IN FEBRUARY 1940. AFTER SEVERAL MONTH'S REFIT AT SAINT JOHN, NEW BRUNSWICK, FEGEN COMMENCED CONVOY ESCORT DUTIES OUT OF HALIFAX. HIS GALLANTRY IN THE FACE OF OVERWHELMING ODDS EARNED HIM THE VICTORIA CROSS, BUT COST HIM HIS LIFE.

Bay Park was established in February 1941. It commemorates the ship's heroic action, as well as the memory of Owen Sound's first Second World War casualty, Stoker Jimmie Johnson, who lost his life when *Jervis Bay* was sunk.

But perhaps the most fitting memorials are in the city where *Jervis Bay* was converted to an armed merchant cruiser—Saint John. The Saint John East Branch of the Royal Canadian Legion on Bayside Drive changed its name to Jervis Bay Memorial Branch and displays memorabilia from the ship, including a white ensign, a clock, crockery and photographs. The branch was instrumental in developing what eventually became Jervis Bay–Ross Memorial Park on Loch Lomond Road. Today it contains memorials to several units connected with Saint John, including a plaque to the 26th (New Brunswick) Battalion (see Chapter 3), which originally stood at Market Slip. In 1941, a three-and-a-half metre granite column was erected in the park commemorating *Jervis Bay*'s gallantry. A bas-relief plaque on the memorial reads:

In Honoured Memory of
Captain E. S. Fogarty Fegen V.C. Officers and Men of H.M.S. Jervis Bay
Who Gave Their Lives in Gallant Action Against Overwhelming Odds with
A German Raider in the North Atlantic November 5 1940 in Order that
36 Ships under Their Care Might be Saved

And what of the German raider? On April 9, 1945, just a month before the war ended in Europe, *Admiral Scheer* came to an end when RAF Lancaster bombers sunk it at the Kiel naval base in northern Germany.

Acting Captain Frederick Thornton Peters
HMS *Walney*, Royal Navy
Oran, Algeria, November 8, 1942

If it were possible to measure bravery on a scale, then Frederick Thornton Peters would have a legitimate claim to the title of one of the bravest Canadians of all time. He certainly became one of the most decorated, earning not only the VC, but also the Distinguished Service Order (DSO) and two Distinguished Service Crosses (DSC), as well as the American DSC and other awards. It is a unique and unrivalled record. Peters is the only Prince Edward Island native to receive the Victoria Cross, as well as the only Atlantic Canadian to earn that medal in the Second World War. As the last person born in the region to earn the VC, he shares a distinction with William Hall, the first recipient—they both served in the RN. There is also another aspect to Peters's life that sets him apart: much of his history is sketchy and the peculiar gaps in the record have led some to speculate about a double life as a spy.

A big, burly man, Peters was born in Charlottetown on September 17, 1889, from United Empire Loyalist stock. His father, Frederick, a lawyer, was called to the Bar of Prince Edward Island and Nova Scotia in 1876; later, he became provincial attorney general and its first Liberal premier from 1891–97. His mother, Bertha, was the youngest daughter of Father of Confederation John Hamilton Grey. Peters received his early education at a private school run by St. Peter's Anglican Cathedral. Then, in 1898, when he was nine, his family left the island, and moved west to British Columbia where his father accepted an appointment with the Alaska Boundary Commission. The family settled first in Victoria and later in Prince Rupert, where Peters completed his schooling.

Even as a young boy the navy fascinated Peters, in particular naval battles, especially those involving the British and Germans. As a result, even before he left PEI he had picked up the nickname "Fritz." Out west, Fritz's passion for the navy continued, coming to fruition in January 1905 when his parents allowed him to enroll in the RN as a sixteen-year-old cadet. By May of the next year he was serving at sea as a midshipman and, for some reason, picked up another nickname, "Tramp." It would prove a fitting name for much of Peters's life.

It seems that a naval career was pre-ordained for Peters. A fellow officer once described him as "a typical Elizabethan gentleman adventurer. His entire soul was in the Navy. It was a fascination with him." Another friend, Commander David Joel, who trained with Peters as a midshipman at HMS *Britannia*, the RN's training establishment for aspiring officers, said, "He was one of the rare 'romantic' Adventurers, one of those complete 'Pirates' that the Navy occasionally produces. These types are completely without fear, dedicated to duty or their own interpretation of it, and tough as old ropes."

In 1908, while still a midshipman, Peters led rescue parties ashore in Sicily to evacuate civilians threatened by the volcanic eruption of Mount Messina. A grateful Italian government decorated him for bravery with the Silver Messina Earthquake Medal, the first of many awards he received during his career. Peters received his commission as a sub-lieutenant in July 1909 and began his first tour of duty in 1910. He served in destroyers on the China Station until December 1913, protecting Britain's many interests in the Far East in the days of gunboat diplomacy. While in China, he became a lieutenant in January 1911.

Forty years later, after his death, Betty Lockhart, the daughter of the British commissioner at Mei Hai Wei, recalled those days in a far outpost of the Empire in her memoir. She described Peters "of the black eyes and white teeth and aloof humour" and wrote: "so mad Peters has gone after all, another delightful link severing our youth from us." She continued, "But is it sadly? Is it not rather triumphantly that we remember that splendid gay youth in the sunshine; the delightful capers, the nonsense and the dancing. How grateful I am for all those sweet delicious memories peopled by such gallant ones." It seems that life was not all hardships for a dashing young officer on the edges of Empire.

Peters resigned suddenly from the navy in December 1913, giving as his only reason the fact that his "family's coffers needed filling" and took a job with Canadian Pacific Ships as a third officer.

Peters rejoined the navy as a lieutenant in September 1914, a month after the First World War started, and saw his first action shortly thereafter. On January 23, 1915, the German battle cruiser squadron under Vice Admiral Franz von Hipper sailed out to raid the English coast and harass the British fishing fleet. The RN, in possession of German code books, intercepted and deciphered the enemy's radio messages and a battle cruiser squadron under Vice Admiral Sir David Beatty steamed forth to meet them. Lighter cruisers and destroyers accompanied both fleets' battle cruisers.

Peters served as first lieutenant in the destroyer HMS *Meteor*, part of the Harwich Force, which was named after its east coast home port. *Meteor* belonged to a flotilla of seven new M-class destroyers: three-funnel vessels displacing about a thousand tonnes carrying a complement of seventy-eight, and mounting three 4-inch guns and four 21-inch torpedo tubes. Attaining a speed of about thirty-five knots, they made a sturdy, hard-hitting addition to the destroyer force.

Shortly after 7 o'clock the next morning, the two fleets met at Dogger Bank in the North Sea, midway between Britain and Germany. After a brief exchange of gunfire, the outnumbered German ships turned to flee, pursued in a running battle by the British. As the RN battle cruisers' speed increased, only the M-class destroyers could keep abreast of them. *Meteor*, under Captain the Honourable Herbert Meade, approached the withdrawing Germans to ascertain their number and disposition. As it did, *Blücher*, the rearmost of the German battle cruisers, fired on *Meteor*. Meade, having gotten the information he wanted, passed it to Vice Admiral Beatty and took up station astern of the fleet.

By 8:52 A.M., the British battle cruisers came within range of the enemy and opened fire. Beatty's flagship, HMS *Lion*, hit *Blücher* for the first time at 9:19 and scored a direct hit on the after turret of the flagship *Seydlitz*, leading the German line. Fire from other British ships hit *Blücher* repeatedly and she began to fall behind, suffering severe damage. It looked as if a British victory were in the making. Unfortunately, Beatty was about to snatch defeat from the jaws of victory. Sighting a signal flying from *Seydlitz* for the German destroyers to launch a torpedo attack, Beatty signaled a turn northward. As *Lion* turned it was struck by a salvo from *Seydlitz*, followed a few minutes later by more direct hits from another German battle cruiser. In serious trouble, *Lion*'s speed dropped rapidly.

Beatty now compounded his earlier error by sending an ambiguous signal. He intended to order his other battle cruisers to pursue the fleeing Germans, while light cruisers and destroyers finished off the damaged *Blücher*, but the other British vessels took Beatty's signal to mean all ships should attack the floundering German battle cruiser. As the German squadron escaped to the southeast, the undamaged British battle cruisers pumped shell after shell into the wounded *Blücher*. Once the battle cruisers finished, the destroyers moved in for the kill. Captain Meade, leading the other destroyers in *Meteor* went in to administer the *coup de grâce*. Although dead in the water and on fire, *Blücher* still had some fight in it and opened fire on the leading destroyer with its main and secondary armament.

Meteor received five hits, including one from an 8.2-inch shell that inflicted severe damage. With the ship's foremost boiler-room wrecked and several men injured, Fritz Peters descended to the boiler room to turn off the steam cocks, a dangerous task to undertake when a ship has been hit. For his gallantry he received a Mention-in-Dispatches from Beatty and the DSO in recognition of his services. He became one of the first Canadians ever to be awarded the DSO, a rare honour for a junior officer, and often called "the poor man's VC" when given to one.

Although fifteen British sailors died in the battle, in German Vice Admiral von Hipper's flagship alone the death toll reached 192. As for *Blücher*, after over seventy shells and seven torpedoes found their mark, the ship rolled onto its starboard side, turned upside down and sank, drowning 782 of her crew. The British battle cruisers then took up the chase of the German squadron, but too late. They turned back to find Beatty steaming towards them in the destroyer to which he had transferred his flag. The opportunity for a decisive victory had passed. As the ships returned to their homeports, another destroyer took the powerless *Meteor* in tow.

The British put the battle to good use for propaganda purposes. A cameraman had captured the sinking of *Blücher* on moving film and a still photograph from it, showing hundreds of sailors sliding off the hull and into the sea, became a popular souvenir item. Some enterprising entrepreneurs even engraved the scene on the side of silver cigarette cases. The kaiser promptly ordered his fleet to avoid the chance of losing any more major warships.

PETERS WAS FIRST LIEUTENANT ON THE DESTROYER HMS *METEOR*, WHICH HELPED SINK THE GERMAN BATTLE CRUISER *BLÜCHER* OFF DOGGER BANK IN JANUARY 1915, WITH THE LOSS OF 782 OF ITS CREW. BEFORE SHE WENT DOWN, *BLÜCHER* DAMAGED *METEOR*.

From November 1915 until June 1919, Fritz Peters successively held the command of four vessels: *Greyhound*, an older and smaller thirty-knot destroyer launched in 1900, which carried a complement of sixty-three and was armed with a 12-pounder and two torpedo tubes; *Christopher* and *Cockatrice*, two 850-tonne K class destroyers launched just before the war, crewed by seventy-four sailors and more heavily armed with three 4-inch guns and two torpedo tubes; and *Polyanthus*, a twelve-hundred-tonne Flower class sloop launched in September 1917 and armed with two 4-inch guns.

In 1917, while commanding *Christopher*, Peters received another award, for rescuing the crew of the Q-ship *Dunraven*, which had been torpedoed by a German submarine and was badly damaged. Gordon Campbell—who had been Ronald Stuart's captain in *Pargust* (see Chapter 2)—was in command of *Dunraven*. Peters arrived on the scene and took *Dunraven* in tow for Plymouth, but as the weather worsened the ship's crew had to be taken off. In the early morning hours of August 9, the Q-ship went down, colours still flying. The man who would earn the VC in the Second World War had just saved the lives of two present and two future VC recipients from the First World War. In addition to Captain Campbell himself and Seaman William Williams (who received the VC in the same action involving *Pargust* and under the same rule as Lieutenant Stuart), two crew members of *Dunraven* would soon receive the VC. Campbell received a second bar to his DSO, while Peters received the DSC for "services in Destroyer and Torpedo Boat Flotillas during the period ending 31 December 1917."

After the war, in June 1919, the RN selected Peters, who been promoted lieutenant commander, for the first post-war course at the RN Staff College. He qualified as a staff officer and did well enough on the course to be offered an excellent appointment for a junior officer as assistant staff officer (operations) in *Queen Elizabeth*, flagship of the Home Fleet. But Peters again resigned from the navy in June 1920, at his own request. While on the Retired List, he advanced to commander in 1929.

Much of Peters's life for the next twenty years remains shrouded in mystery, with hints that he may have been engaged in espionage for the British. He apparently returned to Canada, but then became somewhat of a drifter, tramping around the world. Stories exist of him selling boots to the Russians and of him going to the Gold Coast (modern Ghana) in the 1930s to grow cocoa. Every two to three years his friends in London would see him, spending his money until it ran out and he returned to Africa to make more. He was a warrior without a war. Or was he?

Then, in 1939, the Second World War broke out. Peters worked his way to England in a tramp steamer and re-enlisted in the RN. In October, the navy made him a lieutenant and gave him command of *Lord Stanhope*, leading an anti-submarine flotilla of small ships such as whalers and trawlers. Three months later he took command of *Thirlmere* and the 10th Anti-Submarine Striking Force. Operating out of the Orkney and Shetland Islands off the north coast of Scotland, in the nine months between

October 1939 and June 1940, Peters's force managed to sink two German U-boats. In July he received a bar to his DSC "for good services in the Royal Navy since the outbreak of the war," in particular in command of *Thirlmere*.

At this point, Commander Peters was plucked from relative obscurity and moved to the Directorate of Naval Intelligence, which seconded him to the Secret Intelligence Service, also known as MI5. Was this based on his work between the wars? Peters became commandant of a school established at Brickendonbury Hall near Hertford, for training special agents in the techniques of underground work. Here he came into contact with two of the most famous spies of the twentieth century, who were also two of its most notorious traitors. Guy Burgess and Kim Philby—who had each already been "turned" by the Soviets—were both colleagues of Peters at the school. In fact, the whole idea of creating the school had been proposed by Burgess and fleshed out by Philby.

In his book, *My Silent War*, Philby remembered Peters's "faraway naval eyes and a gentle smile of great charm." The naval officer often took Burgess and Philby to dinner at a London restaurant to listen to their views on the new school. Unfortunately, the navy gave him little guidance as to what the school should do, and even less in the way of useful information to impart to the students. Despite this, the "trainees came to adore him." However, Peters quickly grew to detest the job, and the political intrigues that went with it.

As the summer wore on, his "aspect changed for the worse" without any clear direction from London. He detested paperwork and, according to Philby, "fell into a deep depression" when he learned the school would be disbanded. Peters took it personally, seemingly "conscious of failure and neglect." He spent an entire evening composing his letter of resignation as commandant. It must have been a great weight off his mind, Philby writes, as "he cheered up and the charming smile came back, for the first time in many days. He was clearly happy to be going back to his little ships after his brief baptism of political fire."

Peters worked briefly for the director of the Anti-Submarine Warfare Division from February to April 1941, when he became staff officer (operations) to the Commander-in-Chief at Portsmouth. In August, he became commander of HMS *Tynwald*, an auxiliary anti-aircraft ship, with the acting rank of captain.

However, fate still had greater things in store for Fritz Peters. The RN selected him for a special mission and made him primarily responsible for planning part of a major Allied operation. In October 1942, Peters showed up at the naval base at Greenock, Scotland, with a truckload of explosives. With amazing prescience, he told his friend Joel, "I am probably going to be killed, but it's well worth it." The Allies were planning a major offensive operation in North Africa, and, in spite of wartime secrecy, Peters's friends who were in a position to know suspected his involvement. Peters himself alluded to having received his instructions from Churchill.

Peters's command consisted of four tiny ships which were to undertake the difficult and dangerous task of capturing Oran harbour in Algeria, without damaging the port. Code-named Operation Reservist, it supported the much larger Operation Torch, the Allied landings in North Africa. Torch included the greatest armada the world had seen up to that time. It consisted of three task forces. The Western Task Force of thirty-five thousand men in thirty-nine vessels, supported by a powerful naval squadron, sailed directly from the US under Major-General George S. Patton to capture Casablanca in French Morocco. US Major-General Lloyd Fredenhall commanded the Central Task Force, which came from Britain. It consisted of thirty-nine thousand men in forty-seven ships, escorted by an RN squadron, and had Oran as its objective. The Eastern Task Force, thirty-three thousand men in thirty-four ships, also with a British naval escort, was to take Algiers.

The reaction of Vichy France (which controlled both Algeria and Morocco) to the invasion could only be surmised. Operation Torch marked a turning point in the war in the West—from defensive to offensive operations. Its objectives were to link up with the British Eighth Army in the Western Desert, end the campaign in North Africa and make the Mediterranean Sea safe for future Allied movements, specifically against Sicily and Italy.

A large Canadian naval contingent, consisting of corvettes and landing craft, took part in Operation Torch. As RCN landing craft ferried in American and British troops, they faced generally light opposition from Vichy French forces, resulting in few casualties. This happy state of events continued as the Canadian flotillas brought in reinforcements and supplies over the next week. When the fleet sailed back to England, carrying the wounded and returning men no longer needed in the operation, the heaviest casualties were the result of German subs torpedoing a number of ships.

Peters's part in the overall plan was simple, but extraordinarily danger-ous, bordering on the suicidal. As the Central Task Force landed east and west of Oran, encircling the city, he would attempt to land American com-bat troops and anti-sabotage parties directly in the port. They were to seize the shore batteries covering the harbour and prevent immobilization of the dock and its machinery, or the blocking of the harbour itself, as it was important for the Allies to have the port in full working order for future operations. Two motor launches, *ML 480* and *ML 483*, would lay down a smoke screen, while a pair of fifteen-hundred-tonne former US Coast Guard cutters, *Walney* (ex-*Ponchartrain*) and *Hartland* (ex-*Sebago*)—trans-ferred to the RN under the US Lend-Lease Act in 1941 for use as escorts—would ram the 180-metre boom across the mouth of Oran harbour and smash through it.

The slow, lightly armoured cutters mounted only two 4-inch guns each. Once they broke through the boom and got inside the twenty-seven-hun-dred-metre-long breakwater, with *Hartland* drawing fire, *Walney* would come alongside the quay, unload four canoe teams equipped with self-pro-pelled mines and take the French warships by surprise. *Hartland* would then secure the jetties and ships near the harbour mouth. With the capture of the port and ships, it was expected that the surrender of the town would follow swiftly.

On the night of November 7, 1942, *Walney* (under Lieutenant-Commander Peter Meyrick) and *Hartland* (under Lieutenant-Commander G. P. Billot) steamed towards their objective. Aboard the two ships were American personnel to help with the assault: a battalion of 393 men from 6th Armoured Infantry Division, thirty-five sailors and six marines. Some would man canoes to seize port installations and prevent the Vichy French from destroying them and scuttling French ships in the harbour, while oth-ers were specially trained technicians to operate the harbour once it fell.

One of two elements was necessary for this audacious plan to succeed: surprise or non-resistance by the French. However, surprise evaporated when Peters was ordered to assault the port two hours after Allied troops had landed successfully on the beaches adjacent to Oran against light oppo-sition. By the time *Walney* and *Hartland* approached the port, the French were fully alerted and ready to fight.

Moreover, Allied intelligence had grossly underestimated the Vichy will to fight, counting too much on bad relations between the Germans and their uneasy French collaborators. They also failed to take into account the fact that a French fleet manned by French crews held Oran—a fleet which was still smarting from the British sinking of three battleships there after the fall of France in 1940 (to prevent them from falling into Nazi hands). France's honour demanded satisfaction. When the two Allied cutters approached the boom at 2:45 on the morning of November 8, sirens sounded and all lights in the town went out. Circling off the entrance with *Hartland*, Peters demanded surrender in French over his ship's loudspeaker. In response, a search-light suddenly enveloped *Walney* and heavy, though inaccurate, machine-gun fire followed.

This did not deter Peters. *Walney* and *Hartland* circled around and, in the proudest tradi-tions of the RN's long history, steamed ahead at fifteen knots, partially screened by smoke, head-ing for the boom. At 3:10 A.M., *Walney* broke through and slipped three canoes, but at least one was sunk immediately by gunfire. As *Walney* steamed up the harbour with *Hartland* following astern, a shore battery opened fire and hit her. Then, the French sloop *La*

CAPTAIN PETERS PHOTOGRAPHED SHORTLY BEFORE HE EMBARKED ON THE MISSION THAT RESULTED IN THE AWARD OF THE VICTORIA CROSS AND LED TO HIS DEATH.

Surprise tried to break out and Peters ordered his men to ram her, but *Walney* missed. Two broadsides from the French ship raked the tiny cutter from a few metres, damaging both engines and killing or wounding many of her crew. Under continuous heavy crossfire from several ships and sub-marines at close range, *Walney* somehow managed to limp further into the harbour, making for the quay. Just when it looked as if things could not get worse, they did, as point-blank fire from warships and shore batteries pounded the two valiant little ships.

Another ship, the destroyer *Epervier*, blocked the way, so Peters ordered *Walney* alongside, intending to board the French ship. Then *Walney*'s engine room took a direct hit and her boilers exploded. Another shell scored a direct hit on the bridge, which burst into flames. Of the seventeen men on the bridge, only Peters survived, blown clear by the blast, but blinded in one eye and wounded in the shoulder. With *Walney* a blazing wreck and most of her crew and landing party dead or wounded, a few surviving Americans managed to lob hand grenades at the French ship and throw grapnels onto her deck for boarding. They stormed aboard, firing tommy guns and revolvers. On the tiny cutter, as crewmen carried the injured below to the wardroom, a shell exploded inside. In that confined space, it killed everyone. Then the ammunition stores blew up and depth charges stored below decks began exploding.

Still Peters persisted. He ran fore, then aft, along his ship in an attempt to get mooring lines ashore. He soon realized he faced an impossible task and ordered abandon ship. French sailors machine gunned British and American survivors in the water. As *Walney* drifted into the harbour, explosions continued to rock her. Once he knew all surviving hands had made it overboard, Peters jumped into the water himself. Sometime between 9:00 and 10:00 that morning he watched *Walney* slowly turn onto its side— American and British ensigns still flying—and sink. In the shallow waters of Oran harbour, part of its hull still protruded above the water.

The other cutter, *Hartland*, had also reached the jetty by this time and suffered a similar fate. Intense small arms and shell fire killed or injured many of its crew, not leaving enough men to handle its mooring lines and secure the ship. A broadside from a French destroyer, *Typhon*, stopped it dead in the water. Completely engulfed in flames, the small ship drifted to the centre of the harbour under continuous shelling from other ships and the shore. The few survivors abandoned ship and, at dawn, *Hartland* blew up and sank.

Only fifteen men survived *Walney*'s sinking. Eighty-one of her crew went down with the ship. Among the American soldiers, less than fifty remained alive and unwounded, while five American sailors were killed and seven wounded. Total RN losses were 113 killed and eighty-six wounded. Peters and a few others managed to get on a Carley float, where some Vichy French picked them up and took Peters before the French admiral in charge of the port. The French officer tried to get Peters to admit he fired the first shot, but when he would not do so the admiral threw him into prison.

Meanwhile, the French went about destroying the port facilities and scuttling ships to block the harbour—the very sabotage Peters's mission was supposed to prevent. Some of the remaining French ships in the harbour tried to fight or break out, but British warships sunk them. Two days later, the French released Peters from his prison hospital when encircling American troops of the Central Task Force liberated the town. A grateful civilian populace carried him through the streets in a victory celebration and showered him with flowers in tribute.

Peters flew to Gibraltar for an onward flight to England, there to receive further medical treatment and to report on the attack. On Friday, November 13, he boarded a Royal Australian Air Force Sunderland flying boat for the trip back, along with four other naval officers. Not long into the flight, despite a forecast of calm and clear conditions, the plane ran into forty-knot headwinds accompanied by hail, sleet and lighting. They passed the point of no return and, with insufficient fuel to divert elsewhere, the pilot pressed on.

Eventually, they flew over the breakwater at Plymouth Sound with the fuel gauge showing less than fifteen minutes of flying time left. In thick fog and a pitch-black night, the pilot began to descend by altimeter to the harbour below. As the altimeter passed through two hundred metres, the aircraft crashed into the water and turned turtle at the entrance to the navy's Devonport Dockyard. The pilot and others, some seriously injured, escaped from the downed aircraft and began swimming for shore.

Acting Captain Frederick Thornton Peters was not among them. The effects of the crash or the cold waters of Plymouth Sound, or a combination of both, took his life. Just before take-off from Gibraltar, Peters told the flight engineer, "You know we navy men are a bit suspicious…we shouldn't be taking off on Friday the thirteenth." A mystery even surrounds Peters's death. One version of events maintains that the pilot, Flying Officer Wyn Thorpe, got safely out of his aircraft and began swimming for shore when he discovered Peters's unconscious body, drifting in the icy water in a life jacket. He swam on in the darkness, towing the body, but was not found by a rescue boat for another ninety minutes, by which time Peters was dead. Another version maintains that Peters's body was never found.

It did not take the Americans long to recognize Peters's heroism. On the recommendation of surviving officers, they awarded him their DSC, the highest medal for bravery the United States could bestow on a foreigner. The citation was published in the *London Gazette* on January 19, 1943.

Lieutenant-General Dwight D. Eisenhower, in charge of Operation Torch, sent two senior officers to Peters's mother in Trail, BC, to present her son's DSC to her in a special private ceremony. The British also decided to honour his courage, but dithered about whether or not to announce it publicly for fear of offending the French. In the end, they awarded him the VC. His citation was published in the *London Gazette* on May 18, 1943, six months after the event.

Winston Churchill called Peters's attack at Oran "the finest British Naval engagement since Trafalgar." Admiral of the Fleet Sir Andrew Cunningham, the Allied naval Commander-in-Chief for Operation Torch, said, "The enterprise was one of desperate hazard. Courage and leadership achieved all that could be done against odds that proved overwhelming." At fifty-three, and still married only to his beloved navy, Peters became the oldest Canadian and the second oldest naval recipient of the VC ever. Amazingly, the British did not ceremoniously present their highest award for gallantry in the face of the enemy to Peters's mother. She received it through the mail, accompanied by a standard letter of acknowledgement.

Later, she received a letter from author and war correspondent A. D. Divine who wrote: "I do know that the men who were with him, the survivors of the exploit, spoke of your son in the very highest possible terms. They would, I know, have gone with him again knowing that the same future was in store for them." He acknowledged the "brilliance and dash of this Zeebrugge in miniature," referring to the Belgian port that had been the site of a daring Royal Navy raid in the First World War.

Peters's VC and other medals, after being held by the family for years, came onto the market in the early 1990s, when a nephew offered them for sale. At this point, a number of Islanders formed a committee to buy Peters's medals and bring them to PEI. They established Operation Victoria Cross and asked Jack McAndrew, a Charlottetown television producer, journalist and commentator, to be the campaign's coordinator. Despite a determined effort to raise the $100,000 asking price and buy the medals for display in Peters's home province, the organizers never reached their goal. In 1994, an English collector bought Peters's medals at a Christie's auction and the money collected by Operation Victoria Cross was turned over to the Department of Veterans' Affairs.

Kim Philby later wrote, when he heard of the award of the VC to Peters for "what was probably unnecessarily gallant behaviour in Oran harbour," that he "felt a pang that [Peters] should never have known about it. He was the type of strong sentimentalist who would have wept at such an honour." Supporting the story that Frederick Thornton Peters has no known grave, his name appears on the Naval Memorial in Portsmouth, England, on Southsea Common overlooking the promenade. Part of an inscription on the memorial notes it is in honour of those who "have no other grave than the sea." His name also appears on a plaque at the Trail branch of the Royal Canadian Legion. In his native province, a new building housing HMCS *Queen Charlotte*, the Naval Reserve Division in Charlottetown, was opened in 1997 and named in his honour.

CHAPTER 10

FIRST AND LAST

Flight-Lieutenant David Ernest Hornell
162 Squadron, Royal Canadian Air Force
The North Sea, June 24, 1944

June 24, 1944, dawned bright and clear, the North Sea rough but sunlit. Canso flying boat 9754 "P" from the Royal Canadian Air Force's 162 Squadron patrolled its assigned area between Iceland and Norway, searching for German submarines that were attempting to break through the North Transit Area and attack the huge Allied D-Day invasion fleet off the coast of Normandy. Its navigator, Flying Officer Ed Matheson, described the flying as "95 percent pure boredom and probably two minutes of pure terror and heart-pounding."

At about 7:00 P.M., after twelve long hours on patrol, Flight-Sergeant Joe Bodnoff, one of the Canso's three wireless/air gunners, came on the intercom to the plane's captain, Flight-Lieutenant David Hornell, asking, "Do you see something on the water?" What Hornell saw was a surfaced submarine. Matheson's two minutes of sheer terror were about to begin.

Without hesitation, the Canso's captain turned to commence his attack while the crew sprang into action, sending out a "flash" radio message to squadron headquarters. The submarine, *U-1225*, saw the aircraft, changed its course and opened surprisingly accurate fire at about five and a half kilometres. According to Matheson, "As we were making the run, we were getting hit. One shell went off just outside the hull right behind the radio . . . this one blew holes in the side of the aircraft that wrecked the radio and I got two pieces of shrapnel right behind the ear."

Disregarding the damage, Hornell closed with the enemy submarine and ordered his gunners to return fire, with the flying boat about eleven hundred metres away. One .30-calibre gun jammed, but another scored direct hits on the sub, raking the conning tower, killing most of the crew on its deck and causing the U-boat to turn sharply to starboard. The enemy then reopened fire, tearing two large holes in the plane's starboard wing. Hornell immediately took evasive action, but the Canso became extremely difficult to control.

FLIGHT-LIEUTENANT DAVID HORNELL'S DARING ATTACK ON U-1225 IN THE NORTH SEA IN JUNE 1944 EARNED HIM THE ROYAL CANADIAN AIR FORCE'S FIRST VICTORIA CROSS.

As Hornell manoeuvred for his run-in attack, German fire hit the plane again at about seven hundred metres and the damaged wing burst into flames from leaking fuel and oil. The aircraft began to shake severely—becoming an easy target for fire from the sub. However, even as the flames reached the plane's fuel tank, Hornell courageously pressed home his attack. The valiant pilot flew right up the U-boat's track at only fifteen metres height, dropping his depth charges in a textbook strike, straddling the submarine. When the charges went off, the sub's bows reared high out of the water before she sank.

Now that he had dispatched the sub, Hornell faced an even more serious problem—how to save himself and his crew. As the vibrations worsened, the pilot managed by phenomenal efforts to gain a little height and turn the airplane into the wind. But the flames spread rapidly and the starboard engine fell off. Hornell had done all he could in the air; it was time to bring the Canso down. He landed skillfully on the surface in a heavy swell, bouncing twice before settling down about sixteen hundred metres from the U-boat. Aflame and full of holes, the shattered aircraft quickly sank.

Only one of the airplane's four-man dinghies was undamaged. At best, the dinghy could hold seven of the eight crew members at once, so the men took turns slipping into the frigid sea, hanging onto the sides of the dinghy while their Mae Wests kept them afloat. Matheson guessed the air temperature at about minus ten degrees Celsius. "I know we were just about frozen after three hours," he recalled. According to Flight-Sergeant Syd Cole, another of the wireless/air gunners, "about 20 percent of the time we were all in the water anyway because of the huge waves." He remembers the freezing crewmen periodically rubbing each other's limbs to restore circulation.

Bailing continuously because of rough seas, the crew's freezing ordeal lasted through the night, as Hornell grew weaker and weaker and started to lose his sight from the effects of the salt water. Nevertheless, he continued to encourage his crew and remained unfailingly positive. Then the dinghy capsized, sending everyone into the icy waters. The airmen righted it only with great difficulty, as their strength began to give out. This happened twice more before two of the crew, sergeants Scott and St-Laurent, died of exposure, their bodies lost to the watery depths.

As it happened, 162 Squadron never received the radio message Hornell sent upon encountering the sub. By sheer chance, four hours after they ditched, a homeward-bound Catalina from 333 Squadron sighted the dinghy, as well other dinghies a short distance away which carried the sub's survivors. Unable to land because of increasingly rough seas, a crewman in the flying boat signalled a message on an Aldis lamp: "Congratulations. Sub sank. Help on way." Due to low fuel, the Catalina departed after about two hours.

Meanwhile, the Air-Sea Rescue organization went into action and a Sunderland flew out to the site. Unfortunately, it could not land either and so dropped a lifeboat, which came down about 450 metres away. Matheson said that Hornell, although he was clearly not in any condition to do so, "was going to swim for it, but he had to be restrained." Cole recalled the life raft descending: "It was a bloody beautiful sight. It came down on six parachutes. But five collapsed and the sixth stayed on like a sail. Last we saw it, it was headed for Greenland." Not long after the Sunderland appeared on the scene, Hornell lost his sight completely and seemed "very close to death," in Matheson's words.

At one time, seven aircraft circled overhead, but it took almost twenty-one hours for a rescue launch to arrive. Unfortunately, Hornell, whose efforts helped keep his crew alive, died after being picked up, despite intense medical efforts to revive him. The boat took the surviving aircrew, as well as the submariners, to the Shetland Islands for treatment. It also took David Hornell's body to be buried in the cemetery at Lerwick, the bleak island's wind-swept capital. All eight crewmembers, surviving or dead, received decorations. Hornell was awarded the VC, the first member of Canada's youngest service, the RCAF, to be so honoured. The award of Hornell's VC was published in the *London Gazette* on July 28, 1944.

Although three Canadian pilots had received the VC during the First World War (Billy Bishop, Alan MacLeod and Billy Barker), they served in the Royal Flying Corps at the time.

Pilot Officer Hornell had this photograph taken in Toronto on October 4, 1941, nine days after attaining his pilot's wings at No. 12 Elementary Flying Training School in Goderich.

Hornell became one of only four Canadians to earn the VC in the air during the Second World War, all of them posthumously. Hornell and Andrew Mynarski both served in the RCAF, while Ian Bazalgette served in the RAF and Robert Gray was a member of the Royal Canadian Naval Volunteer Reserve (RCNVR), attached to the RN's Fleet Air Arm (FAA). As well, Hornell was the only person from Coastal Command to achieve this honour. The Earl of Athlone, governor general of Canada, presented Hornell's VC to his widow.

David Ernest "Bud" Hornell, was born in Lucknow, Ontario, near Goderich, on January 26, 1910. A few years later, his family moved to Mimico, a Toronto suburb, where he attended John English Public High School, Mimico High School (graduating with honours) and Western Technical School. When he finished school, he worked for the Goodyear Tire and Rubber Company from 1927 to 1940 in Mimico, where he lived with his wife and won praise for his community work with boys. After the war broke out, Hornell enlisted in the RCAF on January 8, 1941, and received his commission as pilot officer later that year. He took his initial flying training at No. 12 Elementary Flying Training School in Goderich, attaining his pilot's wings on September 25, 1941. Chosen for coastal patrol duties, he then attended Course 19 at No. 31 General Reconnaissance School in Charlottetown, PEI, from mid-October to mid-December. Following completion of this training, Hornell went to RCAF Station Coal Lake on northern Vancouver Island.

In 1943, Hornell joined 162 (Bomber Reconnaissance) Squadron, commanded by Wing Commander C. G. W. Chapman. Part of the RCAF's Eastern Air Command, the squadron had been formed at Yarmouth, NS, on May 19, 1942, from the flying-boat detachment of 10 (Bomber Reconnaissance) Squadron, nicknamed "The North Atlantic Squadron." 162 Squadron provided convoy escorts and anti-submarine patrols over Canada's east coast waters and out into the North Atlantic. Its Latin motto, which translates as "We will hunt them even through the lowest deeps," aptly reflected the squadron's goal.

162 Squadron flew the Canso PBY-5A, which was the Canadian version of the Catalina flying boat in service with American forces. Named after a Nova Scotian strait just as the US model had been named after a Californian one, the Canso was a standard Catalina with a wheeled undercarriage attached, creating an amphibious aircraft. About 225 of these flying

boats were built for the RCAF; Hornell's 9754 was built at Boeing's Sea Island plant near Vancouver. The Cansos played a major role in the Battle of the Atlantic, flying from bases in Nova Scotia, Newfoundland, Labrador, Quebec and Iceland. The long-range, twin-engine amphibian could fly about forty-one hundred kilometres on patrol, carrying a seven-to-nine-man crew. The amphibian's sting came from two .30 calibre machine guns in the bow, two .50 calibre machine guns (one on each side), plus 1,814 kilograms of depth charges.

From Yarmouth, 162 Squadron supported detachments at Mont-Joli, Quebec, as well as Gander and Stephenville, Newfoundland, extending its range of anti-submarine duties over the Gulf of St. Lawrence and the east coast. By March 1943 the squadron was up to full strength and, in October, it moved to RCAF Station Dartmouth—Eastern Air Command's largest and most important base—from where Hornell continued to fly endless hours on anti-submarine patrols. In December, Hornell and unit personnel were advised of an overseas deployment and in January 1944 they went to Reykjavik, Iceland, on loan to the RAF's Coastal Command to help cover the mid-ocean part of North Atlantic convoy routes. During January, squadron personnel and aircraft were dispersed between Dartmouth, Goose Bay and Greenland before finally coming together in their new home in Reykjavik.

Coastal Command, in close cooperation with the navy, controlled a number of British, Canadian and American squadrons based in Iceland and Scotland, charged with patrolling northern waters against the ever-present German submarine threat. Under extreme conditions of ice, snow, sleet and fierce gales these units gave sterling service and accounted for many enemy losses. In late May 1944, a detachment from 162 Squadron began transferring to Wick, Scotland (not far from mainland Britain's most northerly point at John O'Groats) to help deal with heavy U-boat activity off Scotland's north coast. Hornell and his crew arrived on June 3.

That month, 162 Squadron had an outstanding run of victories and became the RCAF's most successful bomber reconnaissance squadron of the war. It sighted seven U-boats, sinking five, sharing in the sinking of the sixth and damaging the seventh. And thirty-four-year old Bud Hornell achieved part of that amazing record. Along with other aircrew, he demonstrated that the Battle of the Atlantic, the war's longest campaign, was not won by sea power alone. While warships of the RCN sank thirty German and three Italian submarines, aircraft of the RCAF sent twenty-three U-boats to the bottom, at a cost of 570 airmen and 126 airplanes.

Hornell's crew also received decorations for this action. His co-pilot, Flying Officer B. C. Denomy, received the DSO; Matheson and wireless operator/air gunner Flying Officer G. Campbell were given the Distinguished Flying Cross; Cole and Bodnoff were awarded the Distinguished Flying Medal; and the two sergeants who perished, engineers Scott and St-Laurent, were Mentioned-in-Dispatches. In 1973, Hornell was among the inaugural inductees to Canada's Aviation Hall of Fame, now located at Wetaskiwin, sixty-five kilometres south of Edmonton. His citation noted, "his winning of the Victoria Cross in aerial combat must be regarded as one of the most outstanding contributions to Canadian aviation."

Other honours commemorate Hornell's courageous feat. In 1961, the David Hornell Junior School was built in Toronto, in the neighbourhood where he grew up. The school's coat of arms depicts his Victoria Cross as well as the RCAF albatross, and a replica of Hornell's VC is on permanent display there. In 1977, the Ontario government placed an historical plaque on the school summarizing his deed. Hornell's memory is evoked annually during the school's Remembrance Day ceremonies, and on November 11, 1999, the school opened the David Hornell Gallery. In Weston, Ontario, two organizations keep Hornell's name alive: 700 David Hornell VC Squadron, Royal Canadian Air Cadets, and 442 David Hornell Wing, Royal Canadian Air Force Association. In Goderich, where Hornell commenced his flight training and not far from where he was born, the Huron County Museum has a display in his memory, as well as a special programme for school children to learn about him.

On November 15, 1979, Canada Post issued a stamp as part of its historic aircraft series. It shows Hornell's Canso banking to attack *U-1225*, seen on the surface in the background. At 14 Wing Greenwood in the Annapolis Valley, the Hornell Centre was opened and named after him on May 29, 1980, in a ceremony attended by Minister of National Defence Gilles Lamontagne—a Second World War aircrew survivor—and the Chief of Defence Staff, General Ramsay Withers. The centre is responsible for air traffic control and tracking at eastern Canada's largest airbase, which is home to maritime patrol aircraft. Hornell's name also appears on the RAF Memorial in St. Clement Dane's Church, London, the RAF church, and on a plaque at the Trail, BC, branch of the Royal Canadian Legion.

In March 1991, in the presence of his brother and some of his crew members, David Hornell's VC was loaned to the Canadian Air Force and placed on permanent display in the Bishop Building in Winnipeg, the site of various Canadian Air Force Headquarters over the years. More recently, on June 24, 2001, the fifty-seventh anniversary of Hornell's valour, the Canadian Warplane Heritage Museum at Hamilton International Airport in Ontario dedicated a Consolidated Canso PBY-5A, restored in the colours and markings of 162 Squadron, to his memory. In attendance were several members of Hornell's family and his squadron, including Graham Campbell, one of Hornell's two surviving crewmen.

Lieutenant Robert Hampton Gray
Royal Canadian Naval Volunteer Reserve,
attached Royal Navy Fleet Air Arm, HMS *Formidable*
Onagawa Bay, Japan, August 9, 1945

Robert Hampton Gray stands among the most tragic of Victoria Cross recipients. Gray's act of valour, in which he gave his life, occurred on the same day as the second atomic bomb was dropped on Japan, essentially ending the Second World War and leading to Japan's surrender six days later.

The Canadian war effort in the Pacific Theatre was minimal; Canada's limited resources were concentrated on winning the war against Germany. Even so, the Canadian Army's first battle of the Second World War was against Japan, and it was one of its most disastrous. Two infantry battalions, the Winnipeg Grenadiers and the Royal Rifles of Canada, plus a brigade headquarters, totalling some two thousand soldiers, were virtually wiped out in the fighting that followed the Japanese attack on Hong Kong in December 1941.

The army was involved in other, less well-known actions against Japan. In August 1943, 13 Brigade Group participated with US troops in the invasion of the Aleutian island of Kiska, off the coast of Alaska. The 1st Canada–US Special Service Force (later nicknamed the "Devil's Brigade" by the Germans during fighting in Italy) led the way in its first operation. Unknown to the Allies, the Japanese had withdrawn three weeks earlier, but the Canadians remained for another three months.

In 1944, top secret No. 1 Canadian Special Wireless Group set up in northern Australia to intercept and decrypt Japanese military messages in the Dutch East Indies (now Indonesia). Their work played an integral part in shortening the war in the Pacific Theatre. Another secret group operating in Southeast Asia was Force 136. The unit's commandos, including

Chinese-Canadians, operated behind enemy lines in Malaya (now Malaysia).

On the air side, three RCAF squadrons served in Southeast Asia: No. 413, a general reconnaissance squadron equipped with Consolidated Catalina flying boats, moved to Ceylon (now Sri Lanka) in 1942, and Nos. 435 and 436, transport squadrons that flew Dakotas in support of the British Fourteenth Army in Burma.

Given the RCN's contribution to the Battle of the Atlantic, Canadian naval involvement in the war in the Pacific was minor. As the war in the Atlantic wore down, the cruiser HMCS *Uganda* joined a Royal Navy task force in the western Pacific in March 1945, and participated in operations against the Japanese.

Once the war in Europe ended, Canada planned to contribute a fleet of sixty ships, a bomber force and an infantry division for the final assault against Japan, some eighty thousand men. Volunteers were assembled and began training, but before the force saw action, the US dropped atomic bombs on Hiroshima and Nagasaki. However, many Canadians did participate in the war against Japan, either as members of the armed forces of other countries, notably Britain, or as Canadian servicemen attached to the British Forces. Among these were some of the two hundred naval aviators and observers serving with the RN's Fleet Air Arm (FAA), including Robert Hampton Gray.

"Hammy" Gray was born in Trail, BC, on November 2, 1917, the middle of three children and the son of Boer War veteran and Scottish immigrant John Gray and his Ontarian wife, Wilhelmina. The family moved to Nelson, where the senior Gray continued his jewellery business and Hammy completed elementary school and high school. In the fall of 1936, he entered the University of Alberta at Edmonton and, after two years, transferred to the University of British Columbia, intending to take a pre-med programme leading to a medical degree at Montreal's McGill University. At university, Gray joined a fraternity, became editor of the student yearbook and participated fully in the social side of campus life. A likeable, friendly, relaxed, slightly chubby young man with a great sense of humour, he studiously avoided sports.

In July 1940, Gray and two friends drove to Calgary, where they enlisted in the Royal Canadian Naval Volunteer Reserve as ordinary seamen at HMCS *Tecumseh* because, in Gray's words, "I was getting a little mad at

Hitler." At the time, the RN was accepting selected RCNVR volunteers as potential officer candidates to help with its manpower shortages. Gray and others in the programme were sent to HMCS *Stadacona* in Halifax—the first of Gray's many connections with the city in the course of the war—to await transport to Britain. At Halifax, Gray and the other candidates lived at the Exhibition Grounds in austere accommodations, their boredom broken only by "seemingly endless route marches around Bedford Basin." However, when transport arrived at Halifax space was unavailable for Gray and a few others, who subsequently sailed overseas from Montreal on September 10.

LIEUTENANT "HAMMY" GRAY, RCNVR, WAS THE CANADIAN NAVY'S ONLY RECIPIENT OF THE VICTORIA CROSS, AS WELL AS THE ONLY CANADIAN FIGHTER PILOT TO EARN THE RARE AWARD.

In Britain, the Canadian candidates were sent to HMS *Raleigh* in Cornwall, where they were dismayed to find they would not even be considered for officer selection by an Admiralty board until completion of nearly six months of training as ordinary seamen—three of them at sea, on the lower deck. Salvation came in December in the form of an offer to transfer to the FAA for pilot training, as the Royal Navy's Fleet Air Arm expanded to meet wartime requirements.

Preparatory seamanship training followed immediately at HMS *St. Vincent* at Gosport, and then basic pilot qualification at No. 24 Elementary

Flying Training School at Luton, near London. Gray completed his flying training back in Canada at No. 31 Service Flying Training School at Collins Bay, near Kingston, Ontario, one of many such schools established in Canada under the British Commonwealth Air Training Plan (BCATP), which eventually trained 131,553 aircrew, including over twenty-six hundred FAA pilots. Gray received his naval wings in September 1941 and his commission as a temporary sub-lieutenant in December, backdated to the previous December.

After graduation, Gray travelled to Halifax to await transportation to Britain. His accommodation was in Y Depot (now the site of Windsor Park), crammed with thousands of others in the same situation. With nothing to do, and armed with a year's worth of officer's back pay, Gray and other pilots indulged in some raucous celebrations. Some of their newfound riches paid for the change from their seaman's "square rig" to officers' uniforms.

From Halifax, Gray returned to Britain in late November for operational flying training, including instruction in advanced night flying and carrier landing operations. By now, the FAA was converting to Hurricanes, which had transferred from the RAF as that service re-equipped with Spitfires. In December 1941, mere days after the Japanese attack on Pearl Harbor, Gray wrote in a letter home to his family: "Do tell me all about how this Japanese affair is affecting you. I expect the people in Vancouver are really worried about things. I do hope that nothing occurs there. I don't want them to go through what went on over here."

After operational training, in late February 1942, Gray was posted to 757 Squadron near Winchester, a second-line unit equipped with the Skua, an obsolete, two-seat, fighter/dive bomber used to train naval wireless operators. On March 4, shortly after his arrival, he received word his twenty-one-year-old younger brother Jack, a flight sergeant and wireless operator/air gunner in 144 Squadron, had been killed along with the rest of his crew during a crash of their bomber at Doncaster, in Yorkshire, on February 27; the bomber had been returning from a mine-laying operation over the estuary of Germany's Elbe River. By the time the misdirected message reached him, Jack's funeral had already taken place. Gray visited his brother's grave at Doncaster's Rose Hill Cemetery later that month.

Gray got his wish for a posting to an operational theatre in May 1942, and he sailed for South Africa. After a brief time flying with 789 Squadron there, he joined 795 Squadron, which was equipped with obsolescent

Fulmars and Martlets, at Tanga, Tanganyika, in August. A posting to 803 Squadron, a first-line unit, followed in September; however, as his transfer coincided with the rainy season, the inclement weather curtailed much of the flying. In December, Gray finally got to sea with his new squadron aboard the aircraft carrier HMS *Illustrious*. The end of the month saw his promotion to lieutenant, followed by re-assignment to a newly formed, ten-aircraft Hurricane squadron, 877, which was preparing for deployment to Ceylon. His new squadron flew out of Tanga, a base he knew well. Promotion meant Gray was now the unit's senior pilot and second-in-command.

In July 1943, 877 Squadron moved to a base near Mombasa, in preparation for their move to Ceylon. However, as the war against Japan had forced the Japanese to concentrate their forces in the Pacific and give up their goal of moving into the Indian Ocean and invading Ceylon, the need for British reinforcement of the island colony was diminished. At the end of the year, 877 Squadron received the order to disband. In February 1944, Gray returned to Britain, visited his brother's grave again and was posted to HMCS *Stadacona* at Halifax for ten weeks leave. As he began his leave, a new FAA squadron was being formed at Brunswick, Maine, under Lieutenant-Commander Richard Bigg-Wither, an experienced naval aviator. (The RN often used the USN air station at Brunswick to work up new FAA squadrons coming into service.)

No. 1841 Squadron flew the Chance-Vought Corsair, an American airplane that eventually became the primary fighter of nineteen FAA squadrons. The Corsair, specifically designed for carrier operations, was the fastest aircraft in the fleet and had the greatest range. The Mark IV, which the squadron received in 1945, had a top speed of over 650 kilometres per hour, with a maximum range of twenty-five hundred kilometres and a service ceiling of ten thousand metres. It carried an impressive bomb load of nine hundred kilograms. By the end of the war, the Corsair had flown more operational sorties and destroyed more enemy aircraft than any other FAA fighter.

During the first week of June 1944, while back in Halifax after a visit home, Gray met his closest boyhood friend from Nelson, Peter Dewdney, who was a lieutenant serving aboard a Fairmile anti-submarine motor launch. Dewdney's uncle was Frederick Thornton Peters, whose VC award had been announced in the *London Gazette* a year earlier for leading the suicide attack on the Algerian port of Oran in November 1942 (see Chapter 9). When Gray left Halifax later that month, it marked the last time he saw Canada.

In Britain, he flew with 748 Squadron at Yeovilton for Corsair conversion. Then, on August 6, Gray joined 1841 Squadron, embarked on HMS *Formidable*, an armoured aircraft carrier that had entered service on October 31, 1940. The mission for *Formidable*'s one Corsair and two Barracuda squadrons was to sink the massive, heavily armoured, 47,708-tonne German battleship *Tirpitz*, which was holed up in Norway's Kaafjord. Before Gray joined the unit, its two previous attempts against *Tirpitz* had been unsuccessful; on each occasion the squadron's senior pilot crashed and was made a prisoner of war. Gray was their replacement. He was ecstatic; after four long years of training he was finally going into action.

On August 18, *Formidable* sailed on its third attempt against *Tirpitz*, in the company of two other carriers, *Indefatigable* and *Furious*, escorted by a battleship and destroyer screen. Several attacks were frustrated by bad weather until August 24, when a strike went in through heavy smoke and flak put up by *Tirpitz*, her accompanying Narvik-class destroyers and shore-based batteries. Gray led his Corsair flight in close strafing runs, his .50-calibre machine guns chattering away against flak locations to draw enemy fire away from the Barracudas and other Corsairs attempting to bomb *Tirpitz*. When this task was finished, he attacked a nearby seaplane base and air-fields. Overall, the attack on *Tirpitz* failed, at a cost of four Corsairs and three Barracudas.

Gray was at it again on August 29, as part of another strike of Corsairs and Barracudas. This time, he led his flight in a low-level strafing run through a storm of anti-aircraft fire against three of *Tirpitz*'s protective destroyers, allowing the Barracudas to bomb the battleship. A 1,600-pound bomb hit the warship just forward of the bridge, penetrated eight decks and then, frustratingly, failed to explode. During his run, a 40-millimetre cannon shell hit Gray's Corsair, ripping off most of its rudder and causing other damage. He made it back to *Formidable* and orbited for forty-five minutes, patiently waiting his turn to land. Flak had shot down one Corsair and damaged eleven others.

Gray received a Mention-in-Dispatches "for undaunted courage, skill and determination in carrying out daring attacks on the German battleship *Tirpitz*." As the new boy, joining a tightly knit group of experienced pilots, he had proven himself and gained their respect. *Formidable* returned to Scapa Flow in the Orkney Islands, Scotland; no further FAA attacks were made against *Tirpitz*. Although it was not known at the time, the battleship had already suffered extensive damage below the waterline during various attacks, limiting her sailing options. *Tirpitz* remained off the Norwegian coast, subjected to RAF Lancaster bomber attacks. On November 12, 1944, the attacks finally succeeded: two Tallboys, giant 12,000-pound bombs developed only a few months earlier, scored direct hits and sent *Tirpitz* to the bottom in three minutes.

Meanwhile, *Formidable* embarked in September on a new mission—to join the Pacific Fleet. She carried three squadrons: 1841 and 1842, each with fifteen Corsairs, and 848, with twenty-one Grumman Avengers. The American-built Avenger had replaced the ugly duckling Barracuda, which was a poorly designed, underpowered and unloved aircraft. By contrast, pilots loved their new Avenger torpedo bombers, one of the outstanding naval strike aircraft of the war. Gray and his fellow Corsair pilots also took delivery of a new aircraft. When they got to Colombo, Ceylon, on February 8, 1945, they received the Mark IV version of the fighter, painted in the midnight blue used by the USN. *Formidable* sailed on to Australia, where she continued air training exercises and commenced workups with other ships. She headed north in the company of the Canadian cruiser *Uganda* and two destroyers, and finally joined the British Pacific Fleet (BPF) on April 14.

The sea-going portion of the BPF, designated Task Force 57, was comprised of First Aircraft Carrier Squadron of four veteran Fleet Class carriers under Rear Admiral Sir Philip Vian, supported by two battleships, six cruisers and fifteen destroyers. Vice Admiral Sir Bernard Rawlings commanded the Task Force, which operated as an independent group under the overall control of Admiral Raymond Spruance, commander of the much larger American Fifth Fleet. Previously, the British carriers had been operating separately from the American ones, as the USN felt the British vessels could not function successfully with their own faster, more mobile and better-supported carriers. It took a direct appeal by Prime Minister Churchill to President Roosevelt before the American Navy agreed to work more closely with the BPF.

The entire BPF was smaller than an American task force. Compared to the USN Essex Class carriers, the RN carriers were slower, smaller, carried fewer aircraft and were more restricted in the operation and handling of aircraft. Additionally, their limitations in fuel and storage capacity, coupled with available British logistical support, meant they could only be kept at sea for a maximum of twenty days. In one area however, the British were the envy of their reluctant American allies. Their seventy-six-millimetre thick armoured flight decks were better able to withstand Japanese *kamikaze* attacks with less structural damage and human injury than the USN carriers, which had unarmoured teak planking over light steel and open hangars. Such attacks on American carriers invariably put them out of action for weeks, while British carriers were able to carry on. An American liaison officer aboard one of the RN carriers summed it up nicely: "When a *kamikaze* hits a United States carrier, it's six months' repair at Pearl. In a Limey carrier it's a case of 'Sweepers, man your brooms.'"

Gray went into action on April 16, two days after *Formidable* joined the fleet, by participating in Operation Iceberg off the Sakishima-gunto, a small group of islands midway between Formosa (modern Taiwan) and Okinawa. While the Americans fought it out on Okinawa to the northeast, where they had landed on April 1, British aircraft attempted to prevent Japanese planes from reaching the invasion area. Gray led his flight against targets of opportunity at two airfields, attacking airplanes on the ground and anti-aircraft gun emplacements. Similar attacks continued against other airfields over the next few days.

No matter how hard they were hit, the Japanese always seemed to be able to repair their airfields overnight, and were ready to send aircraft to the battle raging around Okinawa by the next day. In twelve days of operational flying, *Formidable*'s three squadrons lost twenty-nine aircrew, either killed or missing, with nineteen aircraft downed by flak and another twenty-eight by other causes. This left only four aircraft of *Formidable*'s complement of fifty-one fully operational. In return, the British had neutralized the Japanese airfields for various lengths of time and destroyed forty-five of their airplanes.

Before long, *Formidable* experienced her first *kamikaze* attack, unfortunately as a result of a tactical error by Admiral Rawlings. The *kamikaze* (Japanese for "Divine Wind") had been instituted as a last-ditch effort to protect the Home Islands by sending thousands of young volunteers in virtually anything that would fly to crash into Allied warships. Although *kamikazes* were first employed in late 1944 in the battle for the Philippines, their first mass attacks, known as *kikusui* (literally "floating chrysanthemums"), had only taken place a month earlier.

On one occasion, Rawlings detached the majority of the ships in his protective screen, leaving only one cruiser and six destroyers as plane guard and screen—insufficient to provide adequate radar and anti-aircraft coverage for the carriers. The remainder of the British ships sailed to conduct a surface bombardment of Sakishima-gunto's airfields, in support of air strikes. Rawlings did it with the best of intentions, hoping to improve the morale of the escort force by sending them into action. It was a decision he would regret for the rest of his life.

HMS *FORMIDABLE* EXPERIENCED SEVERAL KAMIKAZE ATTACKS IN WHICH IT SUFFERED SEVERE DAMAGE, BUT WITHSTOOD THEM ALL. SAILORS CLEAN UP AFTER A HEAVY ATTACK, AS THE SHIP MAKES SMOKE TO DISORIENT POTENTIAL ATTACKERS.

In the absence of most of *Formidable*'s protective escorts, a Japanese Zeke dive bomber crashed into the flight deck beside the carrier's island and detonated a 225-kilogram bomb. The force of the explosion drove a piece of shrapnel down through all decks to a fuel tank in her hull, puncturing a steam line on the way. Additional explosions followed, causing fires that blackened the island. By the time damage-control crews managed to check the fires, eleven aircraft were destroyed and eight sailors killed, with another forty-seven injured, many with severe burns. Yet, in less than six hours, *Formidable* was ready once again to launch her aircraft. It was a sobering experience for her ship's company; previously only aircrew had experienced at first hand the devastating results of the determined Japanese defence of their homeland. Rawlings learned an unforgettable lesson about carrier operations as well.

On May 9, *Formidable* suffered another *kamikaze* attack as a Japanese airplane crashed onto the flight deck, causing explosions and fires, some of which spread to the hangar deck. This attack destroyed seven aircraft and damaged another two, while casualties were limited to one dead and several injured. In less than an hour, the carrier was able to launch aircraft. Then, an accidental fire on May 18 further reduced her serviceable air fleet to eleven Corsairs and four Avengers. *Formidable* subsequently returned to Australia for much-needed repairs and aircraft replacement.

After repairs and replenishment, the British Pacific Fleet—less one carrier—rejoined the Americans in July. This time the fleet was designated Task Force 37 and assigned to the USN Third Fleet under the legendary Admiral Bull Halsey, who was the antithesis of the quiet and unassuming Admiral Spruance. Halsey had been given clear instructions to "attack Japanese naval and air forces, shipping, shipyards and coastal objectives." The combined American and British fleets mustered over fifteen hundred aircraft—fighters, dive bombers and torpedo planes.

They faced a battered yet formidable foe. In mid-1945 the Japanese still had over ten thousand available aircraft and five thousand dedicated *kamikaze* pilots. Although they had not been able to prevent the US invasion of Okinawa, *kamikazes* destroyed over thirty ships and damaged two hundred others, inflicting several thousand casualties in the process. Each of *Formidable*'s Corsair squadrons had been increased by two aircraft, while her Avenger squadron was reduced to twelve. A new addition was a detachment of six Grumman Hellcat fighters, a match for every opposing Japanese fighter. Of the sixty-five hundred Japanese aircraft which USN pilots claimed to have shot down, nearly five thousand of these were accounted for by Hellcats.

By mid-July, the combined American and British naval fleets arrived at a launch area some two hundred kilometres northeast of Tokyo, and began air attacks against airfields and targets of opportunity on the Japanese Home Islands. Anti-shipping runs—one of Lieutenant Gray's specialties—were among the more lucrative occasional targets. Gray flew several fighter-bomber missions, known as Ramrods, leading his flight in low-level strafing and bombing runs over Honshu. *Formidable*'s first attack was against Niigata, on the west coast of northern Honshu, and it achieved complete surprise. Several Ramrods took place over the following days, though bad weather interfered with the schedule of missions. Although the attacks were mostly successful, they took a heavy toll in pilots and aircraft from determined Japanese anti-aircraft fire.

During a Ramrod on July 28, Gray was leading a low-level strike against a naval base north of Kyoto when he bombed a Japanese destroyer: his direct hit set it afire and sent it to the bottom. Admiral Vian, commanding the British carriers, sent him a congratulatory message praising his conduct in the action. On August 31, the award of the DSC to Gray for "determination and address in air attacks on targets in Japan on the 18th, 24th and 28th of July 1945" was announced.

Two days later, flying was suspended for more than a week as rough seas and cloudy skies precluded operations. The fleet took the opportunity to carry out replenishment at sea and repair its damaged aircraft in preparation for renewed assaults against the Japanese. On August 6, as Allied flying operations in the area remained curtailed, an American B-29 took off on a mission that changed warfare—and the world—forever. The *Enola Gay* dropped an atomic bomb on Hiroshima, instantly incinerating thousands of people and buildings in a blinding flash of light. The atomic age had begun.

Although it was obvious that the war would shortly end, Allied operations continued against the Japanese, but with a caveat: pilots were instructed not to take unnecessary chances; in particular they were to make only one run at each target. Three days later, on August 9, the British Pacific Fleet was 260 kilometres east of northern Honshu, preparing for operations against several airfields on the island. *Formidable*'s fighter wing was assigned three Ramrods, directed at the airfields of Shiogama and Matsushima. Lieutenant-Commander Bigg-Wither led the twelve Corsairs of Ramrod One, followed by Gray leading the remaining eight in Ramrod Two.

At 8:00 A.M., Ramrod Two started to launch—two flights of four Corsairs, each carrying two 500-pound bombs. They climbed to their flying altitude of three thousand metres, and then headed towards Honshu. The Corsairs made landfall about 9:20 and turned south towards Matsushima Bay, near one of the target airfields. As they flew southwards, they passed over Onagawa Bay, surrounded by steep hills on three sides. Several ships rested at anchor in the bay, including a suspected destroyer.

Ramrod Two flew on to Matsushima airfield, where there was little flak to meet the Corsairs. As earlier Ramrods had already hit the area, Gray decided to make a low-level attack against the shipping in Onagawa Bay. He intended to make his bombing approach from inland at three thousand metres, dive down into the lone valley leading to the bay for maximum cover from Japanese anti-aircraft fire and escape seawards at surface height. After the attack, the Corsairs would rendezvous at Itzu Shima, a small island a few kilometres to the north. The low-level bombing run would only take four seconds.

The Japanese defenders had clearly recognized Gray's approach route as the most likely one and positioned their shore-based anti-aircraft guns accordingly. Similarly, gun crews on the various ships anticipated such an attack and kept their eyes—and their weapons—trained landwards. Gray

WHEN HE FOUND NO TARGETS AT A JAPANESE AIRFIELD ON HONSHU ISLAND, GRAY DECIDED TO MAKE A LOW-LEVEL ATTACK AGAINST THE SHIPPING IN ONAGAWA BAY. HE MADE HIS BOMBING APPROACH FROM INLAND AT 3,000 METRES, DOVE DOWN INTO THE LONE VALLEY LEADING TO THE BAY FOR MAXIMUM COVER FROM JAPANESE ANTI-AIRCRAFT FIRE AND COMMENCED HIS STRAFING RUN.

led the opening attack run, coming in low amid a hail of intense anti-aircraft fire from the nine-hundred-tonne ocean escort *Amakusa*, the destroyer *Ohama*, Minesweeper 33 and Subchaser 42. Bullets and shells streamed towards him, knocking off one of his bombs and setting his airplane on fire. However, Gray kept steady on his course, fifteen metres above the water, and dropped his remaining bomb from only forty-five metres away.

By now, smoke and flames were streaming from Gray's Corsair. As he passed over *Amakusa*, his bomb struck the vessel amidships, below a port gun platform. It smashed through the hull and crashed into the engine room, where it exploded, instantly killing forty sailors in the confined space. The force of the blast ripped into a nearby ammunition magazine, which blew up, taking out a large part of the starboard hull. *Amakusa* listed to that side and began to sink. Gray continued seawards, his Corsair completely enveloped in heavy smoke and flames. Then his aircraft slowly turned to starboard, rolled over on its back and disappeared into the water in a violent burst of spray. Someone called out "There goes Gray" over the radio. As *Amakusa*'s list worsened, a bugle sounded abandon ship, while the following Corsairs strafed the burning wreck and the surviving crewmen. Those who were able leapt into the water. At 9:45, the ship went under, taking another thirty-one crewmen with it.

The seven remaining Corsairs, their pilots badly shaken at the loss of their leader, rendezvoused over Itzu Shima as planned. They made two more attacks on shipping in the bay, contrary to doctrine, but a mixture of anger, apprehension and grief drove them to return. They sank *Ohama*, badly damaged the minesweeper and safely returned to *Formidable*. In all, 157 Japanese perished in the attack. About two hours later, the Americans dropped their second atomic bomb, this time on Nagasaki. The Japanese accepted the Allied terms of surrender the next day.

Admiral Vian, Captain P. Ruck-Keene (*Formidable*'s commander) and Lieutenant-Commander Bigg-Wither met shortly afterwards to discuss how to recognize Gray's gallantry and, by extension, that of all Canadians killed while serving in the BPF. With either a Mention-in-Dispatches or the Victoria Cross as the only possibilities for a posthumous award, they unanimously agreed on the latter as the suitable honour. Vian's recommendation for the award observed, "I have in mind firstly the brilliant fighting spirit and inspired leadership; an unforgettable example of selfless and sustained devotion to duty without regard to safety of life and limb." He went on to note the role of the BCATP in the war, "The award of this highly prized and highly regarded recognition of valour may fittingly be conferred on a native of Canada, which Dominion has played so great a part in the training of our airmen."

The announcement of Gray's VC was published in the *London Gazette* on November 13. In February 1946, the Earl of Athlone, governor general of Canada, presented Gray's VC to his parents in Ottawa. Today it is on loan to the Canadian War Museum. In the museum's Hall of Honour, Gray is one of over forty heroes from Canada's military history who is show-cased. Also in Ottawa, a statue of Gray is one of *The Valiants*, a series of fourteen statues of Canada's greatest war heroes, scheduled tto be unveiled in 2006. Other tributes also mark his bravery. On October 29, 1952, Gray's mother, Wilhelmina, then a widow, opened the Hampton Gray Memorial School for the children of servicemen at the home of Canadian naval avia-tion, HMCS *Shearwater*, outside of Dartmouth.

Naval aviation in Canada had started at the base during the closing months of the First World War, when Acting Lieutenant-Commander Richard E. Byrd, United States Navy—who later gained international renown as a polar explorer—established a seaplane base there to search for German submarines prowling off the Nova Scotian coast. A fledgling, and short-lived, Royal Canadian Naval Air Service used the facilities and equip-ment Byrd left behind. One of his seaplane hangars, known as Y hangar, is still in use today by a naval diving unit.

After the decommissioning of *Formidable* in 1947 and before it was scrapped in 1953, the ship's bell was donated to the Hampton Gray Memorial School. Today, the school is known as the Hampton Gray Memorial Centre and houses various 12 Wing Shearwater organizations, such as a Military Family Resource Centre, French Language Training Centre and Canadian Forces Exchange. *Formidable*'s bell has been relocat-ed to the Shearwater Aviation Museum's Victoria Cross Memorial Gallery, where David Hornell and Hammy Gray, Canada's two naval aviation VC recipients, are honoured.

In Gray's hometown of Nelson, the federal government building was named the Gray Building when it opened in 1956. Some twenty years later, a bureaucratic oversight resulted in it being renamed the Federal Building. However, local citizens complained and, in 1980, it was officially rededicat-ed to Gray. The Gyro Park in Nelson also commemorates Gray's deed in a memorial at the park's entrance, while the city's Sea Cadets and a swimming pool also bear his name. A few kilometres north of Nelson, in Kokanee Glacier Provincial Park, a majestic mountain was named Gray's Peak shortly after the war in 1946, in memory of brothers Jack and Hammy, the first and last Nelson natives to die in the war.

In neighbouring Alberta, where Hammy enlisted, a lake 165 kilometres north of Edmonton was named Gray Lake in 1983. In 1974, Gray was inducted into Canada's Aviation Hall of Fame, the first naval officer to be so honoured, while the Canadian Warplane Heritage Museum, outside of Hamilton, displays a Chance Vought Corsair Mark IV, carrying the markings of Gray's aircraft. In 1988, the Naval Museum of Alberta, the largest museum of its kind in Canada, opened in Calgary. It is based on HMCS *Tecumseh*, where Gray enlisted almost fifty years earlier, and is dedicated to his memory. In 1992, a plaque was unveiled in Collins Bay, near Kingston, in honour of Gray and the twenty-three pilots killed during flying training there. In Ottawa, the local branch of the Canadian Naval Air Group, an organization that perpetuates the traditions and ideals of the Royal Canadian Naval Air Arm, is named the Hampton Gray Chapter. Finally, like all Canadian sailors who lost their lives in the war and who have no known grave, Gray's name is engraved on the Sailors' Memorial in Halifax's Point Pleasant Park.

Other memorials to Gray are far away from Canada. In Elgin, Scotland, the home of the original FAA base, "Gray's Walk" runs through the married quarters. In the churchyard of the village of Brechin, also in his ancestral homeland, a Gray family memorial honours Hammy as well as his brother, Jack.

Today, a simple granite cairn stands on top of a low hill in Sakiyama Peace Park, overlooking Onagawa Bay, directly opposite the site where Gray's Corsair crashed. Erected by the Japanese in 1989, it is the only known instance of a monument honouring an Allied serviceman in all of Japan. It seems somehow fitting that such a memorial should recognize the gallantry of the war's—and Canada's—last Victoria Cross recipient.

EPILOGUE

When the Victoria Cross was instituted there were few means of recognizing courage on the battlefield, and most were unavailable to junior officers, senior NCOs or other ranks. Traditionally, bravery in action could be honoured in one of three ways: promotion by brevet (i.e. without the pay of the higher rank), Mention-in-Dispatches and appointment to the Order of the Bath (available only for officers over a certain rank). The army's Distinguished Conduct Medal and the navy's Conspicuous Gallantry Medal—both established during the Crimean War—were, for the longest time, the only awards that could be given to non-officers for distinguished service. Over the years, a number of additional awards were created such as the Distinguished Service Order, Military Cross and Military Medal. Other awards for bravery not in the face of the enemy, such as the Albert Medal, George Cross and George Medal, were also instituted, along with various life-saving medals.

Many of the deeds for which a VC was awarded in its early days would certainly have been recognized by one of these other medals if they had been in existence at the time. This is not to denigrate the valour of some of the early recipients, but simply to reinforce a point: over the years, the VC has become harder to earn. Perhaps the most telling figures to illustrate this point are those for the Indian Mutiny and the Second World War. Virtually the same number of VCs were awarded for each (182 versus 181 respectively), yet the Indian Mutiny lasted just thirteen months, saw under three hundred thousand British and Indian troops deployed only on land and was confined to a small area of the sub-continent. On the other hand, the Second World War lasted seventy-two months, saw nearly four million troops deployed from the six major countries of the Empire alone (Britain, India, Australia, Canada, New Zealand and South Africa) on land, sea and air and was global in reach. A soldier in the Indian Mutiny had roughly a one in 1,593 chance of earning a VC, while in the Second World War the odds were one in 21,668. Put another way, for every VC awarded during the Second World War, thirteen were awarded during the Indian Mutiny.

It was also generally easier to earn a VC early in a war: the first individual to single-handedly charge an enemy machine-gun nest was far more likely to receive the VC than the fifty-first. An individual was also more likely to earn a VC if he were an officer rather than a soldier. Officers, by virtue of their positions, had much more freedom of movement than ordinary soldiers and more control over their own destinies. An officer could often decide whether or not he was going to be brave, while a man in the ranks was often carried along in an action to whatever fate awaited him. On a lesser scale, the same applied to senior NCOs, especially when acting in an officer's appointment, either due to manpower shortages or because the officers immediately involved were killed or otherwise taken out of action. Table 4, which shows the ranks of Canada's ninety-eight VC recipients, illustrates this point. Although there were thousands more other ranks in combat than officers, fifty-four recipients were officers, while forty-four were other ranks.

ARMY		NAVY		AIR FORCE	
Pte	17				
L/Cpl	3				
Cpl (inc A/Cpl)	9	AS	1		
L/Sgt	1				
Sgt(inc A/Sgt)	10				
CSM/WO II	3				
2Lt	1			Plt Offr	1
Lt (inc Asst Surg & T/Lt	24	Lt (inc T/Lt)	2	Lt	1
Capt (inc Surg, T/Capt & H/Capt)	10			Capt or F/Lt	2
Maj (inc T/Maj & A/Maj)	6			A/Maj or A/Sqn Ldr	2
Lt-Col (inc T/Lt-Col)	4				
		A/Capt	1		
Subtotal	88	4		6	
Total	98				

Table 4. Ranks of Canadian VC recipients.(A/=Acting, T/=Temporary, H/=Honorary)

Although many VC recipients went on to achieve high rank, earning a VC was not a guarantee of success in later life. Some recipients, like Filip Konowal, hit rock bottom. Seventeen committed suicide, eleven spent their final years in workhouses, five died in mental asylums and two, or possibly three, were murdered. After surviving the dangers of combat, another forty-one died in road, railway or riding accidents.

There have been a number of attempts to pinpoint what particular traits or background inspires a man to the bravery that earns a VC, without success. VC recipients have come from throughout the Empire and Commonwealth (as well as the fourteen mentioned in the Introduction who were non-British subjects), from families small and large, high and low. They have been born into families that produced generations of military men and those that have not. Some have been professional soldiers, while many others were conscripts or had joined for the particular war of the moment. Many have been superb athletes, while many more have not.

In short, there is no common link connecting the 1,351 individuals who have earned the Victoria Cross. It could simply be that, somewhat akin to lightning striking, earning a VC is a matter of being at the right place at the right time. How any particular individual will actually react in a real battle situation is not something that can be predicted, although even today it remains a prime objective of all military training. We can only hope that should Canada ever go to war again, our military men and women will display the same gallantry in battle that their forbears did.

Just as the VC has become harder to earn, it should be noted that larger percentages are posthumous. While thirty percent of First World War VCs were posthumous, this number rises to forty-eight percent for the Second World War. Some authorities had even speculated a VC would never be awarded again or, if it were, it would certainly be posthumously. Many did not subscribe to this particular logic—after all, what is the point of having a medal or decoration if it can never be awarded? In any case, the doubters were recently proven wrong by the first award of a Victoria Cross to a living recipient in thirty-six years. On April 28, 2005, Queen Elizabeth pinned the VC on twenty-five-year-old Private Johnson Gideon Beharry for two separate actions during the Second Gulf War in May and June of 2004. At the time, Beharry, of the 1st Battalion, Princess of Wales's Royal Regiment, was the driver of a thirty-tonne Warrior infantry fighting vehicle, and displayed extraordinary courage under fire to save his comrades from ambush. In the violence-wracked town of Al-Amarah, he single-handedly saved thirty fellow soldiers in one attack and, six weeks later, repeated his heroics and successfully backed his vehicle out of another ambush, suffering serious injuries on both occasions.

Perhaps the time has come for Canada to award its own unique Canadianized VC (described in the Introduction) by emulating Britain and the United States. In May 2000, after many years of effort by the Royal Canadian Legion, Canada at long last repatriated the remains of an unidentified soldier of the First World War from Vimy Ridge in France and reinterred him with great ceremony in Ottawa, in front of the National War Memorial. He lies there today as Canada's Unknown Soldier, his tomb a visible symbol of all of Canada's sons and daughters killed in many conflicts, both in war and peace. What more fitting tribute than to award the Unknown Soldier with the first "Canadian" Victoria Cross, in effect honouring the bravery of all who fought for Canada since its creation?

It is a proposal worthy of consideration.

TOMB OF THE UNKNOWN SOLDIER

APPENDIX 1

VICTORIA CROSS RECIPIENTS ASSOCIATED WITH ATLANTIC CANADA

(* denotes posthumous award; A/=Acting, T/=Temporary)

Name/Rank/Unit	Place/Date of Birth	Place/Date of VC	Place/Date of Death
Crimean War			
Commerell, Cdr John Edmund			
HMS *Weser*, Royal Navy	London, England Jan 13, 1829	Putrid Sea, Russia Oct 11, 1855	London, England May 21, 1901
Indian Mutiny			
Hall, Able Seaman William Neilson			
HMS *Shannon*, Naval Brigade, Royal Navy	Horton Bluff, NS Apr 25, 1829	Lucknow, India Nov 16, 1857	Hantsport, NS Aug 25, 1904
McMaster, Asst Surg Valentine Munbee			
78th Regiment of Foot, British Army	Trinchinopoly, India May 16, 1834	Lucknow, India Sep 25, 1857	Belfast, Ireland Jan 22, 1872
Boer War			
Nickerson, Lt William Henry Snyder			
Royal Army Medical Corps attached Mounted Infantry, British Army	Dorchester, NB Mar 21, 1875	Wakkerstroom, South Africa Apr 20, 1900	Cours, Scotland Apr 10, 1954
First World War			
*Bent, T/Lt-Col Philip Eric			
9th Bn, the Leicestershire Regt, British Army	Halifax, NS Jan 3, 1891	Polygon Wood, Belgium Oct 1, 1917	Polygon Wood, Belgium Oct 1, 1917

Name/Rank/Unit	Place/Date of Birth	Place/Date of VC	Place/Date of Death

First World War continued

*Croak, Pte John Bernard

13th Bn, CEF	Little Bay, NL	Amiens, France	Amiens, France
	May 18, 1892	Aug 8, 1918	Aug 8, 1918

Dobson, Cdr Claude Congreve

CMB 31, Royal Navy	Bristol, England	Kronstadt, Russia	Chatham, England
	Jan 1, 1885	Aug 18, 1919	June 26, 1940

Forbes-Robertson, A/Lt-Col James

1st Bn, The Border Regt,	Cheltenham, England	Near Vieux Berquin,	Bourton-on-the-
British Army	July 7, 1884	France	Water, England
		Apr 11–12, 1918	Aug 5, 1955

Good, Cpl Herman James

13th Bn, CEF	South Bathurst, NB	Hangard Wood,	Bathurst, NB
	Nov 29, 1887	France	Apr 18, 1969
		Aug 8, 1918	

Gregg, Lt Milton Fowler

The Royal Canadian Regt,	Mountain Dale, NB	Near Cambrai,	Fredericton, NB
CEF	Apr 10, 1892	France	Mar 13, 1978
		Sep 27–Oct 1, 1918	

Kerr, Pte John Chipman

49th Bn, CEF	Fox River, NS	Courcelette, France	Port Moody, BC
	Jan 11, 1887	Sep 16, 1916	Feb 19, 1963

Metcalf, LCpl William Henry

16th Bn, CEF	Waite Township, ME	Arras, France	South Portland, ME
	Jan 29, 1894	Sep 2, 1918	Aug 8, 1968

Peck, Lt-Col Cyrus Wesley

16th Bn, CEF	Hopewell Hill, NB	Villers-lez-	Sidney, BC
	Apr 26, 1871	Cagnicourt, France	Sep 27, 1956
		Sep 2, 1918	

Ricketts, Pte Thomas

1st Bn, R Nfld R, British Army	Middle Arm, NF	Ledgehem, Belgium	St John's, NF
	Apr 15, 1901	Oct 14, 1918	Feb 10, 1967

Name/Rank/Unit	Place/Date of Birth	Place/Date of VC	Place/Date of Death

First World War continued

*Robertson, Pte James Peter

27th Bn, CEF	Albion Mines, NS	Passchendaele,	Passchendaele,
	Oct 26, 1883	Belgium	Belgium
		Nov 6, 1917	Nov 6, 1917

Ryder, Pte Robert Edward

12th Bn, The Middlesex Regt	Harefield, England	Thiepval, France	Hucknall, Engalnd
(Duke of Cambridge's Own),	Dec 17, 1895	Sep 26, 1916	Dec 1, 1978
British Army			

Stuart, Lt Ronald Neil

HMS *Pargust*,	Liverpool, England	Atlantic Ocean	Charing,
Royal Naval Reserve	Aug 26, 1886	June 7, 1917	England
			Feb 8, 1954

Second World War

*Fegen, A/Capt Edward Stephen Fogarty

| HMS *Jervis Bay*, | Southsea, England, | Atlantic Ocean | Atlantic Ocean |
| Royal Navy | Oct 8, 1891 | Nov 5, 1940 | Nov 5, 1940 |

*Gray, Lt Robert Hampden

Royal Canadian Naval	Trail, BC	Onagawa Bay,	Onagawa Bay,
Volunteer Reserve,	Nov 2, 1917	Honshu, Japan	Honshu, Japan
HMS *Formidable*,		Aug 9, 1945	Aug 9, 1945
attached Royal Navy Fleet			
Air Arm			

*Hornell, F-Lt David Ernest

162 Sqn,	Mimico, ON	Near Faroe Is,	Near Faroe Is,
Royal Canadian Air Force	Jan 26, 1910	North Atlantic	North Atlantic
		June 24, 1944	June 25, 1944

*Peters, A/Capt Frederick Thornton

| HMS *Walney*, Royal Navy | Charlottetown, PE | Oran, Algeria | Plymouth, England |
| | Sep 17, 1889 | Nov 8, 1942 | Nov 13, 1942 |

Appendix 2

Viewing a Victoria Cross
in Atlantic Canada

Details of VCs Held or Displayed
in Atlantic Canada

As of 2005, there were three VCs held in Atlantic Canada, while several museums display replicas. William Hall's VC and other medals are owned by the Province of Nova Scotia but are not usually on public display. An exception was made in February 2005, when they were displayed in the Maritime Museum of the Atlantic for Black Heritage Month. The medals are ordinarily held by the Nova Scotia Museum under the control of the Speaker of the Legislative Assembly. Meanwhile, John Croak's VC is owned by the Army Museum–Halifax Citadel, where it and his other medals are displayed.

One other VC is held in Atlantic Canada, though it did not belong to someone who was born in the region. Captain Coulson Norman Mitchell, from Winnipeg, earned his VC during the First World War on the night of October 8–9, 1918, during an attack near Cambrai, France. He was serving with the 4th Canadian Engineer Battalion, and is the only member of the Royal Canadian Engineers to be so honoured. Mitchell led a small group of sappers ahead of the main infantry assault wave to check out three bridges across a canal. Finding the main bridge prepared for demolition by the Germans, he and a sergeant dashed across it and began cutting the wires. Suddenly, three enemy bridge guards began firing on them. No sooner were these guards dispatched then the Germans attacked, whom Mitchell and his men also repelled. Mitchell then removed the demolition charges and successfully prevented the Germans from blowing up the bridge, maintaining the small bridgehead until reinforcements arrived at dawn. Mitchell's VC is on display at the Canadian Military Engineer Museum located in building J-10, the Mitchell Building (named after him), at the Canadian Forces School of Military Engineering at Canadian Forces Base Gagetown, in New Brunswick.

Several museums in Atlantic Canada have displays honouring the region's VC winners, many of them including replicas of the medal. Besides Croak's medals, the Army Museum–Halifax Citadel displays reproductions of the VCs and medals groups of the other ten VC recipients born in Atlantic Canada. Hall's medals are profiled in the Black Cultural Centre in Preston and the Shearwater Aviation Museum in Dartmouth. The Aviation Museum also contains reproductions of the VCs of David Hornell and Robert Gray in its Victoria Cross Memorial Gallery. Replicas of Milton Gregg's VC and other medals are displayed at the Vimy Branch of the Royal Canadian Legion, Halifax.

The Canadian Forces Base Gagetown Military Museum has a VC Hallway containing drawings of all Canadian VC recipients, along with descriptions of their deeds. In Charlottetown, the Naval Reserve Division, HMCS *Queen Charlotte*, is housed in a building named after and dedicated to Frederick Peters in 1997. It contains a display which relates the story of his life and features a replica of his VC. In St. John's, the Royal Newfoundland Regiment has a display showing the details of Thomas Ricketts's VC and other awards. Additionally, several small museums throughout Atlantic Canada have exhibits about VC recipients.

Image Sources

The Army Medical Services Museum 7, 22, 34, 63

John Boileau 103, 129, 173, 188, 190, 256

Joan Cervin 78

Dolda Clarke 199, 206

Jerry Kean, Army Museum–Halifax Citadel 1, 3, 169

Library and Archives Canada 2, 10, 16, 19, 54, 81, 85, 87, 109, 110, 112, 115, 122, 125, 128, 130, 131, 141, 142, 145, 150, 154, 161, 165, 170, 171, 172, 180 (© Library and Archives Canada. Reproduced with the permission of the Minister of Public Works and Government Services Canada, 2005. Source: Library and Archives Canada/National Film Board of Canada/Phototheque Collection/PA-197736), 213, 233, 239,

Nova Scotia Archives and Records Management 36, 39, 51

PPCLI Museum 14

The Royal Leicestershire Regiment Museum 104

Shearwater Aviation Museum 231, 245, 248

Brenda Wood 95, 98

BIBLIOGRAPHY

Andrews, Allen. *Brave Soldiers, Proud Regiments: Canada's Military Heritage.* Vancouver: Ronsdale, 1997.

Arthur, Max. *Symbol of Courage: The Men behind the Medal.* London: Pan, 2005.

Bacon, D. A. *The History of the 110th Brigade.* Unpublished typescript memoir. Leicestershire Record Office, Wigston Magna, England.

Bishop, Arthur. *Canada's Military Heritage.* Vol. 2, *Courage on the Battlefield.* Toronto: McGraw-Hill Ryerson, 1993.

———. *Canada's Military Heritage.* Vol. 3, *Courage at Sea.* Toronto: McGraw-Hill Ryerson, 1995.

———. *Our Bravest and Our Best: The Stories of Canada's Victoria Cross Winners,* Toronto: McGraw-Hill Ryerson, 1995.

Blakeley, Phyllis R. *Glimpses of Halifax 1867–1900.* Facsimile edition. Belleville: Mika, 1973.

Blatherwick, Francis John. *1,000 Brave Canadians: The Canadian Gallantry Awards 1854–1989.* Toronto: Unitrade, 1991.

Buzzell, Nora, comp. *The Register of the Victoria Cross.* Cheltenham: This England, 1988.

Cave, Joy B. *Two Newfoundland VCs.* St. John's: Creative, 1984.

Cave, Nigel. *Battleground Europe: Somme—Beaumont Hamel.* London: Leo Cooper, 1994.

Collier, Richard. *The Great Indian Mutiny: A Dramatic Account of the Sepoy Rebellion.* New York: E. P. Dutton, 1964.

Dunmore, Spencer. *In Great Waters: The Epic Story of the Battle of the Atlantic 1939-45.* Toronto: McClelland & Stewart, 1999.

Dupuy, R. Ernest, and Trevor N. Dupuy. *The Collins Encyclopedia of Military History from 3500 BC to the Present.* Fourth Edition. London: BCA, 1994.

Eber, Dorothy Harley. *Genius at Work: Images of Alexander Graham Bell.* Toronto: McClelland & Stewart, 1982.

Edwardes, Michael. *A Season in Hell: The Defence of the Lucknow Residency.* London: Hamish Hamilton, 1973.

Farwell, Byron. *Queen Victoria's Little Wars*. New York: Harper & Row, 1972.

Fetherstonhaugh, R. C. *The Royal Canadian Regiment*. Vol. 1, *1883-1933*. Montreal: Gazette, 1936.

———. *The 13th Battalion Royal Highlanders of Canada, 1914—1919*. Toronto: 13th Battalion, 1925.

Fitzgerald, Jack. *Beyond Belief: Incredible Stories of Old St. John's*. St. John's: Creative, 2001.

Fox, Brent. *The Captain Calls: 300 Years of Nova Scotia Military History*. Hantsport, NS: Lancelot, 1993.

Gilbert, Martin. *First World War*. London: Weidenfield & Nicolson, 1994.

Gliddon, Gerald. *The Battle of the Somme: A Topographical History*. Sutton: Stroud, 1998.

Golding, Capt. J. H. "The VC Centenary." *Canadian Army Journal*. Vol. 10, No. 4 (October 1956).

Harris, John. *The Indian Mutiny*. London: Hart-Davis, MacGibbon, 1973.

Harvey, David. *Monuments to Courage: Victoria Cross Headstones and Memorials*. Bahrain: Kevin and Kay Patience, 1999.

Hibbert, Christopher. *The Great Mutiny: India 1857*. London: Allen Lane, 1978.

Hunt, M. Stuart, comp. and ed. *Nova Scotia's Part in the Great War*. Halifax: Nova Scotia Veteran Publishing, 1920.

Kemp, Lt.-Cdr. P. K. *H.M. Destroyers*. London: Herbert Jenkins, 1956.

Lee, Emanoel. *To the Bitter End: A Photographic History of the Boer War 1899–1902*. London: Penguin, 1986.

London Gazette. Various editions.

Luciuk, Lubomyr Y., and Ron Sorobey. *Konowal*. Kingston & Kyiv: Kashtan, 1996.

MacDonald, F. B., and John J. Gardiner. *The Twenty-Fifth Battalion Canadian Expeditionary Force: Nova Scotia's Famous Regiment in World War One*. Sydney: City Printers, 1983.

MacGowan, S. Douglas, Harry Heckbert and Byron O'Leary. *New Brunswick's "Fighting 26th": A History of the 26th New Brunswick Battalion, CEF 1914–1919*. Saint John: Neptune, 1994.

Machum, Col. George C. *Canada's VCs.* Toronto: McClelland & Stewart, 1956.

MacLellan, C. Roger. *Wave an Arm, "Follow Me!" The Wartime Experiences of a CANLOAN Platoon Commander.* Hantsport, NS: Lancelot, 1993.

Malleson, Col. G. B. *History of the Indian Mutiny, 1857–1858.* Vol. 2. London: Allen, 1879.

Manning, Capt. T. D. *The British Destroyer.* London: Godfrey Cave Associates, 1961.

Marteinson, John. *We Stand on Guard: An Illustrated History of the Canadian Army.* Montreal: Ovale, 1992.

Martin, Stuart. *The Story of the Thirteenth Battalion, 1914–1919.* London: Charles, 1918.

McCarthy, A. J. *Bay of Chaleur Forgotten Treasures.* Halifax: Nimbus, 1997.

———. *The Bay of Chaleur at War: From Vimy Ridge to Vietnam.* Halifax: Nimbus, 1998.

McWilliams, James, and R. James Steel. *Amiens: Dawn of Victory.* Toronto: Dundurn, 2001.

Miller, Carman. *Painting the Map Red: Canada and the South African War, 1899–1902.* Montreal & Kingston: McGill-Queen's University Press, 1993.

Morrow, R. A. H. *The Story of the Springhill Colliery Disaster.* Saint John: Morrow, 1891.

Mulholland, John, and Alan Jordan, eds. *Victoria Cross Bibliography.* London: Spink, 1999.

Nicholson, Col. G. W. L. *The Fighting Newfoundlander.* London: Nelson, 1964.

———. *Canada's Nursing Sisters.* Toronto: A. M. Hakkert, 1975.

Pachai, Bridglal. *William Hall: Winner of the Victoria Cross.* Tantallon, NS: Four East, 1995.

Parkin, J. H. *Bell and Baldwin: Their Development of Aerodromes and Hydrodromes at Baddeck, Nova Scotia.* Toronto: University of Toronto, 1964.

Perkins, J. David, comp. and ed. *CC Dobson, VC, DSO, RN.* Dartmouth, NS: Seaboot, 1991.

Philby, Kim. *My Silent War.* New York: Grove, 1968.

Raddall, Thomas H. *West Novas: A History of the West Nova Scotia Regiment.* Liverpool, NS: self-published, 1947.

Richardson, Matthew. *The Tigers: 6th, 7th, 8th & 9th (Service) Battalions of the Leicester Regiment.* Barnsley, UK: Leo Cooper, 2000.

Riddle, David K., and Donald G. Mitchell, comps. *The Distinguished Service Order Awarded to Members of the Canadian Expeditionary Force and Canadians in the Royal Naval Air Service, the Royal Flying Corps and Royal Air Force 1915–1920.* Winnipeg: Kirkby-Marlton, 1991.

———, comps. *The Military Cross Awarded to Members of the Canadian Expeditionary Force 1915-1921.* Winnipeg: Kirkby-Marlton, 1991.

Roberts, T. G., ed. *Thirty Canadian VCs.* Skeffington: Canadian War Records Office, 1918.

Schull, Joseph. *Far Distant Ships: An Official Account of Canadian Naval Operations in World War II.* Toronto: Stoddart, 1987.

Smith, Marilyn Gurney. *The King's Yard: An Illustrated History of the Halifax Dockyard.* Halifax: Nimbus, 1985.

Soward, Stuart E. *A Formidable Hero: Lt RH Gray, VC, DSC, RCNVR.* Toronto: CANAV, 1987.

Spicer, Stanley T. *Maritimers Ashore & Afloat.* Vol. 1. Hantsport, NS: Lancelot, 1993.

States, David W. "William Hall, VC of Horton Bluff, Nova Scotia, Nineteenth-Century Naval Hero." In *Collections of the Royal Nova Scotia Historical Society.* Vol. 44. Halifax: McCurdy, 1996.

Stevens, G. R. *A City Goes to War.* Brampton, ON: Charters, 1964.

———. *The Royal Canadian Regiment.* Vol. 2. *1933–1966.* London, ON: London, 1967.

Swettenham, John, ed. *Valiant Men: Canada's Victoria Cross and George Cross Winners.* Toronto: Hakkert, 1973.

Tascona, Bruce. *From the Forks to Flanders Field: The Story of the 27th City of Winnipeg Battalion 1914–1919.* Winnipeg: Self-published, 1995.

Turner, John Frayn. *VCs of the Royal Navy.* London: Harrap, 1956.

Urquhart, Lt.-Col. H. M. *The History of the 16th Battalion (The Canadian Scottish), Canadian Expeditionary Force, in the Great War, 1914–1919.* Toronto: Macmillan, 1932.

Winton, John. *The Victoria Cross at Sea.* London: Michael Joseph, 1978.

INDEX

Imperial Chinese Squadron 48
Imperial Ottoman Order of the Osmanieh 65
Impregnable, HMS 49
Indefatigable, HMS 242
India 12, 23, 25, 28–52, 65, 68, 105, 253
Indian Army 21
Indian Medical Establishment 12
Indian Medical Service 23
Indian Mutiny 6, 8, 12, 20, 21, 28–53, 57, 205, 253
Indian Mutiny Medal 44
Indian Naval Brigade 8
Indonesia (Dutch East Indies) 25, 178, 237
Infantry Hill 193, 194
Inglis, John 32, 44
Inglis, Julia (Thesiger) 32, 44
Inkerman, Battle of 45, 46
Italian Bronze Medal for Military Valour 97
Italian Campaign 25
Italy 12, 20, 25, 175, 176, 223, 237
Itzu Shima, Japan 248, 249

J

Jacob, Claud 204
Japan 20, 237–52
Jee, Joseph 34, 35
Jervis Bay, HMS 208–16
Joel, David 217, 223
John, Prince 205
Johnson Gideon Beharry 255
Johnson, Jimmie 215

K

Kangsoo, HMS 48, 49
Keiberg, Belgium 200, 201
Keith, Alexander 37
Kemmel Hill Sector 113, 165
Kerr, Ernest 80
Kerr, Gertrude 92
Kerr, Gesner 80
Kerr, John Chipman 80–93, 116, 123, 149, 165, 166
Kerr, Roland 80, 81, 92
Kiggell, Launcelot 99, 100
Kimberley, South Africa 61
King's African Rifles 21
King's Own Royal Lancaster Regiment 163
Kitchener's Wood, Belgium 145
Kitchener, 1st Earl (Horatio Herbert Kitchener) 105
Knott, B. D. 50
Konowal, Filip 17, 18, 255
Korean War 20, 25, 93, 178
Krancke, Theodor 209, 212
Kronstadt, Russia 73–77, 214

L

La Surprise 225
Labrador 235
Ladysmith, South Africa 61
Lamontagne, Gilles 236
Langemarck, Belgium 100, 101, 195, 198
Laurier, Wilfred 153
Lawrence, Henry 31, 32
Le Havre, France 100
Ledeghem, Belgium 183, 201
Leicestershire Regiment (17th Regiment of Foot) 104, 105
Leliefontein, South Africa 8
Lion, HMS 219
Lisle, Beauvoir de 187
Little Bay, Newfoundland 122
Lockhart, Betty 217
Lockhartville, Nova Scotia 50, 51
Lord Stanhope, HMS 221
Lord Strathcona's Horse (Royal Canadians) 23
Louise, Princess 163
Lucknow, India 28–32, 34, 35, 38–44, 51
Ludendorff, Erich 120, 121, 126, 132, 155

M

Macdonald, Angus L. 175
Macdonell, Archie 152
Machum, George 21, 23
Mackenzie King, William Lyon 18, 175, 178
Mackenzie, Alexander 36
MacLeod, Alan 233
MacMechan, Archibald 79
Mafeking, South Africa 61
Magersfontein, South Africa 61
Magicienne, HMS 56
Magnificent, HMS 77
Malaysia-Indonesia Confrontation 25
Marcoing Line 169–71, 198
Marquoin Line 169
Martin-Leake, Arthur 11
Mary, Princess 205, 207
Mary, Queen Consort 50, 205
Matheson, Ed 230, 232, 233, 236
McAndrew, Jack 228
McMaster, Bryce Belcher 38
McMaster, Eleanor Annie (Burmester) 37
McMaster, Valentine Munbee 11, 34–38, 43, 53
Meade, Herbert 218, 219
Medal of Bravery 26
Medal of Honor 19
Medal of Military Valour 26, 27
Memorial University 206
Mercer, M. S. 113
Merchant Navy 104, 212